LITERATURE AGAINST ITSELF

Gerald Graff

LITERATURE AGAINST ITSELF

Literary Ideas
in Modern Society

The University of Chicago Press
Chicago and London

GERALD GRAFF is professor of English and
chairman of the English Department at
Northwestern University. He is the author of
Poetic Statement and Critical Dogma.

The University of Chicago Press, Chicago 60637
The University of Chicago Press, Ltd., London

© 1979 by The University of Chicago
All rights reserved. Published 1979
Printed in the United States of America
83 82 81 80 79   5 4 3 2 1

Library of Congress Cataloging in Publication Data

Graff, Gerald.
    Literature against itself.

    Includes bibliographical references and index.
    1. Literature and society.   I. Title.
PN51.G68   801'.95   78-9879
ISBN 0-226-30600-3

To my mother

Contents

Acknowledgments

The writer of an argumentative book is more than usually dependent on the friends and colleagues to whom he can turn for judgments of his work. If he is lucky, his associates will be astute enough to curb his more erratic hunches and give him confidence in the good ones which lack of faith might otherwise have caused to go unpursued. I feel lucky to have had such associates, though they cannot be blamed for the erratic hunches that remain in the book or for my failure to make more of the better ones.

The following people read portions of my manuscript and made many useful criticisms and suggestions: Tom Costello, Wallace Douglas, Joseph Epstein, Mark Krupnick, Christopher Lasch, Frank Lentricchia, Margaret Rapp, and Pat Story.

Charles Newman read the whole of an early draft and gave me encouragement when I needed it most.

Wayne Booth read the whole manuscript and contributed moral support and shrewd criticism.

I owe a special debt to my student Anton van der Hoven, who not only gave indispensable aid in preparing the manuscript for the press but also went over my final version with great care and was responsible for many improvements.

I am grateful to the Newberry Library and the National Endowment for the Humanities for a six-month grant that enabled me to bring this project near completion.

Finally, for permission to reprint material in which parts of this book first appeared, I want to thank the editors of the following journals: *TriQuarterly, American Scholar, Social Research, Salmagundi.*

The impious maintain that nonsense is normal in the Library and
that the reasonable (and even
humble and pure coherence) is
an almost miraculous exception.
Jorge Luis Borges

I think this is the great sin of the
intellectual: that he never really
tests his ideas by what it would
mean to him if he were to undergo
the experience that he is recommending.
Lionel Trilling

One

Culture, Criticism and Unreality

This is a book about our ways of talking about literature—how they got started, why they have taken the turn they have taken recently, where they go wrong, what we can do about setting them right. More broadly it is about certain contradictions in the languages of the humanities—the terms (or "paradigms") in which we do our thinking in and about humanistic activities. It is also a book about the social context of literature and criticism—how both literature and our ways of talking about it have been conditioned by social pressures and how they have in turn influenced social life. Conceptions of literature and the humanities both reflect and shape our conceptions of humanness and our views of man in society. Most theories of the nature of literature are more or less concealed theories of the nature of man and of the good society. In this sense, literary thinking is inseparable from moral and social thinking.

By "literary thinking" I mean thinking found *in* literary works as well as thinking *about* literature, its nature, its effects, its responsibilities. These two kinds of thinking are not easy to separate, especially at the moment, when so much literature reads as if it were literary criticism and at least some literary criticism tries hard to look like literature. Both the artists and the critics have taken as their subject the problematic status of their own authority to make statements about anything outside the systems of language and convention in which they must write. Nor is it quite so easy as it was only a few decades ago to distinguish the typical thinking of "literary intellectuals" from that of people with no special competence or interest in literary or intellectual matters. One of the defining aspects of the current situation is the penetration of literary ideologies and paradigms into areas heretofore impervious to them—with a consequent loss

1

of oppositional tension between literary culture and general society.*

In a book that spends much of its time objecting to the ideas of the "adversary culture," I should make clear at the outset my sympathy with the view that literature ought to play an adversary role in society. But recent social developments have opened up difficult questions about the adequacy of our ways of conceiving "adversariness." The ease with which attempts at subversive culture are now absorbed and assimilated into the motifs of mass culture suggests that something deeper is at work than a mere immunity to being shocked on the part of the audience. It suggests that the restless, revisionary spirit of the adversary culture actually accords with the underlying temper of society itself. And it suggests that our favorite modes of questioning society are shaped by this society's characteristic modes of thinking. As Irving Howe says in *Decline of the New*, "alienation has been transformed from a serious and revolutionary concept into a motif of mass culture, and the content of modernism into the decor of *kitsch*."[1] With the changed social circumstances, the experimental ethos of modernism no longer has any useful work to do. This is not because there are no longer any entrenched

*Hans Magnus Enzensberger makes the point trenchantly: "the capacity of the capitalist society to reabsorb, suck up, swallow, 'cultural goods' of widely varying digestibility has enormously increased. Today the political harmlessness of all literary, indeed, all artistic products, is clearly evident: the very fact that they can be defined as such neutralized them. Their claim to be enlightening, their utopian surplus, their critical potential has shrivelled to mere appearance.

". . . Even the most extreme esthetic contraventions no longer meet with serious resistance. . . . sooner or later, and usually sooner, by way of detours via advertising, design, and styling, the inventions become part and parcel of the consumer sphere. This means the end of an equivocation which has ruled progressive literature for fifty years: the parallelism or even equation of formal and social innovation" (*The Consciousness Industry: On Literature, Politics, and the Media* [New York: Seabury Press, 1974], 90–91).

In the same vein, Harold Rosenberg says: "Social and/or aesthetic far-outness is a public relations technique aimed at the presumed indignation of a stable middle class that ceased to exist four decades ago" (*Partisan Review*, symposium on "Art, Culture, and Conservatism," 39, no. 3 [Summer 1972], 444).

ideologies to challenge but because the revisionary formulas do
not challenge them—they *are* the entrenched ideologies, or at
least they play into them.

The interrelations between literary culture and the general
society are too complicated for simple formulation, but something of their character can be suggested by this paradox: on the
one hand, literary culture continues to be dominated by a psychology of "alienation"—a legacy of the romantic period, when
the man of letters began to define himself and his aims in explicit
opposition to the new industrial and commercial order. On the
other hand, this very psychology of alienation has itself become so
pervasive, its vocabularies and rhetorics have been so well pub-
licized and assimilated, that the old separation between the adversary culture and its presumably philistine "adversary" has
been closed. Alienation has itself become a defining principle of
community, through a phenomenon I describe in my second and
third chapters as "the power of powerlessness."

By the power of powerlessness, I mean the hold that sophisticated ideologies of alienation exert on the average citizen in his
understanding of himself and the world. But powerlessness and
alienation no longer necessarily call themselves by these unflat-
tering names. They reappear under new titles—autonomy, liberation, even revolution. And of late alienation has taken to
expressing itself in declarations of the end of alienation or in
attempts to go "beyond" alienation, usually by abandoning the
critical point of view.

The Triumph of the Vanguard

When I talk about "literary thinking" in this book, then, I mean
something rather more specialized than any sort of thinking that
happens to be done by anybody in connection with literature. I
mean specifically "advanced" literary thinking, the kind of
thinking expressed in the most sophisticated theories of twentieth-century criticism. A good many of my readers will feel
little affiliation with this vanguard, and these comprise a sizeable
and powerful group, possibly a majority, in the literary culture
at large. Some scholars in this group applaud attacks on de-

constructionism and other fashions as proofs that they need
not bother to read the critics in question. It would be self-
deluding to pretend that in attacking "fashionable" literary
ideas, one is not oneself doing something fashionable. Both the
"conservative" and the "vanguard" factions in current cultural
quarrels use the word "fashionable" as a stick with which to beat
the other side, yet both sides can substantiate their usage con-
vincingly enough.

Nevertheless, the vanguard party—admittedly a very loose and
decentralized entity—commands immense advantages. Its *rhetoric* carries an authority and an assurance that quite belie the
self-doubting tenor of what is said in this rhetoric, while its
would-be opposition sounds homely and threadbare by comparison. The advanced ideas and rhetoric have attained prestige both
within the university and outside, despite the esoteric terms in
which—at the loftiest level—they are couched. The resistance to
the contemporary, the experimental (or "innovative," as we now
say), and the vanguard that used to be a distinguishing mark of
"academic" literary culture has been thrown on the defensive.*
Resistance remains, but it is largely unorganized, without a coherent theoretical position, and unsure of itself; and it is easily
intimidated by charges that it is elitist, dogmatic, dull, reactionary, and hostile to novelty and progress—all of which, of
course, it sometimes is.

There has been no lack of distinguished critical writing that
might lend authority to a constructive resistance movement. One
can list such names as Auerbach, Booth, Lukács, Winters, Wil-
son, Howe, and Hirsch among critics who, in diverse ways, have
challenged prevailing vanguard dogmas. Yet despite these critics'
wide influence, this aspect of their work—its challenge to mod-

---

*As Robert Brustein says, "the image of an embattled group of minority
artists trying to survive in the face of a philistine public and a reactionary
critical establishment is simply unrecognizable in the seventies: it belongs to the twenties" (*Partisan Review*, symposium on "Art, Culture,
and Conservatism," 39, no. 3 [Summer 1972], 444). Yet even in the
twenties, perceptive observers such as George Grosz were writing that
"formal revolution lost its shock effect long ago" ("Art Is in Danger,"
Dadas on Art, ed. Lucy R. Lippard [New York: Prentice-Hall, 1971], 84).

ernist ideas—has not fully registered. This aspect has not entered
into the stream of those ideas critics feel they cannot dismiss or
ignore without being called to account. In the rhetorical world of
current criticism, one is free to write as if "everybody knows" that
mimesis is a dead issue, just as if Auerbach and Lukács had not
written.

The turning point in the self-liquidation of resistance to the
vanguard in the American university occurred at the moment,
hard to fix precisely, when the New Criticism achieved full academic respectability. The New Criticism, to whose formulations I
come back repeatedly in these chapters, seems to me by far the
most significant movement in the history of Anglo-American
criticism in this century. New schools in its wake keep repudiating
it, yet they do so with weapons derived from the New Critical
arsenal. As my fourth chapter argues, the current tendency to
characterize the New Criticism as a party of Tradition and Orthodoxy may be a useful strategy for dramatizing one's own claims of
revolutionary innovation, but it bears little relation to actual
history. The most significant achievement of the New Criticism
was not its dissemination of a new technique of reading (though
this was certainly significant), but its popularization of the modernist idea of literature and along with it modernist assumptions
about language, knowledge, and experience. Or rather, along
with a new technique of close textual analysis, readers educated
by the New Critics also absorbed a number of presuppositions
about the nature of literature and life that had no necessary
connection with this technique.

The New Critics set out—and in this they succeeded wholly—
to expunge from the mind of the educated middle class what
might be called the genteel schoolmarm theory of literature,
which had defined literature as a kind of prettified didacticism,
and to replace it with a theory of the radical "autonomy" of the
imagination. This view of literature went along with a deeply
skeptical view of rational and logical modes of making sense of
the immense complexity of experience—modes invariably associated with the most reductive forms of scientific positivism.

The message of modernism, as the New Critics conveyed it to
the teachers who passed it on to their students, was that "exper-

ience" is always superior to ideas "about" experience, that (as
Yeats had said) man can "embody" truth but he cannot "know"
it, at least not through the generalized concepts of the understanding.[2] This message helped to inject a distrust of the power of
understanding both into mass culture and the intellectual reaction against mass culture. The revolt against the New Criticism
that erupted on the cultural left in the sixties—and continues
today, shorn of much of its specifically political animus—owed its
very conception of politics largely to the modernist doctrines the
New Criticism had purveyed, doctrines which had already made a
political antithesis out of the relations between creative imagination and objective reason. The difference between the older
New Critics and the newer new critics who have repudiated them
are differences between factions of the vanguard. There have
been many attempts to go beyond the New Criticism in the last
two decades, and of course to some extent they have succeeded,
for better or worse. But since these attempts have not challenged
the key principle of the New Criticism, its hostile (or, at best,
equivocal) view of the referential powers of literature, they have
not gotten far. Revolutions *within* the vanguard have become
more frequent than ever, and current "self-consciousness" and
poststructuralism will no doubt soon give way to something else.
Yet the vanguard itself, with its anti-representational esthetic,
survives these changes, weary though it may be of surviving.

It is difficult to mourn the disappearance of the genteel schoolmarm theory of literature, which had little hold on reality, either
the reality of modern literature or of modern life. Yet the theory
of literature popularized by the New Critics had its own difficulties in defining a relation between literature and reality, in
part because of the very vehemence with which it reacted against
anything that faintly resembled the schoolmarm theory. To say
that "a poem should not mean but be" might be a proper enough
answer to an admirer of Edgar A. Guest or a student for whom
reading Shakespeare meant extracting a few moral maxims and
equating them with the message of the play, but it was not very
helpful in suggesting how literary works *do* convey their messages. In a rather ambiguous way, such theories gave the impres-

sion that there is something altogether suspicious about ascribing
any kind of message to literature, whether schoolmarmish or
otherwise. It is easy enough to ridicule the schoolmarms, but
literature *has* seemed to many people, not all of them stupid or
complacent, to make statements, to contribute to man's understanding of how things really are, not merely how they appear to
our consciousness. In fact, more than any literature before it, the
literature of modernism has seemed to make the most aggressive
kind of statements—to make a kind of all-out raid on reality, on
the great and urgent problems of modern society and the modern
self. The interpretations of the New Critics themselves—of alienation and the wasteland and the loss of cultural unity—seemed
repeatedly to call attention to these pressing realities. Yet New
Critical theory did not deal adequately with this reality-centered
aspect of literature, whether ancient or modern. And the theories
that have arisen in their wake have not done so either. The
rhetorics of recent criticism have tended either to overlook this
reality-centered aspect or to deny its existence—on the grounds
that reality cannot be understood at all or that understanding it
objectively is the special job of some other discipline. At the very
moment when the scope of literary culture has increasingly con-
tracted to the university, the educational function of literature
has become increasingly amorphous. The loss of belief—or loss
of interest—in literature as a means of understanding weakens
the educational claims of literature and leaves the literature
teacher without a rationale for what he professes. Students are
quick to perceive that their teachers no longer hold the naive view
that literature can explain anything.

There arises that contradiction in literary culture that I have
tried to suggest in the title of this book. As modern society has
thrown literature on the defensive and forced it to undertake the
most aggressive cultural aims, the same forces have encouraged
definitions of literature that conflict with these aims and turn the
humanists against themselves. The view of literature as the sovereign orderer of reality and our most valuable means of making
sense of the world is strangely licensed by our view that reality is
not susceptible to comprehension and management.

The Unreality of Reality

The difficulty, needless to say, has had much to do with the fact that "reality" itself has become an increasingly problematic concept.* (The word "problematic" is perhaps the one indispensable piece of equipment for anybody wishing to set up shop as a literary critic today.) It is no longer a simple matter, if it ever was, to distinguish between the real and the fictive. It would be difficult to exaggerate the extent to which modern reality seems to render absurd all attempts to understand, define, explain, and formulate it, even through the most tentative and exploratory methods. The very notions of understanding, definition, explanation, and "point of view" have come to seem suspect. They imply rigidity, an inability to swim with the current. When Ortega y Gasset wrote in *The Dehumanization of Art* about "the progressive dis-realization of the world" since the Renaissance, he referred specifically to the rise of philosophic idealism.[3] But his phrase could refer equally well to the effects of modern technology, war, politics, commerce, social engineering, and journalism, which, by promoting continuous discontinuity and upheaval, have assaulted our assurance of reality. The "established order" is itself embarked on the radical disruption of the sense of reality. One of my central arguments is that the real "avant-garde" is advanced capitalism, with its built-in need to destroy all vestiges of tradition, all orthodox ideologies, all continuous and stable forms of reality in order to stimulate higher levels of consumption.

The essence of capitalistic reality is its unreality, its malleable, ephemeral quality, which provides little in the way of a resisting medium against which personal identity can be formed. People in the nineteenth century could see this fact more easily than we can today, for they could perceive the incursion of this capitalist

---

*Like many other essential words, "reality" has been beaten into nonsense. In a recent "personal" ad in *The New York Review of Books,* "UNUSUAL, ATTRACTIVE, academic woman" solicits responses from males "unafraid of growing and open to exploring the life of the mind, body, and spirit in an atmosphere of equality and reality."

reality as a profound change—in contrast to what still remained
of the feudal order. For us, lacking the advantage of such contrasting perspective, unreality threatens to become a kind of
absolute. It can be so overwhelming that we are tempted to see it
as a kind of metaphysical principle—as Kafka's Joseph K. does
at the end of *The Trial*, when he objects that the logic, or illogic,
by which "The Law" operates "turns lying into a universal principle." Joseph K. retains enough perspective to put up feeble
objections, but in his situation it is tempting to abandon resistance. It sometimes seems as if the only way we can keep up—or
get even—with an increasingly unreal reality is by abandoning the
concept of reality itself and seeing to it that everything is labelled
unreal. Only by such a cynical gesture can we avoid being taken
in. Alienation is thus combatted by the completion of alienation.

Paradoxically, it is through this imitative, homeopathic logic
that the idea of fiction as imitation has been undermined. Pro-
ceeding from the valid insight that something has happened to
the sense of reality and that modern technological reality is in
some profound sense unreal, many writers and critics leap to the
conclusion that literature must for this reason abandon its pretensions to represent external reality and become either a self-
contained reality unto itself or a disintegrated, dispersed process.
It is as if we were to decide that, in a world where reality has
become fantastic, only pure fantasy, unhinged from liability to
anything but itself, has a chance to get at the truth. In this way,
mimetic theory actually survives obliquely in the very formulas
that subvert it—as we can see when we look at some of the current
attempts to deconstruct seemingly mimetic works by showing
them to be structures that call attention to their own fallibility.
The assumptions about the world found in such efforts to
demystify mimesis and realism and to proclaim the reign of
indeterminacy and undecidability bear marks of resentment
against conditions that are obviously all too objectively real and
determinate. Anti-mimetic theories derive from an understandable but distorted reaction to the loss of the sense of reality.

Take, for example, this statement from William Gass's trea-
tise, *Fiction and the Figures of Life:*

And has not the world become, for many novelists, a place not only vacant of gods, but also empty of a generously regular and peacefully abiding nature on which the novelist might, in large, rely, so to concentrate on cutting a fine and sculptured line through a large mass taken for granted, and has it now also seemed to him absent of that perceptive and sympathetic reader who had his own genius and would undertake the labor, rather easy, of following the gracious turns that line might take; so that, with all these forms of vacantness about him, he has felt the need to reconstitute, entire, his world. . .?[4]

Gass's point is not dissimilar to that made by Lukács in *Theory of the Novel*: having lost touch with an epic world that presents itself as a "rounded totality," the modern novelist is forced back in on his subjectivity, the subject being forced to make "itself the sole ruler of existence."[5]

For Lukács, however, this alienation of the writer from external reality is itself a consequence of events in the external world, of a history whose traces do not disappear from the novel. The "transcendental homelessness" of the novel does not destroy the novel's mimetic function but becomes the basis of it. Gass, by contrast, having ascribed the crisis of the novel to historical and social changes—the disappearance of a harmonious nature and of a homogeneous, trained reading public—proceeds to remove these changes from the scope of the novel itself. From the novelist's point of view, as Gass presents matters, the world has not merely changed but disappeared entirely, leaving the novel to "reconstitute" itself as a world unto itself. Instead of seeing the novel as an exploration of those "forms of vacantness" that have come to dominate the modern world, Gass lets his figure of speech beguile him into talking as if the novel can have no subject except its own internal forms.

Of course what Gass describes has been noted many times: the breakdown of agreed-upon systems of belief has forced upon the writer the necessity to devise his own myth, or to view his business as one of experimenting with various myths, none of which can ever achieve full authority. Even so, to describe such a situation is merely to point to an objective state of affairs that the writer will need to take into account, not to suspend the writer's mimetic responsibilities. To say that "forms of vacantness" surround the writer and frustrate his attempts at belief or understanding is itself to express a set of beliefs—one that has achieved an impressive degree of integration and complexity in modern writing. The claim that writing has been dispossessed of preestablished belief-systems is a preestablished belief-system in its own right, and one that draws on firmly established theories of history and politics.

There is thus a contradiction somewhere in the anti-mimetic position. Even to call attention to the radical unintelligibility of our unreal reality is to propose a kind of *understanding* of the way things really are, and to propose it as an objective hypothesis, not as a myth. Modern literature is no exception to the rule that writing, to be effective, has to spring from a coherent and convincing philosophy of life—or at least of that part of life with which the writer deals. There seems no getting away from the fact that literature must have an ideology—even if this ideology is one that calls all ideologies into question. The very act of denying all "naive" realisms presupposes an objective standpoint. Such denials can only be stated in language, and language, it seems, is an incorrigible realist. Far from discrediting the mimetic view of literature, the fact that reality has become problematic seems only to demand it more strongly, for the perception that reality is problematic is itself a mimetic perception, presupposing an objective distance between the observer and what he observes. For that matter, the argument that the observer and what he observes are not separable also presupposes that such a separation *is* possible after all.

But my thesis should not be mistaken for a plea for documentary realism, or for any other convention of representation. Propagandists of the realist movement in the nineteenth and early twentieth centuries did their cause a disservice by insisting that the nature of reality could be successfully probed only through a limited stock of conventions—illusionistic presentation of circumstantial particulars, usually in a linear narrative concentrating on everyday events and naturalistic probabilities. By narrowing the range of mimetic effects to these prescribed conventions, the partisans of realism made it easy to dismiss all pretensions of literature to be answerable to the objective world. And by frequently overlooking the fact that realism is itself a set of arti-ficial conventions, spokesmen for realism left themselves open to the kind of demystification that reduces this mode, like all others, to the level of arbitrary creation.

The representation of objective reality cannot be restricted to a single literary method. Fantastic or nonrealistic methods may serve the end of illustrating aspects of reality as well as conven-tionally realistic methods, and even radically anti-realistic meth-ods are sometimes defensible as legitimate means of representing an unreal reality. Knowing just where to draw the line is the problem. Lucien Goldmann, for example, is not persuasive when he praises Alain Robbe-Grillet's fiction on the grounds that it represents the reified social relationships characteristic of ad-vanced capitalism.* Such a justification could be given for vir-tually any piece of nonsense-writing (though this is not to equate Robbe-Grillet with nonsense). The critical problem—not always attended to by contemporary critics—is to discriminate between anti-realistic works that provide some true understanding of non-reality and those which are merely symptoms of it.

One of the most useful functions that literature and the hu-manities could serve right now would be to shore up the sense of reality, to preserve the distinction between the real and the fic-tive, and to help us resist those influences, both material and intellectual, that would turn lying into a universal principle. A good deal of twentieth-century literature does serve these pur-poses, but it might serve them better were it not for the terms in which we have been taught to understand it, the theoretical categories through which it is mediated to us. Where a mimetic perspective survives in twentieth-century literature—and admit-tedly it often survives only in the most fugitive and elusive ways, if it survives at all—it tends to go unnoticed. This is because our critical vocabulary either has no place for it or is committed to

---

*Lucien Goldmann, *Toward a Sociology of the Novel,* trans. Alan Sheri-dan (London: Tavistock Publications, 1975), 145. Goldmann writes that "the theme of [*Les Gommes* and *Le Voyeur*], the disappearance of any importance and any meaning from individual action, makes them in my opinion two of the most realistic works of contemporary fiction."

denying that it is there at all. Unlike the words for talking about
things like "intertextuality" and "reflexive structure," the words
for describing what literature *says*, what it is "about," are all
marked with the stigmata of squareness and banality. There is no
up-to-date jargon for talking about the referential values of literature. The jargon assists chiefly in other enterprises—questioning
the possibility of literary truth, or translating that truth into psychology, epistemology, myth, or grammar. What gets lost in the
translation as modern literature is assimilated, taught, and popularized, is its critical and explanatory power.

Formalists and Visionaries

There are many theoretical strategies for eliminating literature's
referential functions. One is to say that literature is not about
reality but about itself. Another is to say that "reality" itself is
indistinguishable from literature.* One can arrange prominent
literary theories on a spectrum between these complementary positions, the formalist (or "estheticist") view and the visionary view.
The formalist view separates the literary work from objective
reality, science, and the world of practical, utilitarian communication and defines it as an autonomous, self-sufficient "world"
or law unto itself, independent of the external world. It is this
formalist notion of the self-sufficient work that usually comes to
mind when the term "autonomy" is employed. But the visionary
view demonstrates that quite another use of the term is possible.
In this view, literature does not withdraw from objective reality
but appropriates it, calling into question the entire opposition
between the imaginative and the real, the world of the work and

---

*Robert Alter makes this point well: "There seem to be two complemen-
tary strategies for dissolving the connection between literature and the
real world. One. . . is to exorcise the other-than-literary presence of the
real world by reducing everything to text. The other is to emphasize the
nature of the literary text as a collocation of arbitrary linguistic signs that
can be joined together only on the basis of internal principles of coherence even as they pretend to be determined by objects outside themselves
to which they supposedly refer" ("Mimesis and the Motive for Fiction,"
TriQuarterly, 42 [Spring 1978], 234).

the world of reality. In this view, "reality" itself possesses order
and meaning only insofar as these qualities are imposed on it by
the human imagination. The visionary view is thus a kind of
formalism on the offensive, projecting the autonomous imagination and its categories outward onto the practical world, elevating
the imagination into the status of a universal legislator. In the
visionary view, the real world does not disappear so much as
become a kind of malleable raw material, to be shaped, transformed, and "ordered" by consciousness. The extreme instance
of this view is that all our "ideas of order" are essentially fictions
projected on a world that, in itself, is without order.

I can recall being puzzled when I first started reading intellectual journals in the early fifties at the fact that words such as
"myth" and "fiction" seemed to change their meaning depending
on whether they appeared in the literary or political sections.
When they appeared in the political pages of such journals, these
words were invariably synonymous with lying and untruth. Yet
when they made their appearance in the literary pages of the
same journals, they became synonymous with truth and wisdom—of a higher kind than that which is expressible in rational
or logical formulations. Eventually I began to understand that
there were two separate epistemologies, a "realistic" one that
applied to everyday practical affairs and to public matters and a
literary one that applied to "values" and to the mysteries of
personal experience. As long as one was concerned with everyday
matters and with politics, it was permissible to talk as if reality
were an objective thing intelligible to rational understanding, and
as if truth and falsity, fact and fiction, were distinguishable.
When one shifted to literary discussion, this way of talking was
considered naive or vicious. The commonsense rules one lived by
and by which one formed one's political judgments (if one formed
any at all, as in those days one often did not) were revoked when
one entered the literary frame of reference. There was no need to
be troubled by this state of affairs, since it was understood on all
sides that the literary epistemology held good only for literature
and private experience—and even then it was only a circum-
scribed group of intellectuals who theorized about such matters.
Later on, however, as once esoteric modes of thought began to

spread, the boundaries became blurred. With the rise of the New Left and the "cultural revolution" of the sixties, the literary epistemology began to penetrate into popular political discourse, as well as elsewhere, and the view that "objective reality" is a myth ceased to be a merely literary doctrine. Hearing an idea referred to as a fiction, one could no longer be sure whether it was being attacked or endorsed.

Twenty years ago, the formalist opposition between literature and science was in the ascendancy, so much so as to help provoke alarms about the "two cultures" division and other forms of cultural fragmentation. The tendency since that time has been the quest for reconciliation, the quest to cross boundaries and close gaps. Salutary as such a tendency obviously is, it tempts us to take an uncritical view of the *terms* in which reconciliation is achieved. It makes some difference *how* you reconcile fact and value, science and the humanities, the empirical and the imaginative. Whenever I hear anybody talk about reconciling science and literature, I have learned that what is likely to be coming next is some assertion of the fictionality of everything, some essentially "visionary" strategy of transcendence. We reconcile science and literature not by rehabilitating the truth-claims of literature but by undermining those of science. That is, instead of saying something like: "Literature and science are one, in that both give us objective knowledge about the world," we say: "Literature and science are one, in that both are essentially fictions by which we make sense of the world; the objectivity of science is itself a fiction, a myth, a paradigm, a framework, an ideology, a model, etc."

No critical theorist was more symptomatic of the transition from the dualistic opposition between literature and science in the fifties to the merger of these two in the sixties than Northrop Frye. Frye dissented from the New Critical doctrine of the autonomy of literature by extending this concept beyond the boundaries of the single, atomized, literary text to the "total" universe of literature itself. For Frye, it is not the individual literary work that is autonomous but the whole vast body of literary creation. (Eliot had anticipated this move in his view of literary tradition as an organic "ideal order.") But Frye went even farther: the auton-

omous universe of literature is only a heightened expression of
that creative spirit that all the forms of human culture and all
acts of human valuing exemplify. Frank Lentricchia notes that
Frye's "Aesthetic Humanism" bridges the New Critical gap between literature and reality by subsuming both under the esthetic:
"all human acts [for Frye] are creative (hence, centripetal, literary, and nonreferential). No human act, no human discourse can
be mimetic. With a suspect generosity we welcome as poets our
colleagues from other disciplines."[6] Reasserting Blake's and Shelley's vision of the poet as the exemplary orderer of all experience,
Frye's theory asserted that poetic vision is the paradigm and
model of all our attempts to impose a human significance and
pattern on the brute and inhuman world of nature. Yet as in
Blake and Shelley, it was not only unclear how this "vision" was
to be translated into action, in a society where those in power
seemed not even to notice that it existed, but also how this vision
was to be made responsible to the demands of the real world.
Since Frye claimed that the poetic way of "ordering" reality is not
to be confused with *beliefs* about objective matters of fact, and
indeed is independent of objective truth, his visionary theory of
literary autonomy was finally not so different from the theory of
the formalists after all.

The opposing archetypes of the poet as hypersensitive weakling
and the poet as prophet (or revolutionary) represent the social
correlatives of these contrasting theories of autonomy. Just as the
poet as weakling and the poet as prophet frequently merge in the
same figure, the formalist and the visionary theories can often be
found in the same theorist. Kant appears to write as a formalist
when he calls art "another nature" that makes no truth-claims
and has no practical purpose; he writes as a visionary when he
says that this other nature "emulates the play of reason" in its
quest "to go beyond the limits of experience and to present
[ideas] to sense with a completeness of which there is no example
in nature."[7] Whereas the first of these views strips art of knowledge and separates it from life, the second assigns art a cognitive
function as a lawgiver, the closest thing to Kant's pure reason
itself. Similarly, Mallarmé and the Symbolists persistently vacil-
late between the view that poetry is an alternative to real life and

that poetry is all there is to life—that "in the final analysis, all
earthly existence must ultimately be contained in a book."[8] And
again, Oscar Wilde uses formalist rhetoric when he says in *The
Decay of Lying* that "art never expresses anything but itself,"[9]
and that "art finds her own perfection within, and not outside of,
herself. She is not to be judged by any external standard of resemblance. She is a veil rather than a mirror."[10] He switches to
visionary rhetoric when he says in the same essay that "life
imitates art far more than art imitates life,"[11] a view which
defines art neither as a veil *nor* a mirror but as a mode of seeing
which reorganizes life in its own terms.

The tension or confusion between these contradictory interpretations of the concept of literary autonomy reflects the uncertainty of modern theorists about the relationship of literature to
the objective world. It also dramatizes the social ambivalence of
the modern literary intellectual, who is tempted equally to withdraw from society and politics and to try to take them over. On
the one side, "alienation" withdraws to the margin; on the other,
it imposes itself (and its sense of marginality) on the whole,
transforming itself into a utopian politics. What these polar views
share, however, is their repudiation of art's—or the mind's—
dependence on external reality, their insistence that reality takes
its orders from consciousness more than consciousness takes its
orders from reality. Thus to argue that modern esthetic theories
fail to do justice to the reality-centered activity of literature is not
to make the familiar simplification of equating these theories with
"art for art's sake," though of course art for art's sake is one such
theory. To repudiate art's representational function is not necessarily to leave no link between art and reality, but it is to reduce
reality to a trivial role in the partnership. Reality has no excuse
for existing except to supply inchoate raw materials, which art
proceeds to shape and order according to its own unconditioned
designs.

The contradictions of the poetics of autonomy—which simultaneously exalt and estrange the creative imagination—suggest a
striking parallel with "the triumph of the therapeutic" social type
as described by Philip Rieff. Indeed, Rieff himself, in his book of
this title, declares that the modern esthetic ethos has become an

expression of the "therapeutic mode."[12] The essence of the therapeutic outlook is the assumption that there are no objective ends
or imperatives to which human beings can subordinate themselves. To speak of a self (or a community) as dedicated to some
objectively "high" or "worthwhile" purpose, or indeed to speak
of it as conforming its activity to "reality," is absurd. The self is
liberated from preestablished determinants, yet this liberation is
empty, since its free-floating constructions cannot locate their
relation to anything real. This indulgent view of the self, which we
seem now to concede ourselves as a kind of compensation for the
many difficulties of modern urban existence, at once frees the
individual from obligation and strands him without any way of
measuring the "self-fulfillment" he has been freed to pursue.
Like the creative writer, the therapeutic individual (or collective)
is encouraged to underrate the ability of his consciousness to take
orders from external reality so as to understand and master it
rationally. On the other hand, as a consolation, he is encouraged
to overrate the power of his consciousness to remake the raw
material of reality according to strictly subjective forms. This
combination of resignation and euphoria carries over into political thought, the man of power being understood in terms reminiscent of those which define the visionary poet: the power of both
figures consists in the ability to get their self-created myths
publicly accepted. The ordinary individual, lacking any hope of
acquiring such power, is urged to cultivate the autonomy of his
personal self as a kind of "performance," which is to say, to make
a virtue of the necessity of his dispossession from substantial
external goals.

The Uses of Structuralism

The concept of literary autonomy has come under fire recently
from structuralist criticism, which attempts to demystify literature by showing that literary language, linguistic conventions,
and "textuality," not the imagination or consciousness of the
writer, are the constitutive agents of writing. This view is promising in several ways, the chief of which is its challenge to the New
Critical exaggeration of the difference between literary and non-

literary forms of language. There is even a suggestion in certain passages of structuralist criticism that we make sense of (or "naturalize" or "recuperate") literary works by organizing them in terms of thematic propositions—a view that seems to me of great value in explaining how it is that literature actually carries out its mimetic operations. But structuralist literary theory and its more recent offshoots have chosen to interpret their own discoveries in a way that not only fails to challenge earlier anti-mimetic theories but actually perfects them.

Nothing tells us more about our current dispositions than the way structuralism, ostensibly a humble method of analysis, has come to be widely taken as a kind of ultimate refutation of philosophical and literary realism. That structuralism has discredited mimetic models of thought and language is a proposition now so well established that it requires no argument—merely a wave in the direction of Saussure. As Gerard Genette says, "*it is well known* that from the linguistic standpoint the motivation of the sign, and particularly of the 'word,' is a typical case of realist illusion"[13](italics added). Or in Edward Said's formulation, "language as differentiation and as knowledge bears no necessary correspondence to reality."[14] J. Hillis Miller draws the literary corollary—in an essay entitled "The Fiction of Realism"—as follows:

> One important aspect of current literary criticism is the disintegration of the paradigms of realism under the impact of structural linguistics and the renewal of rhetoric. If meaning in language rises not from the reference of signs to something outside words but from differential relations among the words themselves, if "referent" and "meaning" must always be distinguished, then the notion of a literary text which is validated by its one-to-one correspondence to some social, historical, or psychological reality can no longer be taken for granted. No language is purely mimetic or referential, not even the most utilitarian speech. The specifically literary form of language, however, may be defined as a structure of words which in one way or another calls attention to this fact, while at the same time allowing for its own inevitable misreading as a "mirroring of reality."[15]

Miller does not quite eliminate mimesis from literature—he acknowledges its presence, but only as an inevitable temptation to
"misreading" which the work itself always exposes as illusory.
The claims of mimesis are entertained only so that they can be
overthrown.

Miller's statement conveniently illustrates several more critical
strategies by which the claims of literary referentiality are dis-
patched. First, the concept of reference is stripped of whatever
richness it might possess and reduced to something trivial. This is
done by equating reference with "one-to-one correspondence,"
that is, to a crudely Platonic or Lockean conception of words as
pointers to things. Secondly, the critic assumes that the way
meanings *originate* determines their ability or lack of ability to
refer to external reality. *If* meanings originate merely "from the
differential relations among the words themselves" within purely
artificial sign systems, *then* their reference to external reality can
no longer be taken for granted. In other words, literature must be
fiction because all language is fiction—though it is only literature
that calls attention to its fictive nature. Of course, Miller and
other anti-mimetic critics may be right in all these contentions.
But what is illustrated in his passage is how little pressure is felt
by such critics to *argue* or *give reasons* for their logical and
interpretive moves.

From the thesis that language cannot correspond to reality, it is
a short step to the current revisionist mode of interpretation that
specializes in reading all literary works as commentaries on their
own epistemological problematics. To call attention to the "blindness" of its own language is of course a potential of any text, and
many twentieth-century authors make use of this potential. Yet
one might think it possible for an author to choose *not* to actu-
alize this potential, *not* to call attention to the problematics of his
own language. If one ignores the intention of the author, however, which one can do by claiming that it is either irrelevant or
unknowable, and if one at the same time invokes the doctrine that
language is inherently incapable of corresponding to any external
object, then any critic can "prove" that any text is really "about"
its own fictive nature. A generalization about language that the
critic possesses in advance before he even reads the particular
work in question is permitted to determine his interpretation.

Thus Miller—in an analysis to be examined in a later chapter—
reads Dickens's ostensibly realistic *Sketches by Boz* as a self-
deconstructing work that calls attention to the falsity of its own
pretensions to realism.[16] Since this mode of interpretation assumes at the outset that language is incapable of reference to
external reality, this premise applies to Dickens's and to other
texts virtually by tautology. It remains only to "validate" this a
priori insight by showing that the text in question employs artificial conventions. Since all texts do, any text can be read as
putting its own referentiality in question.

I have said enough to suggest that structuralist and poststructuralist critics do not get rid of the concept of autonomy so much
as transfer it from the narrow realm of literature to the larger
realm of *écriture*. This move resembles what I have called the
visionary strategy, but it differs from this strategy insofar as it
translates the human categories of consciousness into the inhuman categories of grammar and linguistic structure. It is no
longer the writer who writes, but writing itself—and "to write,"
we are told, is an intransitive verb. Yet the writing—as in earlier
theories—remains unaccountable to external reality. Writing becomes the determinant of what that "external reality" is, as it is
in the visionary view, and it ceases to be responsible to any test
except that of internal "coherence," not of the single work or the
internal network of literary conventions, but of the total sign
system.

The concept of literary autonomy is not without valid uses for
technical criticism. From the point of view of a critic concerned
with the question of how a literary work is put together, the
knowledge that literature possesses an intertextual "grammar" of
myths and other structural forms is indispensable. The development of modern criticism is hardly conceivable without the enabling discovery that, just as we can study the syntax of a sentence
without regard to the sentence's truth-functions, we can study the
structure of a narrative without regard to its referential aspect.
Yet the very success of the structural method for this limited
purpose seems to have encouraged critics to leap to conclusions.
The fact that literature possesses an internal grammar of forms
does not mean that this grammar cannot or ought not be answerable to anything outside itself. The fact that meanings in general

are products of artificial systems of signs does not necessarily discredit the enterprise of inquiring into the reference of these meanings to nonlinguistic states of affairs. And the fact that a critic does not have to be concerned with the truth-claims made by a literary work in order to proceed with his analysis—and produce a certain kind of critical article—does not necessarily mean that these truth-claims can be dismissed or turned into nonclaims. Useful as it is as a methodological principle enabling critics to perform technical analysis, the concept of autonomy becomes a source of mystification when it presents itself as the final word on the relations between literature and the world.

The New Moralism

We must respect the honesty of thinkers who decline to go along with claims about language and literature which they do not believe can be substantiated. But there is more to their attitudes, I think, than principled skepticism. The modern anxiety that sign and meaning, meaning and referent, do not correspond is often accompanied by another emotion—a desire that they not correspond. It is often unclear in modern critical polemics whether we have no choice but to remain in our prison-houses of language or consciousness, or whether we might depart from these prison-houses but *ought not to want to,* lest we compromise the autonomy of human consciousness. Underlying our programmatic skepticism there is frequently a programmatic moralism that assumes man is somehow demeaned if he imitates nature or takes his cues from sources outside his own mind. This romantic view, which has its principal origins in Kant, Hegel, and Blake, heralds the subjection of all thinking to a simple political analogy: insofar as man tries to make nature the reference point and motive of his thought (and his art), he is enslaved to a tyrant outside himself—either a theocratic authority or an empiricist order of material objects; insofar as man creates his own world of culture, independent of preestablished nature, he is free. The half-truth that "man creates his own reality," with its assumption that freedom consists in the elimination of external determinants, informs most of the anti-mimetic literary doctrines of our day.

Such a philosophy comes across in some observations by Said
on the two approaches to textual interpretation between which we
are often asked to choose today. One approach, resting on "the
idea of a 'classical text,' " sees this text as a "system of boundaries and inner constraints, held intact by successive generations," which is to say, as a preestablished object that controls
and determines the responses of the interpreter. The other kind
views the text as "an invitation to unforeseen estrangements from
the habitual, an occasion for unconditional voyages into what
Conrad so aptly called 'the heart of darkness.' "[17] Already one
can see that a morality play is being organized in which the forces
of smug Classical Order will line up against the forces of the
unforeseen, the unconditional, and the risky. Classical Order will
be routed, but apparently not so thoroughly that we shall not have
to guard vigorously against its return.

What goes for critical interpretation clearly goes double for
literature itself: "with the discrediting of mimetic representation," Said continues, taking it for granted that mimesis *has* been
discredited, "a work enters a realm of gentile history, to use
Vico's phrase for secular history, where extraordinary possibilities of variety and diversity are open to it but where it will not be
referred back docilely to an idea that stands above it and explains
it."[18] Said's *docilely* gives the clue to the moralism embedded in
the very structure of this rhetoric, a moralism that equates mimetic representation with conformism and with easy explanations
that have all been made up in advance. To reject these mimetic
models, on the other hand, is to place oneself on the honorable
road to the heart of darkness.

A rhetorical scorecard for this melodrama might look something like this:

	Bad	*Good*
representation		creation
text as determinate object		text as open, indeterminate "invitation"
boundaries and constraints		voyages into the unforeseen
docility, habit		risk
truth as correspondence		truth as invention, fiction
meaning as "product"		meaning as "process"

Frequently "bad" and "good" line up correspondingly with political "right" and "left," but they need not necessarily. Nevertheless, the essentially political nature of these oppositions ought to
be clear.

The challenge of skepticism as a philosophical position must
be answered on its own terms, not explained away as a displacement or sublimation of a moral or political attitude. Nevertheless,
when the moral or political attitude advertises itself so obtrusively
in the way skepticism is formulated, an extra-philosophical inves-
tigation does not seem out of line. As I shall suggest often below,
a great deal of our critical and cultural argument operates on a
principle of guilt-by-association. Realistic and objectivistic ways
of thinking about language and thought are persistently identified with things nobody would want to be associated with if he
could help it: with amoral science, positivism, mechanism, venal
commercial calculation, stifling respectability, inhuman technology, class exploitation, imperialism, manipulative propaganda
and advertising, bureaucracy, regimentation, in short, just about
everything anybody ever found to dislike about "bourgeois culture," as characterized in the crudest sociological stereotypes.
Not that these stereotypes need to be particularly consistent with
one another: "stifling respectability" belongs to an earlier phase
of bourgeois culture than "inhuman technology." The phrase
"bourgeois culture" can obviously mean anything you want it to
mean, depending on which of its bad qualities you wish to invert
in order to derive your definition of art.

The logic which associates objective thinking with social domination and exploitation is not difficult to reconstruct. To appre-
hend something objectively is to separate oneself from that something and thus to view it as an "object" or "thing" distinct from
oneself. It follows—or it is made to follow—that the objective way
of looking at the world is necessarily detached, uninvolved,
"value-free," and, from the point of view of human interests and
needs, inhuman. It follows in turn that there is a necessary link
between the objective point of view and the military, political, and
technological suffering of twentieth-century humanity. If anybody is inclined to doubt these logical equations—to object, say,
that it is *some uses* of objectivity that bear the liability for this

suffering, not objectivity itself—he is referred to results of objective thinking ranging from organized death camps to computer-processing of student records. The mere weight of historical evidence of the terrible consequences of technological reason gives categorical force to the indictment. Thus a critic like George Steiner needs to make no qualifications when he says that "analytic thought has in it a strange violence. To know analytically is to reduce the object of knowledge, however complex, however vital it may be, to just this: an object. It is to dismember."[19] By a simple series of equations that do not have to be defended by argument, analytic thought equals dismemberment.

But the equation of objectification—and hence of mimesis—with technocratic violence is but one of a vast series that discredits mimetic modes of thinking and writing. To think in mimetic forms is necessarily to give priority to the bad side of an endless series of dialectical opposites, many of which are not parallel: it is to favor the head over the heart; the mechanical over the spiritual *or* the natural; the human being as "object" or "thing" or "it" over the human being as "person" or "thou" or authentic end in himself; the inertly impersonal over the richly personal; the sentimentally or gushily personal over the richly impersonal; the banal collective over the uniquely individual; the dissociated, anomic individual over the organic collective; the dead tradition over the living experiment; the positivistic experiment over the living tradition; the static product over the dynamic process; the monotony of linear time over the timeless recurrence of myth; dull, sterile order over dynamic disorder; chaotic, entropic disorder over primordial order; the forces of death over the forces of life.

The need of the humanities to dissociate themselves from anything that might be associated with bourgeois culture not only requires the liquidation of mimetic literary models but virtually anything suggestive of an objective truth-claim, whether in literature, criticism, or any other form of discourse. It is as if the humanities had to divest themselves of intellectual authority in order to escape the bad conscience of bourgeois society. Literature, criticism, all humanistic discourse have to be emptied of content lest somebody accuse them of being bourgeois, autocratic, or elitist. The aim of literary theorizing becomes not to understand the distinctive ways in which literature deals with experience so much as to exonerate literature (and the literary theorist) from social complicity. This exoneration is accomplished by divesting the literary work of its objective truth-claims, usually by the strategy of claiming that literary propositions do not present themselves as genuine beliefs, which is to say, claiming that they are not really propositions at all. If we refuse to extend belief to any proposition (outside as well as inside literature), if we treat such propositions as myths or fictions, then both literature and we ourselves presumably remain innocent of all the crimes our culture has committed in the name of this or that belief, this or that form of objective knowledge. By such logical strategies, well-intentioned humanists argue themselves into a corner: at the very moment when external forces have conspired to deflate the importance and truth of literature, literary theory delivers the final blow itself.

The paradoxical effect of these modes of avoiding complicity is that the humanities end up mirroring the very society they seek to oppose. The refusal to assume authority, the suspicion of "privileged positions," the exaltation of process over ends, the equation of the concepts of mastery and prowess with domination, the effort to establish innocence by remaining aloof from beliefs, and the impulse to undo the reality principle in the name of a liberating perceptual novelty—all these motifs are played out in both the literary culture and the larger society. The sophisticated skepticism of the literary culture is mirrored in the popular desire to be told that our knowledge and perceptions cannot be trusted, that we—as opposed to the technocratic controllers to whom we surrender objective knowledge and power —are lovably mixed-up people who therefore cannot be blamed for the horrors of modern history.

In all sorts of ways, the adversary strategies mirror the established society. The permanent technological revision of the physical and spiritual landscape mirrors the literary vanguard's revisionary assaults on realism while rendering these assaults superfluous. On another level, the artistic attempt to immunize the work against being assimilated as a commodity only produces

a new kind of commodity. By divesting itself of the presumed
elitism of rhetoric, statement, point of view, and mimetic representation, literature aims to resist the "packaging" that tames
and domesticates virtually all cultural products. But this strategy
not only fails to achieve its purpose, it deprives the work of its
critical voice in the process. By rebelling against mimesis, literary
culture aims to repudiate technological thinking. Yet the real
technological thinking may be the kind that politicizes the mental
world in just this way, drawing a sharp antithesis between
individual autonomy and imitation of preestablished models.

Increasingly, the critical perspective expresses itself through a
style of argument that has come to be known as "demystifying."
In the tradition of the great nineteenth-century unmaskers of
myths—Marx, Freud, Nietzsche, Darwin, and so on—contemporary demystifying seeks to disclose once and for all the
artificial and thus alterable nature of the beliefs and usages that
have for so long been regarded as part of the law of nature. As
now practiced, however, demystifying consists in an assault not
only on certain conceptions of reality but on the idea that there is
any such thing as a knowable reality independent of ideology and
myth. Following this line of argument, the demystifiers can
hardly help universalizing mystification in the very process of
trying to drive it away.

The view that we behave in a "radical" or even "revolutionary"
fashion when we insist on the ideological nature of all thinking
remains a powerful motif of left-wing culture, which does not
perceive the kinship between itself and the cynicism and resignation of mass society. The problem is that literature (or any other
mode of writing or thinking) can be an instrument of demystification only so long as we are able to draw a distinction between the
mythical and the nonmythical. The notion, then, that there exists
an objective reality "out there," independent of our perceptions
of it, far from being an ideological rationalization for the existing
order, is a prerequisite for changing the existing order, which has
to be understood as it is before it can be altered.

Yet these very confusions over ideology suggest why it is not
sufficient to make simple appeals to "reason," "objective truth,"
"realism," "humanism," and other such terms. Appeals like

these fall flat because they are spoken in what is virtually a different language—in which reason, objective truth, and so on mean something very different from the degraded meanings they have acquired by virtue of their guilt-by-association with technocratic institutions. The "reason" of most classical, Renaissance, and Enlightenment thinkers is moral and evaluative *and* objective. It bears little resemblance to the value-free, instrumental, purely calculative reason of positivistic science and industrial engineering. This change in the concept of reason reflects a transformation of the structures of social authority in which reason (and other concepts denoting authority) seem, in the eyes of many, to have been objectified. Before we can even argue about such concepts it seems necessary to free them from false politicization—to separate the concepts themselves from the degraded political and social ends in whose name they have been invoked. Until this is done, debate can hardly get off the ground, since what is being attacked is not "reason" or "realism" itself but a caricature that has been set up in order to be quickly disposed of. The notion that "reason has failed," that "objective truth is a lie," that ideals such as "humanism," "culture," "meaning," "tradition," and the like are but so many rationalizations for oppression exemplifies this premature politicization of terms, which can only lead to a repudiation of ideals as such or to the embrace of inverted ideals that defeat our own purposes.

This book, then, seeks to understand why it is that we as literary intellectuals have defined our enterprise in ways that implicitly trivialize it. Shaped by a love-hate relation with science, commerce, and practical life, our definitions of literature unwittingly concede the advantage to the adversaries. Almost as if a formal partition-treaty had been negotiated, the creative faction (or the creative side of the individual) has renounced its claim to be a seeker of rational understanding and identified itself with an outlook that makes rational understanding sound contemptible. There is no deterministic theory of degeneration at work in my diagnosis. Our literary thinking has gone wrong because we have,

by our own free will and our own conscious reasoning, sold
ourselves a certain conceptual bill of goods.

At the same time, there are historical reasons that explain why
this transaction has looked attractive. The conditions in which
literary intellectuals have had to work out their analyses and
strategies have frequently been hard. In many ways, the artist has
been a victim of indifference and contempt, and this indifference
and contempt do not necessarily go away when the artist is
venerated as a celebrity rather than despised as an outcast. Yet
what Edgar Wind has pointed out is still true: "it would be an
illusion to suppose that art suffered these developments as a
victim. Its role has been that of an active partner."* The
adversary culture has carried out the will of its adversary. As if our
society had not rendered literature unimportant enough already,
literary intellectuals have collaborated in ensuring its inef-
fectuality.

*Edgar Wind, *Art and Anarchy* (New York: Vintage Books, 1960), 17.
Wind adds that "art has been displaced from the center of our life not
just by applied science, but above all by its own centrifugal impulse"
(18). Yes, but this needs qualification: as I argue here, art's very loss of
centrality makes it "central" in a centerless society.

Two

The Myth of the
Postmodern
Breakthrough

The postmodern tendency in literature and literary criticism has been characterized as a "breakthrough," a significant reversal of the dominant literary and sociocultural directions of the last two centuries. Literary critics such as Leslie Fiedler, Susan Sontag, George Steiner, Richard Poirier, and Ihab Hassan have written about this reversal, differing in their assessments of its implications but generally agreeing in their descriptions of what is taking place. What is taking place, these critics suggest, is the death of our traditional Western concept of art and literature, a concept which defined "high culture" as our most valuable repository of moral and spiritual wisdom. George Steiner draws attention to the disturbing implications of the fact that, in the Nazi regime, dedication to the highest "humanistic" interests was compatible with the acceptance of systematic murder.[1] Sontag and Fiedler suggest that the entire artistic tradition of the West has been exposed as a kind of hyperrational imperialism akin to the aggression and lust for conquest of bourgeois capitalism. Not only have the older social, moral, and epistemological claims for art seemingly been discredited, but art has come to be seen as a form of complicity, another manifestation of the lies and hypocrisy through which the ruling class has maintained its power.

But concurrent with this loss of confidence in the older claims of the moral and interpretive authority of art is the advent of a new sensibility, bringing a fresh definition of the role of art and culture. This new sensibility manifests itself in a variety of ways: in the refusal to take art "seriously" in the old sense; in the use of art itself as a vehicle for exploding its traditional pretensions and for showing the vulnerability and tenuousness of art and language; in the rejection of the dominant academic tradition of analytic, interpretive criticism, which by reducing art to abstractions tends to neutralize or domesticate its potentially liberating energies; in

31

a less soberly rationalistic mode of consciousness, one that is more congenial to myth, tribal ritual, and visionary experience, grounded in a "protean," fluid, and undifferentiated concept of the self as opposed to the repressed Western ego.

I want here to raise some critical questions about the postmodern breakthrough in the arts and about the larger implications claimed for it in culture and society. I want in particular to challenge the standard description of postmodernism as an overturning of romantic and modernist traditions. To characterize postmodernism as a "breakthrough"—a cant term of our day—is to place a greater distance between current writers and their predecessors than is, I think, justified. There are distinctions to be drawn, of course, and both here and in the final chapter of this book I shall try to draw them. But this chapter argues that postmodernism should be seen not as a break with romantic and modernist assumptions but rather as a logical culmination of the premises of these earlier movements, premises not always clearly defined in discussions of these issues. In the next chapter I question the utopian social claims of the postmodernist sensibility by questioning the parallelism they assume between social and esthetic revolution.

In its literary sense, postmodernism may be defined as the movement within contemporary literature and criticism that calls into question the traditional claims of literature and art to truth and human value. As Richard Poirier has observed, "contemporary literature has come to register the dissolution of the ideas often evoked to justify its existence: the cultural, moral, psychological premises that for many people still define the essence of literature as a humanistic enterprise. Literature is now in the process of telling us how little it means."[2] This is an apt description of the contemporary mood, but what it neglects to mention is that literature has been in the process of telling us how little it means for a long time, as far back as the beginnings of romanticism.

It is clear why we are tempted to feel that the contemporary popularity of anti-art and artistic self-parody represents a sharp break with the modernist past. It does not seem so long ago that writers like Rilke, Valéry, Joyce, Yeats, and others sought a kind of salvation through art. For Rilke, as earlier for Shelley and other romantics, poetry was "a mouth which else Nature would lack," the great agency for the restitution of values in an inherently valueless world. Romantic and modernist writing expressed a faith in the constitutive power of the imagination, a confidence in the ability of literature to impose order, value, and meaning on the chaos and fragmentation of industrial society. This faith seemed to have lapsed after World War II. Literature increasingly adopted an ironic view of its traditional pretensions to truth, high seriousness, and the profundity of "meaning." Furthermore, literature of the postwar period has seemed to have a different relation to criticism than that of the classic modernists. Eliot, Faulkner, Joyce, and their imitators sometimes seemed to be deliberately providing occasions for the complex critical explications of the New Critics. In contrast, much of the literature of the last several decades has been marked by the desire to remain invulnerable to critical analysis.

In an essay that asks the question, "What Was Modernism?" Harry Levin identifies the "ultimate quality" pervading the work of the moderns as "its uncompromising intellectuality."[3] The conventions of postmodern art systematically invert this modernist intellectuality by parodying its respect for truth and significance. In Donald Barthelme's anti-novel, *Snow White*, a questionnaire poses for the reader such mock questions as, "9. Has the work, for you, a metaphysical dimension? Yes ( ) No ( ) 10. What is it (twenty-five words or less)?"[4] Alain Robbe-Grillet produces and campaigns for a type of fiction in which "obviousness, trans-parency preclude the existence of *higher worlds*, of any tran-scendence."[5] Susan Sontag denounces the interpretation of works of art on the grounds that "to interpret is to impoverish, to deplete the world—in order to set up a shadow world of 'meanings.'"[6] Leslie Fiedler, writing on modern poetry, char-acterizes one of its chief tendencies as a "flight from the platitude of meaning."[7] As Jacob Brackman describes this attitude in *The Put-On*, "we are supposed to have learned by now that one does not ask what art means."[8] And, as Brackman shows, this deliberate avoidance of interpretability has moved from the arts into styles of personal behavior. It appears that the term "meaning" itself, as applied not only to art but to more general experience, has joined "truth" and "reality" in the class of words which can no longer be written unless apologized for by inverted commas.

Thus it is tempting to agree with Leslie Fiedler's conclusion that "the Culture Religion of Modernism" is now dead.[9] The most advanced art and criticism of the last twenty years seem to have abandoned the modernist respect for artistic meaning. The religion of art has been "demythologized." A number of considerations, however, render this statement of the case misleading. Examined more closely, both the modernist faith in literary meanings and the postmodern repudiation of these meanings prove to be highly ambivalent attitudes, much closer to one another than may at first appear. The equation of modernism with "uncompromising intellectuality" overlooks how much of this intellectuality devoted itself to calling its own authority into question.

The Religion of Art

The nineteenth century's elevation of art to the status of a surrogate religion had rested on paradoxical foundations. Though in one sense the religion of art increased enormously the cultural prestige and importance of art, there was self-denigration implicit in the terms in which art was deified. Consider the following statement by Ortega y Gasset, contrasting the attitude of the avant-garde art of the mid-twenties, that art is "a thing of no consequence" and "of no transcendent importance," with the veneration art had compelled in the previous century:

> Poetry and music then were activities of an enormous caliber.
> In view of the downfall of religion and the inevitable relativism
> of science, art was expected to take upon itself nothing less
> than the salvation of mankind. Art was important for two
> reasons: on account of its subjects which dealt with the
> profoundest problems of humanity, and on account of its own
> significance as a human pursuit from which the species derived
> its justification and dignity.[10]

Ortega attributes the prestige of art in the nineteenth century to
the fact that art was expected to provide compensation for the
"downfall of religion and the inevitable relativism of science."
But the downfall of religion and the relativism of science were
developments which could not help undermining the moral and
epistemological foundations of art. Once these foundations had
been shaken—and the sense of their precariousness was a condition of the romantic glorification of the creative imagination—art
could scarcely lay claim to any firm authority for dealing with
"the profoundest problems of humanity" and for endowing the
species with "justification and dignity." It is only fair to add that
Ortega's own philosophical writings are profound commentaries
on this crisis of authority in modern experience.

From its beginnings, the romantic religion of art manifested
that self-conflict with its own impulses which Renato Poggioli, in
The Theory of the Avant-Garde, identifies as a defining characteristic of avant-garde thought.[11] The ultimate futility and
impotence of art was implicit in the very terms with which
romantic and subsequently modernist writers attempted to deify
art as a substitute for religion. The concept of an autonomous
creative imagination, which fabricates the forms of order, meaning, and value which men no longer thought they could find in
external nature, implicitly—if not necessarily intentionally—concedes that artistic meaning is a fiction, without any corresponding
object in the extra-artistic world. In this respect the doctrine of
the creative imagination contained within itself the premises of
its refutation.

Recent literature forces us to recognize the precariousness of
the earlier religion of art, to see that the very concept of a *creative*
imagination on which it depended contains an unavoidable
difficulty. For an order or pattern of meaning which must be
invented by human consciousness out of its inner structure—
whether it is thought to derive from the private subjectivity of the
individual, from some intersubjective *Geist* that is assumed to be
common to all minds, or from the humanly created forms of
custom and convention—is necessarily uncertain of its authority.
Old-fashioned textbook descriptions of romanticism stressing the

affirmative flights of the romantic priests of art ignored the
ambivalence pervading romantic writing. Wordsworth, for
example, celebrating the spirit in nature which "rolls through all
things," pauses self-consciously to consider that this celebration
may rest on "a vain belief," justifiable only on pragmatic
grounds. And his affirmation of this spirit is haunted by his
difficulty in determining whether man actually perceives it as an
external reality or creates it out of his own mind. The Shelleyan
stereotype of the poet as the "unacknowledged legislator of the
world," a godlike creator who brings forth a new cosmos *ex nihilo*
and soars beyond the range of commonsense reality, is, from
another perspective, only an honorific reformulation of the
alternate stereotype of the poet as a marginal person, a hapless
trifler or eccentric who inhabits a world of autistic fantasy and
turns his back on objective reality. The secret and unacknowledged collaboration betwen rebellious literati and their philistine
detractors remains an unwritten chapter in the social history of
art. Both poetolatry's glorification of the artist as a demigod and
philistinism's denigration of him as an irresponsible social devi-
ant share a common definition of the artist as a special kind of
person, one who perceives the world in a fashion different from
that of ordinary objective judgment. An inner connection links
the doctrine of imaginative autonomy and the philosophical and
social alienation of art.[12]

   For the romantic belief in the power of the autonomous
imagination was chastened by the recognition that the order and
truth generated by this imagination are no more than arbitrary
and subjective constructions. If imaginative truth is determined
from within rather than without, how can a poet know whether
one myth prompted by his imagination is truer than any other?
And what basis has he for claiming that his particular myth is or
should be shared by others? In the very assertion that poetry
endows the universe with meaning—the proposition of Shelley's
Defence—there lay an implied confession of the arbitrary nature
of that meaning. Romantic esthetics typifies the more general
crisis of modern thought, which pursues a desperate quest for
meaning in experience while refusing to accept the validity of any
meaning proposed. The paradox of the sophisticated modern

mind is that it is unable to believe in the objective validity of
meanings yet is unable to do without meanings. The ambiguous
status of the concept of meaning in modern esthetic theory is one
outcome of this paradox. For the last two centuries, theorists have
engaged in a tightrope act in which the significance which must
be ascribed to art in order to justify its importance has had to be
eliminated from art in order to guarantee its innocence and
authenticity. Thus we have the numerous self-contradictory
attempts in the twentieth century to define art as a discourse
somehow both referential and nonreferential, closed off from the
external world yet embodying profound knowledge of the external
world.[13]

The Appeal to Consensus

The equation of romanticism with "subjectivism" is, of course, a
misunderstanding of the intentions of the major romantic thinkers, who glorified not the idiosyncratic subjectivity of the private
ego but the transcendental subjectivity of universal man, sometimes identified with the Absolute itself. Thus for Shelley, "a
poem is the very image of life expressed in its eternal truth"
according to "the unchangeable forms of human nature, as
existing in the mind of the creator, which is itself the image of all
other minds."[14] By assuming the unity and universality of "all
other minds," this view makes it possible to do without an
external ground of order and value. Henry David Aiken notes
that nineteenth-century thinkers came "increasingly to recognize
that objectivity is not so much a fact about the universe as it is a
matter of common standards of judgment and criticism." Objectivity, in other words, was redefined as intersubjectivity: "Intersubjective norms are not agreed to by the members of a society
because they are objective, but, in effect, become objective
because they are jointly accepted."[15]

In other words, societies do not abide by certain rules because
these rules are, by some preestablished standard, normative.
Rather, societies *choose* to regard certain rules as normative, and
these rules then become established as such. This reasoning refers
normative judgments to what we now call an "existential" act of

choice. In doing so, however, it begs the question of *how* this choice is made. On what basis does society choose? To take a provocative but nevertheless pertinent example, suppose one faction of society prefers a policy of genocide against certain minorities while another prefers a policy of democratic freedom. Is there no standard of *good reasons* that can be invoked to show that democratic freedom constitutes a wiser choice than genocidal extinction? (I have translated the problem into one of values, but the case is not altered when the question is one of what to regard as objectively true.) The notion that choices *determine* norms rather than *obey* them does away with the idea that there are certain norms that *ought* to be chosen by societies and thus precipitates a radical cultural relativism. It is true, of course, that force, not good reasons, *has* governed most societies. Yet if we give up the notion that such reasons can exist prior to choice, we deny the legitimacy of resisting force.

To argue that the nature of a concept is whatever people *believe* it to be may be an adequate strategy as long as everybody in the relevant group believes the same things. It becomes a nonanswer when the nature of the concept has become a contested issue. The appeal to what people believe breaks down as soon as the question arises of whether they *ought* to believe it. The appeal to intersubjective consensus begs the question at hand; it was the breakdown of such consensus, when the literary and the commercial-utilitarian factions of society began to inhabit opposed mental worlds, that in large degree occasioned the cultural problem. It is this dilemma that may have induced Kant himself, in at least one passage, to swerve from his customary position and assert that our mental acts of constituting reality must be controlled by an external object. In the *Prolegomena to Any Future Metaphysics,* Kant poses the question of how we can assure ourselves that our judgments are shared by others. His answer is surprising: "there would be no reason for the judgments of other men necessarily agreeing with mine," Kant says, "if it were not for the unity of the object to which they all refer and with which they accord; hence they must all agree with one another."[16] This answer is surprising because elsewhere Kant insists that it makes no sense to speak of a "unity of the object" as if it were prior to our thinking, because unity inheres not in the object but in the conditions of our common understanding, specifically in the *category* of unity by which our minds constitute the object. Here Kant seems to undo his Copernican revolution by making our ability to consitute the object as a unity depend on the unity of the object in itself prior to our apprehension. In order to account for the universality of our perceptions, Kant is forced to lapse into the sort of "correspondence" theory of truth that his philosophy has presumably done away with.

But of course the great influence of Kant's thought—whether Kant intended it or not—was precisely to discredit this correspondence theory of truth, and to rule out any talk about the way reality *coerces* our judgments. And in the absence of any appeal to such a coercive reality to which the plurality of subjectivities can be referred, all perspectives become equally valid. The romantic Absolute degenerates into a myth or, as we now say, a fiction. The logic of romantic transcendental philosophy led to a relativism that was certainly antithetical to what most romantic thinkers intended, yet which furthered the loss of community they were seeking to redress.

This distinction between the intent of romantic argument and its consequences makes it possible to resolve some recent scholarly controversies over whether the romantics were humanists or nihilists. In a sense, both sides are right. The opposing theories of romanticism do not really conflict, since they are not talking about the same aspects of the subject. Those who see romanticism as positive and optimistic (notably, M. H. Abrams in *Natural Supernaturalism* and René Wellek in "Romanticism Reconsidered") base their view largely on what the romantics themselves consciously intended—to respect common truth and the artist's responsibility to his community. Those who by contrast see romanticism as nihilistic (critics such as J. Hillis Miller, Morse Peckham, and Harold Bloom), base their views on the logical consequences of romantic ideas, independent of intentions. Certainly neither Kant nor any of the thinkers and poets who were influenced by his ideas thought they were proposing a radical relativism that would reduce all values and all reality to a set of fictions. In this sense, Wellek is right when he objects to

Peckham's statement that "Romanticism learns from Kant that it can do entirely without constitutive metaphysics and can use any metaphysic or world hypothesis as supreme fiction." Wellek replies, rightly, that one "learns" nothing of the kind from Kant: "I am not aware of a single writer in the late eighteenth or early nineteenth century to whom this description would apply. Who then rejected the possibility of metaphysics or treated it as supreme fiction?"[17] Nevertheless, in fairness to Peckham's view, there is warrant for arguing that the effect of the romantic argument was to do just this.

The Dehumanization of
Reason: $0 = 0$

The developments we have been discussing have their origins in the social and philosophical crises of modern culture. The critical and scientific philosophies of the seventeenth and eighteenth centuries severed the ancient connection between rational, objective thought and value judgments. Not only values, but all ideas of order which went beyond factual sense-data became increasingly viewed as inherently subjective, a fate which would overtake objective fact itself at a later date. There set in the condition which Erich Heller has described as "the loss of significant external reality," the sense that the objective world and the realm of meanings and values are irreparably divided.[18] Regarded by most thoughtful men up to the end of the Renaissance as a support for the eternal ethical, metaphysical, religious, and esthetic absolutes, "reason," in its empiricist and Cartesian forms, appeared as a threat to the survival of absolutes. As soon became clear, this new reason undermined not only received certainties and traditions but eventually the axioms of rationalism as well. Left to progress without check, reason threatened to yield up a universe in which the result of ethical inquiry, as William James would put it, "could only be one of those indeterminate equations in mathematics which end with $0 = 0$," since "this is as far as the reasoning intellect by itself can go. . . ."[19] This was the "universe of death" encountered by many romantic writers and their protagonists—Goethe's Faust, Coleridge's Ancient Mariner, and Carlyle's Teufelsdröckh among them. In such a universe, choice and action were paralyzed, and literature was deprived of its moral function.

A number of social developments immensely deepened this skepticism toward reason. Industrialism intensified the separation of fact and value by institutionalizing objective thought in the form of technology, commerce, and, later, bureaucracy, administration, and social engineering. "Reason" thus became equated with amoral mechanism, with the commercial calculus of profit and the laissez-faire economy, with *means* and instrumental efficiency over ends, with a regimented, overorganized society which destroys ritual, folk customs, and the heroic dimension of life. In this kind of society, reason appears commonly as a cause of alienation rather than a potential cure: a value-free, depersonalized, finally aimless and *irrational* mode of calculation that serves the goals both of arbitrary terror and dull commercialism.

At the same time, the fragmentation of the emerging democratic and urbanized society generated an awareness of the private interests and prejudices motivating the use of reason. The recognition that thought serves "ideological" purposes gradually gave rise to the view—at first a suspicion, later a programmatic theory—that all thinking is ideological, that there is no disinterested basis on which the competing claims of different nations, classes, and individuals can be compared and judged. As shared forms of social experience disappeared, the belief in the possibility of shared experience weakened. Reason, which from one point of view was inhumanly neutral, was from another as relativistic, partial, and "human" as passion. And as the growth of class consciousness threatened the stability of established order, reason was associated with blind fanaticism, with a demented overconfidence in the ability of theory alone to reform reality. As advances in knowledge became more spectacular, society was plagued by a sense of the discrepancy between the pervasiveness of intellectual analysis and the poverty of its results, between the avidity with which knowledge was pursued and its inability to answer questions of pressing human importance. With the proliferation of scientific knowledge, men felt oppressed, rather than enlightened, by "explanations."

All these developments helped shape an outlook which sees modern history as a kind of fall from organic unity into the original sin of rationality and which thus longs to escape or "transcend" the burden of reflective consciousness. By his fall into reason, man had apparently lost the harmony of subject and object, self and nature, senses and reason, individual and society, play and work—all this for the sake of the questionable benefits of progress. As Schiller put it in a moving statement, "we see in irrational nature only a happier sister who remained in our mother's house, out of which we impetuously fled abroad in the arrogance of our freedom. With painful nostalgia we yearn to return as soon as we have begun to experience the pressure of civilization and hear in the remote lands of art our mother's tender voice. As long as we were children of nature merely, we enjoyed happiness and perfection; we became free, and lost both."[20] Schiller believed that the compensations of freedom and progress were ultimately sufficient to justify the loss, and that at any rate there could be no going back: "That nature which you envy in the irrational is worthy of no respect, no longing. It lies behind you, and must lie eternally behind you."[21] Nevertheless, he cannot help conveying the implication that the advent of rational consciousness and the critical spirit represents a great fall from grace.

One consequence of these developments was to weaken further the classical ideal of an integrated unity of man based on the hierarchical subordination of the "lower" to the "higher" faculties. Even in those German thinkers who glorified Greek culture, this hierarchical view of man, which it was natural enough to associate with tyrannical monarchy, gave way to an "organic" ideal of unity. Reason was not necessarily excluded from this organic unity, but its primacy was usurped by another faculty—sometimes called "Reason" but actually closer to imagination, myth, and fantasy, since it does not conform to "conceptual" or "theoretical" reality, but dictates its laws to reality through an autonomous human consciousness. Mere passive understanding was associated with conformity to traditional authoritarian political systems. Again, this rethinking was necessitated by the fact that understanding had been dehumanized through a kind of guilt-by-association: with soulless technology, with hierarchical social authority, with amoral political economy, with ideological fanaticism, and with a useless and oppressive machinery of explanation.

Given the circumstances, it was inevitable that the crisis of the industrial order would be diagnosed as a case of excess of reason at the expense of the inner life, or in Shelley's phrasing, "an excess of the selfish and calculating principle" and "the materials of external life" over "the power of assimilating them to the internal laws of human nature."[22] It would have to follow that the "human" goals of personal fulfillment, feeling, values, and creativity are arrived at only by overcoming objective consciousness. As Northrop Frye points out, in a statement on Shelley that reveals Frye's own guiding philosophy, "Shelley puts all the discursive disciplines into an inferior group of 'analytic' operations of reason. They are aggressive; they think of ideas as weapons; they seek the irrefutable argument, which keeps eluding them because all arguments are theses, and theses are half-truths implying their own opposites."[23] In other words, reason cannot take us beyond 0=0. Worse still, it is arrogant, aggressive, and divisive. With objective reason thus dehumanized, the autonomous creative imagination becomes the only hope for cultural salvation.

From this era dates one of the commonplaces of modern social criticism. This is the view that progress in objective knowledge and its practical applications has far outstripped progress in the moral and human sphere. Though this complaint seems correct to the point of obviousness, the way it is stated unobtrusively insinuates that moral and human concerns are fundamentally independent of the search for objective knowledge. From this it is a mere step to the idea that objective understanding of the world and human values (including the values expressed through the arts) are inimical, or that the best one can hope to do is to combine these opposing impulses in an uneasy alliance. In this alliance, objective thinking is to be controlled, directed, and humanized by a morality which is implicitly understood to be nonobjective and thus of dubious status right from the beginning. Even when romantic thinkers such as Shelley, Wordsworth, and Carlyle view science as potentially beneficial and capable of harmonizing with literature, the division of labor they adopt equates literature with the "internal," science and objectivity with the "external" phases of existence. This paves the way for the sharp separation of function that we find in so much subsequent literary and cultural criticism, and finally for the outright assault on objective reason that characterizes the recent cultural left.

The Fortunate Fall into
Esthetic Autonomy

In their very reaction against the scientific reduction of experience, the humanists conceded certain premises of science. W. H. Auden describes this underlying agreement between science and romantic humanists as follows:

> Modern science has destroyed our faith in the naïve observation of our senses: we cannot, it tells us, ever know what the physical universe is *really* like; we can only hold whatever subjective notion is appropriate to the particular human purpose we have in view.
> This destroys the traditional conception of *art* as *mimesis*, for there is no longer a nature "out there" to be truly or falsely imitated; all an artist can be *true* to are his subjective sensations and feelings. The change in attitude is already to be seen in Blake's remark that some people see the sun as a round golden disc the size of a guinea but that he sees it as a host crying Holy, Holy, Holy. What is significant about this is that Blake, like the Newtonians he hated, accepts a division between the physical and the spiritual, but, in opposition to them, regards the material universe as the abode of Satan, and so attaches no value to what his physical eye sees.[24]

As described here by Auden, Blake's position converts a seeming disaster into a victory for the spirit: the spirit has lost its basis in objective nature and reason; but this is no misfortune, since

it is better that the spirit not be "enslaved" to nature and
reason anyway. What looks at first like the alienation of literature
from its source of philosophical (and social) authority is actually a
liberation. In this fashion, the new esthetics of romanticism made
a virtue of necessity, or what was perceived as a necessity, by
construing literature's dispossession of an objective world view as
a fortunate fall into "autonomy." Humanists, from this point
on, freely and happily choose to embrace a conception of
art's station which has been forced upon them by the constraints
of the historical situation. From the perception enforced by
science that literature has no objective truth, one moves to the
conclusion that this is for the best, since objective truth is merely
factual, boring, and middle-class.

This strategy of redeeming a bad situation by redescribing it is
seen in the various theories of "disinterestedness" that arose in
eighteenth-century esthetics and were perfected by Kant in the
Critique of Judgment. For Kant the judgments of taste peculiar
to art constitute a "pure disinterested satisfaction," as opposed to
judgments that are "bound up with an interest." The judgment of
taste is "merely *contemplative*," that is, it is "indifferent as
regards the existence of an object." It is "not a cognitive
judgment (either theoretical or practical), and thus is not *based*
on concepts, nor has it concepts as its *purpose*." Art embodies
"the mere form of purposiveness" without aiming at a practical
purpose, just as art incorporates the raw material of the concepts
of the understanding without being itself conceptual.[25] It can
hardly be accidental that this insistence on separating art from
practical interests began to gain popularity at the very moment
when the concept of "interest" was losing its metaphysical
authority on the one hand, and acquiring derogatory commercial
connotations on the other. Nor can it be accidental that art began
to be defined as "purposeless" at the very moment when it was in
fact losing its traditional social purpose as a means of understanding experience. A new class was arising that did not look to
art for an explanation of things as they are and saw no useful
purpose in art. How better to answer this class (while accepting its
assumption) than to deride the concept of "useful purpose" and

to excuse art from any responsibility to it? Thus art came to be celebrated for a freedom from purpose that had been thrust upon it by default.

Over and over, we find that modern esthetic concepts come about as rationalizations of states of affairs that art had little to do with bringing about. From the perception that "poetry makes nothing happen," as Auden in our century has said,[26] we move to the imperative that poetry *ought* to make nothing happen, and finally to the axiom that it is not real poetry if it aims at practical effect. By this logical route, the alienated position of literature ceases to be an aspect of a particular historical condition and becomes part of literature's very *definition*. Of course this pose of withdrawal from practical effect continues to be highly ambiguous. In its very adoption of a "purposeless" stance, literature performs the practical purpose of combatting philistinism. The very retreat of literature into formalism constitutes an assault on the utilitarians and an attempt to counteract their social and personal influence.

Yet the conditions which had brought about the need to conceive the antidote in these terms made its success unlikely. The strategy of promoting art to the status of universal legislator rested on an implicitly defeatist acceptance of art's disinheritance from its philosophical and social authority. The high claims made for art by writers like Shelley and Kant made the attenuated social and philosophical authority of art seem like a form of power rather than of weakness. These claims rationalized art's already marginal social position. The terms in which the literary imagination was praised converted it into a sentimental compensation while imperceptibly conceding literature's loss of explanatory power. The way in which art was supposed to overcome the division between the rational or the practical and the creative— through a projection of "the internal laws of human nature"— only tended to deepen this division and to make it seem part of the very nature of things. Enemies of the fragmentation, specialization, and dissociation of modern society, the romantics themselves dissociated art from practicality and objective reason and paved the way for later theorists who would regard it as a specialized mode of discourse. These arguments reinforced the

division of labor which made "imagination" the province of the
artist and abstract thought, logic, and common sense the monopoly of other people.*

From Deification to
Demystification

Having been dispossessed of a rational world view, literature
must be conceived as an "organism" that somehow, in a fashion
infinitely described but never successfully explained by several
generations of literary theorists, "contains" its meaning imma-
nently within its concrete symbols or processes. Esthetic theory
embarks on the attempt to explain how the concrete artistic
structure can *mean* even though the structure does not rely on
the now-discredited discursive, conceptual, referential forms of
thought and expression. Though this appeal to nonconceptual
models is supposed to help heal the divisions within culture, its
actual tendency is to reinforce the isolation of art and its
withdrawal from public accessibility.

The definition of literature as a nondiscursive, nonconceptual
mode of communication has been proposed in a great variety of
forms, closed, open, and mixed. It is a continuous impulse from

*An example of this division of labor is seen in this statement by Lewis
Mumford: "Art, in the only sense in which one can separate art from
technics, is primarily the domain of the person: and the purpose of art,
apart from various incidental technical functions that may be associated
with it, is to widen the province of personality, so that feelings, emotions,
attitudes, and values, in the special individualized form in which they
happen in one particular person, in one particular culture, can be
transmitted with all their force and meaning to other persons or to other
cultures. . . . Art arises out of man's need to create for himself, beyond
any requirement for mere animal survival, a meaningful and valuable
world. . . .

"Because of their origin and purpose, the meanings of art are of a
different order from the operational meanings of science and technics:
they relate, not to external means and consequences, but to internal
transformations" (*Art and Technics* [New York: Columbia University
Press, 1952], 16-17). Mumford sees the arts as a means of reconciling
the social and psychological split between art and technics. But if one
defines art as concerned purely with "internal transformations," not
"external consequences," this reconciliation becomes improbable.

the beginnings of romanticism to the latest postmodernisms. From Coleridge and his German predecessors to recent formalists, there runs a common theory of art as a *symbol* that contains or "presents" its meanings intransitively, by contrast with discursive *signs* or concepts, which make statements "about" external states of affairs. Despite mounting attacks, the theory shows no sign of losing confidence even today. Thus a recent critic, Leonard B. Meyer, can write with assurance: "There is a profound and basic difference between scientific theories, which are *propositional*, and works of art, which are *presentational*"[27]—as if it were necessary to choose between the propositional and the presentational, as if a work of art could not be both at the same time.

The denial of the propositional nature of literature makes it difficult for literary theory to make a place—as most theorists still wish to do—for a defensible notion of artistic *significance*. Rejecting the idea that literature is propositional, the critic is forced into a dilemma: on the one hand, he tries to elaborate a description of literary meaning that does not appeal to propositions, and plunges into obscurity and mystification; on the other hand, he tries to clarify that description by bringing it into line with our familiar notions of meaning and contradicts himself, since those notions are propositional. Furthermore, every time the critic tries to speak of the meaning or "theme" or "vision" of a particular, concrete work, he can hardly help sliding into a propositional conception of literature. Despite these difficulties, the critical refusal to see literature as propositional remains strong. In the main tradition of modern esthetics—which includes such figures as Croce, Richards, Dewey, Cassirer, Langer, Eliot, Jung, Frye, Jakobson, and Ingarden—literature and art deal with experience only as myth, psychology, or language, not as an object of conceptual understanding. A number of these theorists define art as the experiential complement of understanding without its content—as does Langer in her theory of art as "virtual experience" or Eliot in his view that poetry does not assert beliefs but dramatizes "what it feels like" to have them—again as if experience and ideas "about" experience were incompatible.[28] The intention of these theorists is not to make art irrelevant to life; art in its own ways allegedly gives order and form to life. But this artistic ordering is not supposed to offer itself as understanding, and it does not solicit verification by anything external to the work or to the autonomous consciousness out of which the work arose.

It often follows that the *content* of a literary work, assuming it is even valid to attribute content to literary works, has no interest in itself but serves merely as a pretext, the "bit of nice meat," according to Eliot, that the burglar holds out to the house dog while going about his real work.[29] Consequently, the reader need "believe" only provisionally, if at all, in the truth of the picture of reality presented by the work. Behind this thesis that belief is an inappropriate frame of mind in which to approach literature is the feeling that either there are no beliefs one can legitimately risk affirming, or that the belief-affirming modes of thought and expression have been hopelessly discredited. Often these theorists claim that art is a higher form of "knowledge," but since this knowledge is not conceptual knowledge "about" the world, since it does not invite belief, its credentials are not clear. The various theories of art as nonconceptual knowledge fail to provide art with any stronger cognitive function than was provided by I. A. Richards's logical positivist theory of art as pseudo-statement.[30]

From the position that the literary symbol means no more than itself (autotelic art), it is only a step to the position that literature has *no* meaning (anti-teleological art), or that its meaning is totally indeterminate and "open" to interpretation. The theory of the nondiscursive symbol, though capable of supporting Coleridge's affirmation of literature's transcendent truth, is equally capable of supporting the bleakest, most naturalistic denial of transcendence. Consider a brief illustration. Emerson, in a famous passage in "Self-Reliance," says that "these roses under my window make no reference to former roses or to better ones; they are for what they are; they exist with God to-day. There is no time to them. There is simply the rose."[31] Emerson's rose is a Coleridgean symbol—self-sufficient, complete in itself, untranslatable, yet an embodiment of the immanence of God in nature. Though the feeling-tone of Emerson's statement is far different, the underlying logic is the same as that of the following statement by Robbe-Grillet: "the world is neither significant nor absurd. It *is* quite simply."[32] Both Emerson and Robbe-Grillet are concerned with the intransitivity of natural objects, but the analogy with artistic objects is obvious. Neither nature nor art means anything apart from itself—they simply *are*. Behind Emerson's rose there is the Over-Soul, whereas behind Robbe-Grillet's inexpressive objects there are only hysteria and paranoia—the demystified postmodern equivalent of the Over-Soul. Emerson's object is intransitive because it means everything, Robbe-Grillet's because it means nothing. But whether it is affirmatively or negatively expressed, the esthetic of self-contained meaning is symptomatic of an intellectual situation in which intelligibility is being emptied from the world, so that objects and artworks appear only in their simple presence. The logic underlying the romantic glorification of literature as an autonomous lawgiver is identical to that underlying the postmodern repudiation of literature and its pretensions to interpret life.

The theorists who have adopted these positions rarely suppose that they are draining literature of meaning or cutting it off from life. Charged with doing so, they offer disclaimers: "We are not draining literature of meaning but trying to get at the special character of that meaning; we don't mean to sever literature from life, only to redefine this extremely complex relation." Such disclaimers are largely rhetorical, however, since the critics do not make clear how it is possible to avoid the apparent implications of what they say. The fact that we do not *want* a certain implication to follow from our statements does not in itself prevent it from following. If a critic asserts that literature is an autonomous creation that is not obliged to conform to any preestablished laws, he does not disarm the charge of irresponsibility by adding, "of course I do not mean to suggest that 'anything goes' in literature and that writers are totally free to violate fundamental dictates of common sense." For one has to answer, "Why *shouldn't* anything go, if your original proposition is taken seriously?"

Having overthrown the mimetic theory of art, romantic and postromantic theories soon became the targets of the skepticism they had helped popularize. Their inability to define the cognitive function of art in any but the most equivocal terms has made earlier twentieth-century theorists vulnerable to the kind of attack from more recent critics which they themselves once levelled against traditional mimetic theory. This vulnerability emerges in current attacks on the New Criticism, a subject treated at length in my fifth chapter. With a kind of poetic justice, the New Criticism has been dethroned from its position of preeminence by arguments perfected by itself. The New Critics engaged in quixotic endeavor to defend poetic meanings by arguing that "a poem should not mean but be." In this effort they manifested the ambivalence about meaning and representation that is endemic to modern thinking about art. It demands only a moderate amount of historical sense to see that when Susan Sontag or Roland Barthes indicts the reductive nature of New Critical interpretation they revive the very charge which the New Critics had levelled against their own opponents, namely, "the heresy of paraphrase." We now see the same kind of accusation levelled against "organic" concepts of literature that the New Critical organicists levelled against mimetic concepts—the accusation of reducing the work to a determinate formula. Adepts of interpretation with a profound skepticism toward interpretation, the New Critics proposed a theory of literature that conflicted with their analytical method. While their close readings of texts called attention to the importance of meaning in literature, their theories aroused suspicion of the idea that a literary work can be said to have anything so discursive as a meaning, or that that meaning can be formulated by criticism. That the New Critics in the seventies are routinely disparaged as meaning-mongers and hyper-intellectualizers testifies to the continuing power of the skepticism they themselves helped to popularize. Here we see an example of the way the terms of the modern critical heritage inform the postmodern denigration of this heritage.

A logical evolution, then, connects the romantic and post-romantic cult of the creative self to the cult of the disintegrated, disseminated, dispersed self and of the decentered, undecidable, indeterminate text. Today's cultural battlefield is polarized between traditional humanists on one side and nihilistic "schismatics," in Frank Kermode's term, on the other.* Yet the humanists who celebrate the arts as the sovereign orderer of experience often seem nihilistic in their view of life. This nihilism is particularly overt in a critic like Northrop Frye, who praises Oscar Wilde for the view that "as life has no shape and literature has, literature is throwing away its one distinctive quality when it tries to imitate life."[33] How Frye came to know with such assurance that "life has no shape" is not clear, but if he is right one wonders what difference it should make if literature throws away its distinctive quality, or how literature—or anything—can have a distinctive quality. But those like Frye and Kermode, who defend humanism as a necessary fiction that somehow permits us to make sense of a reality known in advance to be senseless, share the same presuppositions as schismatics such as Artaud, Foucault, Derrida, Barthes, and Robbe-Grillet. The schismatics conclude, with better logic, that, if humanism is indeed a fiction, we ought to quit this pretense that it can be taken seriously.[34]

From Modern to Postmodern

If postmodern literature extends rather than overturns the premises of romanticism and modernism, we should expect this relation to be visible not only in the themes of literature but in its forms. Consider as an example the following passage from Barthelme's *Snow White*:

> "Try to be a man about whom nothing is known," our father said, when we were young. Our father said several other interesting things, but we have forgotten what they were. . . . Our father was a man about whom nothing was known. Nothing is known about him still. He gave us the recipes. He was not very interesting. A tree is more interesting. A suitcase is more interesting. A canned good is more interesting.[35]

*Frank Kermode, *The Sense of an Ending* (New York: Oxford University Press, 1965), 103. See my discussion of Kermode below, 186ff. Kermode himself seems to have become a "schismatic" in his recent writings on textual interpretation.

Barthelme here parodies Henry James's advice to the aspiring
fiction writer: "Try to be one of the people on whom nothing is
lost."[36] Barthelme inverts the assumptions about character,
psychology, and the authority of the artist upon which James, the
father of the modernist "recipe" for the novel, had depended. In
postmodern fiction, character, like external reality, is something
"about which nothing is known," lacking in plausible motive or
discoverable depth. Whereas James had stressed the importance
of artistic selection, defining the chief obligation of the novelist as
the obligation to be "interesting," Barthelme operates by a law of
equivalence according to which nothing is intrinsically more interesting than anything else.[37] Such a law destroys the determinacy of
artistic selection and elevates canned goods to equal status with
human moral choice as artistic subject matter. In place of
Jamesian dedication to the craft of fiction, Barthelme adopts an
irreverent stance toward his work, conceding the arbitrary and
artificial nature of his creation. Retracting any Jamesian claim to
deal seriously with the world, Barthelme's work offers—for
wholly different reasons—the sort of confession of the merely
"make-believe" status of fiction to which James objected in
Thackeray and Trollope. The novel's inability to transcend the
solipsism of subjectivity and language becomes the novel's chief
subject and the principle of its form.

It would seem that the Jamesian esthetic could not be stood on
its head more completely. But only a surface consideration of the
comparison can be content to leave it at that. James himself, in
both his fiction and his criticism, contributed to the skepticism
which Barthelme turns against him. T. S. Eliot wrote that Paul
Valéry was "much too sceptical to believe even in art."[38] The
remark applies, in greater or lesser degree, to all the great modernist worshippers at the shrine of high art, not excluding James.
Consider James's view of the infinite elusiveness of experience,
which is "never limited, and . . . never complete,"[39] an elusiveness
he dramatized in the interminable ambiguities of his later fiction.
James combined an intense dedication to unraveling the secrets of
motive and action with an acutely developed sense of the ultimate
impossibility of such an enterprise.

Conflicting with James's insistence on the importance of artis-

tic selection and shaping is the curiously subjectivistic justification James came to accord to this process. He frequently asserts,
in his later reflections, that the orderings of the artist cannot
derive from or be determined by the raw material of life itself. As
he observes in *The American Scene*:

> To be at all critically, or as we have been fond of calling it,
> analytically minded . . . is to be subject to the superstition that
> objects and places, coherently grouped, disposed for human use
> and addressed to it, must have a sense of their own, a mystic
> meaning proper to themselves to give out: to give out, that is, to
> the participant at once so interested and so detached as to be
> moved to a report of the matter. That perverse person is
> obliged to take it for a working theory that the essence of
> almost any settled aspect of anything may be extracted by the
> chemistry of criticism, and may give us its right name, its
> formula, for convenient use. From the moment the critic finds
> himself sighing, to save trouble in a difficult case, that the
> cluster of appearances can *have* no sense, from that moment he
> begins, and quite consciously, to go to pieces; it being the
> prime business and the high honour of the painter of life
> always to *make* a sense—and to make it most in proportion as
> the immediate aspects are loose or confused. [40]

James seems to be saying there are no objective determinants
guiding the act of "making a sense" of experience. The "mystic
meaning" of events is not in the events themselves, or controlled
by them, but in the observer. James perceives that in these
circumstances there is danger that the observer may "go to
pieces" unless he is adequate to the artist's task of fabricating his
own sense. But though James assigns "high honour" to the
fabricator and shame to the person who surrenders to confusion,
one might question his valuations. Could one not say that the
artist who saves himself by inventing fictions of order he knows to
be arbitrary is engaging in a deception of which the confused
observer is innocent? Is it less honorable to "go to pieces" in
honest confusion than to create forms of coherence whose truth is
admitted to be mythical? James rests his claims of honor for the
artistic process on the damaging admission that artistic order is
not grounded on anything outside itself.

Perceiving that the modernist's seriousness rests on admittedly
arbitrary foundations, the postmodern writer treats this seriousness as an object of parody. Whereas modernists turned to art,
defined as the imposition of human order upon inhuman chaos—
as an antidote for what Eliot called the "immense panorama of
futility and anarchy which is contemporary history"—postmod-
ernists conclude that, under such conceptions of art and history,
art provides no more consolation than any other discredited
cultural institution. Postmodernism signifies that the nightmare
of history, as modernist esthetic and philosophical traditions have
defined history, has overtaken modernism itself.[41] If history lacks
value, pattern, and rationally intelligible meaning, then no
exertions of the shaping, ordering imagination can be anything
but a refuge from truth. Alienation from significant external
reality, from *all* reality, becomes an inescapable condition.

The Two Postmodernisms

In carrying the logic of modernism to its extreme limits, postmodern literature poses in an especially acute fashion the critical
problem raised by all experimental art: does this art represent
a criticism of the distorted aspects of modern life or a mere
addition to it? Georg Lukács has argued persuasively that the
successful presentation of distortion as such presupposes the
existence of an undistorted norm. "Literature," he writes, "must
have a concept of the normal if it is to 'place' distortion correctly,
that is to say, to see it *as* distortion."[42] If life were really a
solipsistic madness, we should have no means of knowing this fact
or representing it. But once the concept of the normal is rejected
as a vestige of an outmoded metaphysics or patronized as a myth,
the concepts of "distortion" and "madness" lose their meanings.
This observation provides a basis for some necessary distinctions
between tendencies in postmodern writing.

In Jorge Luis Borges's stories, for example, techniques of
reflexiveness and self-parody suggest a universe in which human
consciousness is incapable of transcending its own mythologies.
This condition of imprisonment, however, though seen from the
"inside," is presented from a tragic or tragicomic point of view

that forces us to see it *as* a problem. The stories generate a pathos at the absence of a transcendent order of meanings. As Borges's narrator in "The Library of Babel" declares, "Let heaven exist, though my place be in hell. Let me be outraged and annihilated, but for one instant, in one being, let Your enormous Library be justified."[43] The library contains all possible books and all possible interpretations of experience but none which can claim authority over the others; therefore, it cannot be "justified." Nevertheless, Borges affirms the indispensable nature of justification. As in such earlier writers as Kafka and Céline, the memory of a significant external reality that would justify human experience persists in the writer's consciousness and serves as his measure of the distorted, indeterminate world he depicts. Borges's kind of postmodern writing, even in presenting solipsistic distortion as the only possible perspective, nevertheless presents this distortion *as* distortion—that is, it implicitly affirms a concept of the normal, if only as a concept which has been tragically lost. The comic force of characters like "Funes the Memorious" and of solipsistic worlds such as those of "Tlön, Uqbar, Orbis Tertius" lies in the crucial fact that Borges, for all his imaginative sympathy, is *not* Funes, is not an inhabitant of Tlön, and is thus able to view the unreality of their worlds as a predicament. His work retains a link with traditional classical humanism by virtue of its sense of the pathos of this humanism's demise. The critical power of absence remains intact, giving Borges a perspective for judging the unreality of the present. His work affirms the sense of reality in a negative way by dramatizing its absence as a deprivation.

Whatever tendency toward subjectivism these Borges works may contain is further counteracted by their ability to suggest the historical and social causes of this loss of objective reality. Borges invites us to see the solipsistic plight of his characters as a consequence of the relativistic thrust of modern philosophy and modern politics. If reality has yielded to the myth-making of Tlön, as he suggests it has, "the truth is that it longed to yield." The mythologies of "dialectical materialism, anti-Semitism, Nazism" were sufficient "to entrance the minds of men."[44] The loss of reality is made intelligible to the reader as an aspect of a social and historical evolution. At its best, the contemporary wave of self-reflexive fiction is not quite so totally self-reflexive as it is taken to be, since its very reflexivity implies a "realistic" comment on the historical crisis which brought it about. Where such a comment is made, the conventions of anti-realism subserve a higher realism. Often, however, this fiction fails to make its reflexivity intelligible as a consequence of any recognizable cause. Estrangement from reality and meaning becomes detached from the consciousness of its causes—as in the more tediously claustrophobic and mannered experiments of Barthelme and the later Barth.[45] Even in these works, however, the loss of reality and meaning is seen as a distortion of the human condition.

Far different is the attitude expressed in the more celebratory forms of postmodernism. Here there is scarcely any memory of an objective order of values in the past and no regret over its disappearance in the present. Concepts like "significant external reality" and "the human condition" figure only as symbols of the arbitrary authority and predetermination of a repressive past, and their disappearance is viewed as liberation. Dissolution of ego boundaries, seen in tragic postmodern works like *Invitation to a Beheading* as a terrifying disintegration of identity, is viewed as a bracing form of consciousness-expansion and a prelude to growth. Both art and the world, according to Susan Sontag, simply *are*. "Both need no justification; nor could they possibly have any."[46] The obsessive quest for justification which characterizes Borges's protagonists is thus regarded, if it is noticed at all, as a mere survival of outmoded thinking.

It is symptomatic of the critical climate that Borges has been widely read as a celebrant of apocalyptic unreality. Borges's current celebrity is predicated to a large degree on a view that sees him as a pure fabulator revelling in the happy indistinguishability of truth and fiction. Richard Poirier, for example, urges us in reading Borges to get rid of "irrelevant distinctions between art and life, fiction and reality."[47] But if distinctions between fiction and reality were really irrelevant, Borges's work would be pointless.

But then, in a world which simply *is*, pointlessness is truth. There is no ground for posing the question of justification as a question. We can no longer even speak of "alienation" or "loss" of perspective, for there never was anything to be alienated from, never any normative perspective to be lost. The realistic perspective that gives shape and point to works of tragicomic postmodernism, permitting them to present distortion *as* distortion, gives way to a celebration of *energy*—the vitalism of a world that cannot be understood or controlled. We find this celebration of energy in the poetry of the Beats, the "Projective" poets, and other poetic continuators of the nativist line of Whitman, Williams, and Pound, in the short-lived vogue of the Living Theater, happenings, and pop art, and in a variety of artistic and musical experiments with randomness and dissonance. It is also an aspect of the writing of Mailer, Burroughs, and Pynchon, where despite the suggestion of a critical or satiric point of view, the style expresses a facile excitement with the dynamisms of technological process.[48] Richard Poirier states the rationale for this worship of energy, making energy and literature synonymous: "Writing is a form of energy not accountable to the orderings anyone makes of it and specifically not accountable to the liberal humanitarian values most readers want to find there."[49] Literature, in short, is closer to a physical force than to an understanding or "criticism of life," both of which are tame and bourgeois. This celebration of energy frequently seems to hover somewhere between revolutionary politics and sophisticated acquiescence to the agreeably meaningless surfaces of mass culture.

The acquiescence seems to have the upper hand over the politics in the esthetics of John Cage. Susan Sontag says that "Cage proposes for our experience a world in which it's never preferable to do other than we are doing or be elsewhere than we are. 'It is only irritating,' he says, 'to think one would like to be somewhere else. Here we are now.' "* Cage, she writes, "envisages a totally democratic world of the spirit, a world of 'natural

*Sontag, *Styles of Radical Will* (New York: Delta Books, 1969), 94. Sontag seems recently to have recanted these enthusiasms. In *On Photography,* she attacks photography because of its tendency "to rule out a historical understanding of reality" (New York: Farrar, Straus and

activity' in which 'it is understood that everything is clean: there is
no dirt.' . . . Cage proposes the perennial possibility of errorless
behavior, if only we will allow it to be so. 'Error is a fiction, has no
reality in fact.'"[50] Elsewhere Cage puts it this way: "We are
intimate in advance with whatever will happen."[51] Both nostalgia
and hope are impossible because history has disappeared, replaced by an immanent present which is always, at every changing moment, the best of possible worlds. We are "intimate" with
this present, not because it has any meaning or potential direction, but precisely because it is so pointless that to *expect* any
meaning or direction would be out of the question. If one feels
estrangement in contemplating this pointless world, it is because
one has not yet abandoned the anthropocentric expectations
that are the real source of our problem.

   Alienation is thus "overcome" by the strategy of redescribing it
as the normal state of affairs and then enjoying its gratifications.
Political intransigence, from this point of view, is but a symptom
of inadequate adjustment—the inability to get beyond old-
fashioned alienation and immerse oneself in the unitary stream of
things. Calvin Tomkins, admiring Robert Rauschenberg for his
"cheerful and nearly total acceptance" of the materials of urban
life, quotes the artist as follows: "I really feel sorry for people who
think things like soap dishes or mirrors or Coke bottles are ugly,
because they're surrounded by things like that all day long, and it
must make them miserable."[52] What is interesting in Rauschenberg's statement is the way it endows urban commercial ugliness
with the permanence and unchangeability of nature—one might
as soon do something about it as do something about rain or wind.
Whatever one may think about the urban anti-culture, the thing
is *real* and is not going to go away because a few intellectuals
happen not to like it, so therefore one had better learn to love it.
One does not try to change the world but rather alters one's
perspective (or "consciousness") so as to *see* the world in a new
way.

Giroux, 1977, 33). In her earlier work, Sontag tended to see things like
"historical understanding of reality" as poor substitutes for immediate
experience.

The Normalization of
Alienation

The assumption that alienation is the normal and unalterable
condition of human beings has gained strength from structuralist
theories of language described in my introduction: since meaning
arises wholly from the play of differences within artificial sign
systems, it follows that meanings are arbitrary and that everything we say in language is a fiction. Sometimes this assertion
that everything is a fiction immunizes itself from criticism by
claiming *itself* to be no more than a fiction. Thus Sontag tells us
that "one can't object" to Roland Barthes's exposition of structuralist ideas "simply because its leading concepts are intellectual
myths or fictions."[53] Robert Scholes summarizes this poststructuralist outlook as follows:

> Once we knew that fiction was about life and criticism was
> about fiction—and everything was simple. Now we know that
> fiction is about other fiction, is criticism in fact, or metafiction.
> And we know that criticism is about the impossibility of
> anything being about life, really, or even about fiction, or,
> finally, about anything. Criticism has taken the very idea of
> "aboutness" away from us. It has taught us that language
> is tautological, if it is not nonsense, and to the extent that it is
> about anything it is about itself. Mathematics is about mathe-
> matics, poetry is about poetry and criticism is about the
> impossibility of its own existence.[54]

The doctrine is particularly widespread in discussions of recent
fiction. Raymond Federman, a theorist of "surfiction," informs
us that the authentic fiction writers of our day "believe that
reality as such does not exist, or rather exists only in its
fictionalized version."[55] As William Gass puts it, "the novelist, if
he is any good, will keep us kindly imprisoned in his language—
there is literally nothing beyond."[56]

No doubt structuralism, properly understood, is only a method
of analysis and need not carry the dismal ontological conclusions
which such critics have derived from it. But one of its exponents,
Perry Meisel, after reassuring us that "structuralism is a method,
not a program or an ideology," goes on to say that "structuralism

realizes that alienation is the timeless and normative condition of humanity rather than its special modern affliction."[57] For, according to Meisel, "semiotics is in a position to claim that no phenomenon has any ontological status outside its place in the particular information system(s) from which it draws its meaning(s)." From the proposition, unexceptionable in itself, that no signifier can mean anything apart from the code or sign system which gives it significance, one infers the conclusion that no signifier can *refer* to a nonlinguistic reality—that, as Meisel puts it, "all language is finally groundless." There is, then, no such thing as a "real" object outside language, no "nature" or "real life" outside the literary text, no real text behind the critical interpretation, and no real persons or institutions behind the multiplicity of messages human beings produce. Everything is swallowed up in an infinite regress of textuality.

Meisel does not hesitate to draw the social moral of all this: "the only assumption possible in a post-Watergate era," he writes, is "that the artifice is the only reality available."[58] Since artifice is the only reality, the old-fashioned distinctions between "intrinsic" and "extrinsic," literature and life, are abolished. Literature and life are thus reconciled, but only by the strategy of enclosing "life" itself in an autonomous process of textuality which cannot refer beyond its structuring activity. The gulf imposed by romantic esthetics between literary and practical discourse is closed, not by ascribing objective truth to literature, but by withdrawing it from all discourse. Fact and value are reconciled by converting fact along with value into fiction. These reconciliations are dictated not only by philosophical and linguistic theory but by "the post-Watergate era." One wonders whether the moral of the Watergate episode might not actually be that some degree of penetration of artifice, some detection of the hidden facts *is* after all possible. But structuralist skepticism does not wait to be questioned on such points. Its method of demythologizing thinking ends up teaching that no escape from myth-making is possible.[59]

The position of structuralism and poststructuralism, however, on the postmodern spectrum of attitudes is equivocal. On the one hand there is Derrida's influential invocation of "the joyful

Nietzschean affirmation of the play of the world and the innocence of becoming, the affirmation of a world of signs which has
no truth, no origin, no nostalgic guilt, and is proffered for active
interpretation."[60] On the other hand, there is the insistence on
the *risk* involved in the enterprise of doing without a truth and an
origin as anchoring points outside the infinite play of linguistic
differences. As Derrida puts it, "*this affirmation then determines
the non-center otherwise than as a loss of the center. And it plays
the game without security.*"[61] As he does often, Derrida here
seems to be echoing Nietzsche, who stated that "the genuine phi-
losopher. . .risks *himself* constantly. He plays the dangerous
game."[62] However, neither the joy nor the risk invoked by this
view seems fully convincing. The joy of affirmation is a diluted joy,
since it comes about as a consequence of the absence of any
reality or meaning in life to which effort might be directed. And
the element of risk in the "dangerous game" becomes minimal
when (a) relativistic philosophy has eroded the concept of error,
and (b) the culture of pluralism and publicity has endowed
deviation and eccentricity with "charisma."

The postmodern temper has carried the skepticism and anti-
realism of modern literary culture to an extreme beyond which it
would be difficult to go. Though it looks back mockingly on the
modernist tradition and professes to have got beyond it, postmodern literature remains tied to that tradition and unable to
break with it. The very concepts through which modernism is
demystified derive from modernism itself. The loss of significant
external reality, its displacement by myth-making, the domes-
tication and normalization of alienation—these conditions constitute a common point of departure for the writing of our period.
Though for some of this writing they remain conditions to be
somehow resisted, a great deal of it finds them an occasion for
acquiescence and even celebration. Unable to imagine an alternative to a world that has for so long seemed unreal, we have begun
to resign ourselves to this kind of world and to learn how to
redescribe this resignation as a form of heroism. And for some
observers, to whom I turn in the next chapter, this loss of a reality
principle is not a loss at all but a condition of political revolution.

Three

The Politics of
Anti-Realism

As the political radicalism of the sixties has waned, cultural radicalism has grown proportionately in influence. "Cultural radicalism" and "cultural revolution" are vague terms, of course. They denote no particular school of thought but rather a style of thinking, a pattern of typical oppositions and identifications whose rationale is often unformulated. This style of thinking can be found in structuralists and poststructuralists, phenomenologists, post-Freudians and Jungians, existential and Hegelian Marxists, and innumerable other manifestations of the vanguard spirit in art, criticism, and social thought. More broadly still, the patterns of radical cultural thought have become part of the folk mythology of intellectuals as a group—and of those whose outlook is shaped by intellectuals. The names and the movements come and go, but the structures of thought persist. Anybody today who endeavors to think politically advanced thoughts about culture and society is likely to do so using at least some of the patterns I try to describe in this chapter.

Radical Parallelisms

The central premise of cultural radicalism is that there exists a parallel or correspondence between psychological, epistemological, esthetic, and political categories of experience. Repression in psychology, objectivism in epistemology, representationalism and the elitism of high culture in esthetics are parallel expressions of bourgeois social domination. A statement by Joyce Carol Oates, in an essay entitled "New Heaven and Earth," illustrates the neatness of alignment sometimes attained by this parallelism:

> We have come to the end of, we are satiated with, the "objective," valueless philosophies that have always worked to pre-

> serve a status quo, however archaic. We are tired of the old
> dichotomies: Sane/Insane, Normal/Sick, Black/White, Man/
> Nature, Victor/Vanquished, and—above all this Cartesian
> dualism I/It. . . . They are no longer useful or pragmatic.
> They are no longer *true.*[1]

Political domination is the correlative both of the epistemological
separation of the knower from his object and the psychological or
medical differentiation of sanity from insanity. Objective thought
is the psychological and epistemological counterpart of political
tyranny. This is true in several ways: objective thought requires us
to repress our emotions, to take a "valueless" stance in the
interests of operational efficiency. This "reification" destroys the
unity between ourselves and what we perceive and turns the
"other" into an alien thing, ripe for domination and manipulation. In a parallel fashion, Western civilization turns both nature
and human beings into manipulable things through technological
mastery on the one hand and colonialism and exploitation on the
other. Then too, by taking for granted the existence of a stable
world "out there," objective thought presupposes a reality that is
essentially unchangeable. By acknowledging the reality principle,
we reconcile ourselves to the established order as if it were an
eternal law of nature. Thus Roland Barthes can assert that the
"disease of thinking in essences. . .is at the bottom of every
bourgeois mythology of man."[2]

Far from representing the culmination of man's struggle
against ignorance and superstition, then, objective thought
emerges as at best a means of bringing about the expanded
material basis on which the nonaggressive society of the future
will rest, a stage in the evolution of consciousness toward a
reunified sensibility. At worst, it does not even have this justification. Susan Sontag cites "the damage that Western 'Faustian
man,' with his idealism, his magnificent art, his sense of intellectual adventure, his world-devouring energies for conquest,
has already done, and further threatens to do."[3] And Theodore
Roszak writes that "objective consciousness is emphatically *not*
some manner of definitive, transcultural development whose
cogency derives from the fact that it is uniquely in touch with the
truth. Rather, like a mythology, it is an arbitrary construct in

which a given society in a given historical situation has invested its
sense of meaningfulness and value."[4] As Richard Gilman puts it,

> The old Mediterranean values—the belief in the sanctity of the
> individual soul, the importance of logical clarity, brotherhood,
> reason as arbiter, political order, community—are dead as
> *useful* frames of reference or pertinent guides to procedure;
> they are even making some of us sick with a sense of lacerating
> irony.[5]

The counterculture may have departed, but these doctrines
remain in force.*

The cultural revolution is conceived as a revolt against the
reality principle in the name of the pleasure principle, as the
overcoming of repressive reason by imagination—or by a new
"reason" based on eros, fantasy, nonaggressive desire. The
struggle, as Herbert Marcuse defines it, is "between the logic of
domination and the will to gratification. Both assert their claims
for defining the reality principle. The traditional ontology is
contested: against the conception of being in terms of Logos rises
the conception of being in a-logical terms: will and joy. This
countertrend struggles to formulate its own Logos: the logic of
gratification."[6] By undermining the epistemological and instinc-
tual bases of domination, this logic of gratification prepares the
way for the political transformation of society, though the precise
nature of this transformation may as yet be only vaguely fore-
seeable. At present, it may only be possible to say, with Richard

---

*". . .for many 1960s radicals. . .the sentimental reasoning behind this
self-exculpation went something like this: White Americans and Western
Europeans, from whom I am descended, have imposed their will on other
peoples in terrible ways. What they have done to others is analogous to
what they have done to their own instincts, justifying such oppression
and repression by appeals to reason and law. It is the ego that has done
this; away with it, therefore, and with reason and law, which are its
instruments. If I side with the instincts and the unconscious, I declass
myself, and my guilt falls away. In such a view, all culture, all social and
political institutions, and all attempts to govern human affairs according
to reason are nothing but shams, designed to aid the despotic ego in its
work of repression. This caricature of New Left thinking has survived
into the 1970s" (Paul Breslin, "How to Read the New Contemporary
Poem," *American Scholar,* 47, no. 4 [Summer 1978], 365-66).

Poirier, that any political solutions "will require a radical change in the historical, philosophical, and psychological assumptions that are the foundations of any political or economic system. Some kind of cultural revolution is therefore the necessary prelude even to our capacity to think intelligently about political reformation."[7]

Art plays a key role in the social vision of the cultural revolution, but not as propaganda art or as socialist realism. For though realistic art may be radical in content, its formal modes of perception are conventional and reactionary. Radical reform requires the shattering of the realist form of sensibility. Art, defined as Kant defined it as an autonomous expression of the imagination, not passively receiving its laws from nature but freely dictating them to nature, is thus the epitome of liberated sensibility. The romantic opposition between discursive and creative meaning, between language used as a practical or referential *sign* and language used as a constitutive *symbol*, corresponds to the distinction between tyranny and liberation. The imagination's independence of preestablished reality exemplifies the human spirit's break with entrenched political oppression and psychic repression. By refusing to hold a mirror up to nature, by exploding the very idea of a stable "nature," art strikes at the psychological and epistemological bases of the ruling order. This revolt against realism and representation is closely tied to a revolt against a unitary psychology of the self. As Leo Bersani argues, "the literary myth of a rigidly ordered self," a myth perpetuated by realism, "contributes to a pervasive cultural ideology of the self which serves the established order."[8]

Radical art shatters not only the unity of the self but also the linguistic "contracts" which certify orthodox social assumptions and reassure us that reality is safely known and catalogued. Alain Robbe-Grillet says that "academic criticism in the West, as in the Communist countries, employs the word 'realism' as if reality were already entirely constituted (whether for good and all, or not) when the writer comes on the scene. Thus it supposes that the latter's role is limited to 'explaining' and to 'expressing' the reality of his period."[9] In a similar vein, Roland Barthes disparages the conventions of narrative fiction as part of "a security

system for Belles-Lettres," as "formal pacts made between the
writer and society for the justification of the former and the
serenity of the latter."[10] "Classical language," says Barthes, "is a
bringer of euphoria because it is immediately social."[11] Applying
a kind of literary economics, Barthes holds that the classical,
mimetic model of writing presupposes a world packaged, as it
were, for the convenience of the consumer, known and agreed
upon in advance. Literature "remains the currency in use in a
society apprised, by the very form of words, of the meaning of
what it consumes."* Preestablished codes imply a myth of preestablished reality and order, and "the content of the word
'Order' always indicates repression."[12]
    The move beyond the mimetic view of literature entails a move
beyond the mimetic view of criticism. Just as literature ought to
explode the bourgeois myth of a stable reality independent of
human fantasy, so criticism ought to explode the professional
academic myths of "the work itself," the "intention" of the
author, and the determinate nature of textual meaning. The
theory that literature "defamiliarizes" our perception of reality
generates the corollary that criticism ought to defamiliarize our

*Roland Barthes, *Writing Degree Zero*, trans. A. Lavers (New York: Hill
and Wang, 1953), 32. Barthes's portrait was best drawn in 1925 by André
Gide, in his characterization of the literary terrorist Strouvilhou, who
outlines his program as follows: " 'To tell the truth, my dear count, I
must own that of all nauseating human emanations, literature is one of
those which disgust me the most. I can see nothing in it but compromise
and flattery. And I go so far as to doubt whether it can be anything else—
at any rate until it has made a clean sweep of the past. We live upon
nothing but feelings which have been taken for granted once and for all
and which the reader imagines he experiences, because he believes
everything he sees in print; the author builds on this as he does on the
conventions which he believes to be the foundations of his art. These
feelings ring as false as counters, but they pass current. And as everyone
knows that "bad money drives out good," a man who should offer the
public real coins would seem to be defrauding us. In a world in which
everyone cheats, it's the honest man who passes for a charlatan. I give you
fair warning—if I edit a review, it will be in order to prick bladders—in
order to demonetize fine feelings, and those promissory notes which go
by the name of *words*' " (*The Counterfeiters*, trans. Dorothy Bussy [New
York: Vintage Books, 1973], 331–32). Unlike Barthes, Strouvilhou com-
bines the literary brand of counterfeiting with the real thing.

perception of literature, smashing our static, canonical interpretations. These moves beyond realism and beyond objective interpretation are paralleled in turn by a third impulse, which seeks to go beyond elitist hierarchies of high and low culture. These impulses may not coexist in all radical esthetic theories, but they form a logical unity. I propose to examine them in turn.

Beyond Realism

One of the more systematic attempts at an anti-realistic theory of radical esthetics has been made by Herbert Marcuse, whom I shall treat at some length here. Unlike Barthes, Marcuse resists equating "classical language" and classical form with bourgeois domination; he attacks Herbert Read and other avant-garde irrationalists for assuming that "classicism is the intellectual counterpart of political tyranny." Bourgeois art, including bourgeois realism, according to Marcuse, "transcends all particular class content...."[13] Even in expressing specifically bourgeois concerns, this art achieves a "universal meaning" that may be liberating for all classes.[14] Agreeing with Trotsky's strictures against an exclusively proletarian culture, Marcuse holds that the cultural revolution should not repudiate bourgeois culture but should try to "recapture and transform" its "critical, negating, transcending qualities."[15] Marcuse's own esthetic theory exemplifies this *Aufhebung*: it draws on concepts from Kant, Schiller, and Freud while overcoming their bourgeois limitations.

There is, then, a "classical" element in Marcuse's theory which distinguishes it from that of Barthes. But Marcuse defends classicism only by translating it into anti-representational terms, opposing art to classical rationality and to anything resembling mimesis. As thoroughly as any romantic theorist, Marcuse identifies art with the pleasure principle and denies its dependence on the reality principle. Following Kant and Schiller, Marcuse defines art as a "non-conceptual truth of the senses."[16] Though art may *use* concepts as part of its raw material, it is not answerable to theoretical criteria of truth. Marcuse thus rejects Lukács's praise of bourgeois critical realism for depicting "the

basic laws which govern capitalist society." This requirement, he
says, "offends the very nature of art." For "the basic structure
and dynamic of society can never find sensuous, esthetic expression: they are, in Marxian theory, the essence behind the
appearance, which can only be attained through scientific
analysis, and formulated only in the terms of such an analysis.
The 'open form' cannot close the gap between the scientific truth
and its esthetic appearance."[17] Such a passage suggests how
ambivalent Marcuse can be with respect to classical rationality,
how he hovers on the edge of romantic irrationalism without ever
quite taking the plunge. On the one hand, he calls for a new
"conception of being in a-logical terms: will and joy," a "logic of
gratification," a revolt of Eros against the reality principle. On
the other hand, he does not reject Marxist "scientific analysis."
The important point is that though Marcuse does not wholly deny
the possibility or desirability of an objectivist or realistic epistemology, he distinguishes this epistemology from that of art,
contrasting art with science in the fashion of many romantics.
For the creative imagination, he says, summarizing Kant, "the
experience in which the object is thus 'given' is totally different
from the everyday as well as scientific experience; all links
between the object and the world of theoretical and practical
reason are severed, or rather suspended."[18] Presumably, these
oppositions between the esthetic and the theoretical and practical
realms are "transcended" by the work of art itself, or by the
revolutionary realization of artistic vision in the society of the
future. But art remains for Marcuse a nonconceptual mode of
experience. It does not reflect reality.

A similar, though more equivocal, rejection of realism characterizes much of the current revival of Marxist criticism.
Commenting on the disparity between postmodern cultural revolutionaries and Marxism, Leslie Fiedler observes that "the
Marxists are last-ditch defenders of rationality and the primacy
of political fact, intrinsically hostile to an age of myth and
passion, sentimentality and fantasy."[19] Neo-Marxist criticism,
however, seems to have taken steps to remedy this deficiency in
Marxism. Siding with Brecht over Lukács, and often overlooking
the realistic leanings of Brecht, the new Marxism favors the kind

of analogical reasoning—long common in bourgeois avant-garde
circles—which regards "open" forms as progressive, "closed"
ones as reactionary. Thus Terry Eagleton, in *Criticism and Ideology*, opposes "Lukács' nostalgic organicism, his traditionalist
preference for closed, symmetrical totalities," to "open, multiple
forms which bear in their torsions the very imprint of the
contradictions they lay bare."[20] But how can open, multiple
forms "lay bare" contradictions when they are, so often, themselves expressions of a viewpoint distorted by alienation? Where
does literature get the perspective that permits it to present
distortion *as* distortion? How does it make itself a criticism of
ideological contradictions rather than a symptom of them?

In another book, *Marxism and Literary Criticism*, Eagleton
hedges on these questions. He says that art can "yield us a kind of
truth," but this truth is "not, to be sure, a scientific or theoretical
truth, but the truth of how men experience their conditions of life
and of how they protest against them."[21] A footnote attempts to
clarify this point: "Though art is not in itself a scientific mode of
truth, it can, nevertheless, communicate the *experience* of such a
scientific (i.e., revolutionary) understanding of society. This is the
experience which *revolutionary* art can yield us."[22] This sounds
rather like a left-wing version of Susanne Langer's theory that art
yields a "virtual experience" of understanding without the
content of understanding, or like T. S. Eliot's view that poetry
does not solicit beliefs but shows us "what it feels like" to have
beliefs. Like earlier critics in the formalist tradition, Eagleton is
forced into contortions by his refusal to grant a theoretical truth
to art: the problem is to explain how art can provide the
experiential complement of an understanding of reality without
actually *saying* anything about reality. The separation between
the conceptual and the experiential, so familiar in bourgeois
esthetic theory, is not overcome.

Or is it? Eagleton does suggest that art somehow communicates
a critical perspective toward ideology:

> Science gives us conceptual knowledge of a situation; art gives
> us the experience of that situation, which is equivalent to
> ideology. But by doing this, it allows us to "see" the nature

of that ideology, and thus begins to move us towards that full
understanding of ideology which is scientific knowledge. *

But it is not clear how a work of art lets us "see" the nature of an
ideology (and why the quotation marks?) without communicating
a conceptual apprehension of the ideology. Either the audience
perceives the ideology *as* an ideology, in which case it con-
ceptualizes it, or it does not see the ideology at all. Here again we
find the theorist trying to ascribe a critical function to art but not
quite succeeding because he commits the formalist renunciation of "conceptual knowledge" to science.

The same equivocations over mimesis and over the propositional function of art can be found in other current Hegelian and
existential Marxists, but I cannot dwell on their theories here.
One appreciates the determination of the neo-Marxists to avoid
the crudities of vulgar Stalinist realism with its dismissal of
modernist experimental forms.† But in their sympathy with the
anti-realistic premises of modernism, the neo-Marxists may have
abandoned the critical standpoint which makes Marxism a
corrective to conventional modernist literary positions. Marcuse
avoids these vacillations by unequivocally denying the realistic
and theoretical nature of art. But Marcuse, too, has problems
when he attempts to account for the subversive power of art.

Marcuse says this subversive power resides not in the content of
art but in its form. It is art's freedom from conceptual reality, in

*Terry Eagleton, *Marxism and Literary Criticism* (Berkeley: University
of California Press, 1976), 18. Drawing on the theories of Pierre Mach-
erey, Eagleton says "it is by giving ideology a determinate form, fixing it
within certain fictional limits, that art is able to distance itself from it,
thus revealing to us the limits of that ideology" (19). Why the act of
fictionalization should induce a critical view of ideology rather than a
further degree of mystification is not made clear.

†See, for example, Fredric Jameson's treatment of the question of realism
in *Marxism and Form: Twentieth Century Dialectical Theories of Literature* (Princeton: Princeton University Press, 1971). Jameson tends
to equate realism with "positivism" and "empiricism," to which he
counterposes the Marxian dialectical position (see particularly, 359–
416). How Jameson's dialectical position resolves the idealist-realist
opposition eludes me.

fact, its ability to create out of the autonomy of the imagination that "other nature" which, as Kant theorized, supplies a "completeness of which there is no example in nature," that makes art a criticism of the existing order.[23] By freely projecting new possibilities of desire that have never been embodied in the actual world, art gives us a measure of the unsatisfactory reality around us. In this sense, *all* art for Marcuse is formalistic art—even realism. For though the world of a work of art may, as he says, be "derived from the existing one," it transforms this raw material according to the esthetic laws of art and the psychological laws of the mind.[24] In other words, though a work of art may employ "realistic" conventions, it cannot serve a realistic ontology. "The norms governing the order of art are not those governing reality but rather norms of its *negation*."[25] This negation is implicit in the form and style of art as such. Marcuse connects Kant's idea of the imagination and Schiller's idea of art as play with the Freudian concepts of the pleasure principle, Eros, and "the return of the repressed."[26]

Art then, regardless of its specific content, evokes "the power of the negative." Its very structure evokes "the words, the images, the music of another reality, of another order repelled by the existing one and yet alive in memory and anticipation."[27] One implication of this view is that even the artist who sets out to write an apology for the existing order may actually end up subverting it—indeed, if he is a true artist he cannot help doing so. Thus, like earlier Marxist critics, Marcuse provides a theoretical defense for art created from a consciously reactionary point of view, but his strategy is different. When Marx, Engels, and Lukács praised the novels of Balzac as "progressive" despite their overtly legitimist message, they did so on the grounds that Balzac's presentational realism contradicted that message. Despite his conscious intentions to the contrary, Balzac was too good a realist not to give a true picture of the direction in which history was moving. Marcuse, by contrast, finds explicitly reactionary art progressive not because it reveals the real world but because it negates it. Even an artistic idealization of the existing order will, by virtue of its presentation of an esthetic world, stand as an implicit critique.

   Though Marcuse attributes subversive effects to all forms
of art, he at the same time argues that the purely esthetic
nature of artistic negation limits and often neutralizes these
effects: "the critical function of art is self-defeating. The
very commitment of art to form vitiates the negation of unfreedom in art." In order to be negated, Marcuse says, unfreedom has to be represented "with the semblance of reality,"
yet this "element of semblance necessarily subjects the represented reality to aesthetic standards and thus deprives it of its
terror."[28] This explains why societies have often been able to
domesticate radical art and render its rebellion harmless. There is
a dialectic, then, between the negations of art and the negation of
these negations by the society which assimilates them. Marcuse's
esthetic writings are studded with warnings against overestimat-
ing the power of art *by itself* to precipitate a revolution. Nevertheless, despite these cautions, Marcuse does not cease affirming
that art embodies the very spirit of human liberation. And in his
Essay on Liberation, a manifesto of the late sixties, Marcuse
judges that the "disorderly, uncivil, farcical, artistic desublimation of culture constitutes an essential element of radical politics:
of the subverting forces in transition."[29]
   In the esthetic of the cultural left, one of the chief means by
which art presumably exercises a subversive political effect is by
shattering familiar modes of perception. This esthetic of "defamiliarization," to use a term of the Russian formalists,[30] has its
roots in the romantic idea that art strips away the veil of
customary perception and permits us to see the world in a new
light. At first sight, this doctrine appears anti-formalistic, and
indeed a version of it was espoused by nineteenth-century realists,
who saw themselves as unmasking conventional false appearances
and official moralities. But the concept of defamiliarization may
be put to formalist or anti-realist uses. Defamiliarization may
mean exploding *all* perceptual categories, including those inevitably left intact by the most uncompromising realism. This
formalist strategy attempts to defamiliarize not in order to expose
some truer reality behind the veil of customary perception but in
order to dislodge from us the expectation that we can ever locate
such a reality at all. It is by means of this radical concept of

perpetual esthetic defamiliarization that Marcuse is able to
combine two modes that are usually opposed—Kantian formalism and surrealism.

Marcuse writes of "surrealistic forms of protest and refusal" as
the needed solvent of "repressive reason" in one-dimensional
society.[31] He celebrates the verbal disruptions of experimental
literature, which break the oppressive rule of the established
language and images over the mind of man. He stresses that art
dissolves the film of familiarity and cliché which, in advanced
society, intercedes between reality and our perceptions:

> Non-objective, abstract painting and sculpture, stream-of-
> consciousness and formalist literature, twelve-tone composi-
> tion, blues and jazz: these are not merely new modes of
> perception reorienting and intensifying the old ones, they
> rather dissolve the very structure of perception in order to make
> room—for what? The new object of art is not yet "given," but
> the familiar object has become impossible, false. From illusion,
> imitation, harmony to reality—but the reality is not yet "given";
> it is not the one which is the object of "realism." Reality has
> to be discovered and projected. The senses must learn not to
> see things anymore in the medium of that law and order which
> has formed them; the bad functionalism which organizes our
> sensibility must be smashed.[32]

Art in this way brings into being a "new sensorium." In the
universe of art, Marcuse says, "every word, every color, every
sound is 'new,' different—breaking the familiar context of perception and understanding, of sense certainty and reason in
which men and nature are enclosed."[33]

It is only a short step from these concepts of radical perceptual
disruption, defamiliarization, and "making strange" to the
esthetic theories advanced in defense of self-reflexive fiction,
science fiction, and other current fantasy genres. The radical
credentials of fantasy have never before been so widely respected.
David Ketterer writes of the "radical disorientation" produced in
the reader by science fiction conventions, and Darko Suvin calls
this effect one of "cognitive estrangement."[34] Might not the effect
of radical disorientation and cognitive estrangement be to confuse
or disarm critical intelligence rather than to focus it? The

question is never asked. The epistemology of science fiction, according to Ketterer, tends to "destroy old assumptions and suggest a new, and often more visionary reality."[35] A similar view is advanced by Robert Scholes. Science fiction, says Scholes, "can regenerate a criticism of present life...through the construction of models of the future."[36] Science fiction can serve this "model-making" critical function, according to Scholes, precisely because it is not burdened by the reactionary constraints of realistic probability but is "freed," as he says, "of the problem of correspondence or noncorrespondence with some present actuality or some previously experienced past."[37] A similar rationale has been proposed by Scholes and others for self-reflexive fiction: by putting in question the referential claims of language, this fiction shakes us loose from our convictions of the inevitability of the established order.

Structuralist theorizing has contributed to radical esthetics by emphasizing that language is an affair of conventions, purely human contracts that are not "motivated" by the nature of reality. Sign-systems are not closed and predetermined but infinitely open to interpretation. As Barthes suggests, the departures of modern poetry from the "naturalized" cultural norms of prose have an exemplary value, shattering the link between conventions (and the ideologies they conceal) and nature. Barthes contrasts realistic prose, which presupposes a closed, completed universe, with "the terror of an expression without laws" evoked by modern poetry, where "the Word is no longer guided *in advance* by the general intention of a socialized discourse."[38] "Each poetic word is thus an unexpected object, a Pandora's box from which fly out all the potentialities of language"—a discourse "terrible and inhuman."[39] The modern experimental poet exposes the bankruptcy of bourgeois "currency," for underwriting it is only the fiction of an eternal order of reality.

Both Barthes and Marcuse are aware of the paradoxical and equivocal nature of artistic negation. In *One-Dimensional Man*, Marcuse cites Barthes's *Writing Degree Zero* as an example of the kind of vanguard theory which reacts against "the total mobilization of all media for the defense of the established reality" by recommending a "break with communication" itself.[40] Like Barthes, Marcuse recognizes that such anti-art may be politically innocuous, along with the art that expresses a "fashionably desublimated, verbal release of sexuality."[41] He condemns the irrationalism and mysticism of Norman O. Brown, Charles Reich, and the counterculture. He argues that the "revolution in perception" is vitiated when, through drugs or other stimulants, "its narcotic character brings temporary release not only from the reason and rationality of the established system but also from that other rationality which is to change the established system."[42]

In the early seventies, moreover, Marcuse seemed to retract some of his former sympathy for the irrationalistic ruptures of vanguard art. In *Counterrevolution and Revolt* (1972), Marcuse attacks the Artaudian Theater of Cruelty, the Living Theater, and rock culture as symptoms rather than criticisms of one-dimensional society: "To the degree to which it makes itself part of real life," he says, this art "loses the transcendence which opposes art to the established order."[43] The criticism seems well-taken. What is not clear, however, is why Marcuse's own endorsement of formalism and surrealism, indeed Marcuse's definition of all art, should be immune to it. The shattering of the reality principle Marcuse calls for, the overcoming of the subject-object distinction, the emergence of a "new sensorium"—these things would seem to entail the one-dimensional merging of art and life which Marcuse here deplores.

Radical esthetics without realism has been expounded by several recent American critics in a form that at first glance appears anti-political. In *The Confusion of Realms*, Richard Gilman attacks all artistic theory and practice that take literature to be "an employment of language for ends beyond itself. . . ."[44] Invoking recent self-reflexive experimental fiction (Barthelme, Gass, Updike) and the criticism of Susan Sontag, Gilman argues that literary works are self-sufficient, self-justifying universes, not second-order representations of some already existing reality. Literature is properly an "increment," not a "complement,"[45] a new reality rather than a reflection of the old one. Art, says Gilman, need not communicate "experience of any kind except an esthetic one," and it has "no reason for being other than to test and exemplify new forms of consciousness, which, moreover, have had to be invented precisely because actuality is incapable of generating them."[46] In a more recent essay, Gilman applauds the "secularization of art, its chastening and the removal from it of the 'values' that ought to be obtained elsewhere, i.e., the moral, social, and philosophical values which literature and art were once expected to communicate."[47] Richard Poirier, on whose esthetic of "the performing self" I commented in chapter 2, shares these sentiments. Poirier endorses Gilman's attack on those who "confuse realms" by subordinating art to political ends and holds that "literature has only one responsibility—to be compelled and compelling about its own inventions."[48] In *A World Elsewhere*, Poirier argues that this is especially the case for American literature, which, in its classic embodiments, constitutes a series of attempts to create fictive worlds of pure "style" against the alien worlds of politics, morality, and social behavior. These American works create "an imaginative environment that excludes the standards of that 'real' one to which most critics subscribe."[49] A similarly anti-political formalism appears in the theories of Susan Sontag, Leo Bersani, and many others. These critics suggest that the psychic experimentalism of modern art is incompatible with the collective goals of humanitarian social reform, whether liberal or socialist. For these critics, the cultural revolution speaks for energies which cannot be domesticated within the organized forms of politics, for an antinomian self (or loss of self) which cannot be tailored to fit the requirements of any imaginable society, however ideal.

In its very disengagement from society and politics, however, this formalism reveals its political animus. The ostensibly chastened renunciation of humanistic pretensions for literature serves the aggressive aim of subverting the bourgeois mentality. Gilman's assertion that literature ought not be "an employment of language for ends beyond itself" conflicts with his assertion that literature's purpose is to "test and exemplify new forms of consciousness," for the end of these new forms of consciousness is clearly social and extraliterary. Like Marcuse, Gilman proposes formalism as a weapon, as the epistemological solvent of the bourgeois reality-principle and of those "old Mediterranean values" which have become so oppressive. In the very process of

divorcing literature from politics, this characterization of literature as a "world elsewhere" betrays political resentment. But the
same impulse that turns formalism against society turns it against
radical politics, for this politics is seen as a mere extension of the
overrationalized, overorganized social order.

Beyond Objective Criticism
Textual Politics

Among the evidences of elitism and repressive rationalism in
established humanistic studies, none has been more widely
assailed than the academic ideal of objective interpretation. If
their imagery can be taken seriously, some recent commentators
see the strangulation of art by critical objectivity as a kind of
literary counterpart of imperialism or of industrial pollution.
Thus Susan Sontag: "Like the fumes of the automobile and of
heavy industry which befoul the urban atmosphere, the effusion
of interpretations of art today poisons our sensibilities." Interpretation, Sontag says, "has become reactionary, impertinent,
cowardly, stifling." It represents "the revenge of the intellect
upon the world" and "the revenge of the intellect upon art." It
follows that art can maintain its innocence only by defining itself
as the revenge of sensibility against the intellect, which is to say
against "a culture whose already classic dilemma," according to
Sontag, "is the hypertrophy of the intellect at the expense of
energy and sensual capability."[50] Similarly, Richard Poirier sees
"repressive analysis" as a threat to literature, which, as we have
seen, he defines as "a form of energy not accountable to the
orderings anyone makes of it."[51] In this spirit also, Leslie Fiedler
calls for a postmodern criticism that abandons hollow pretensions
to correctness and asserts itself unabashedly as creative writing:
"the newest criticism must be aesthetic, poetic in form as well as
substance."[52] As if in response to Fiedler's call, Ihab Hassan
advances "paracriticism," something that "is not mimesis of art
or science or life," and which, "like so much current literature, . . . is self-reflexive—up to a point!" Following in the path of
this literature, paracriticism makes "mixed use of disconfir-

mation and discontinuity, of space, silence, self-query, and surprise."[53]

Objective analysis is repudiated not only because it is reactionary but because it is impossible. In the previous chapter we looked at the theoretical premise of the current revolt against objective analysis—the view that, as Robert Scholes summarized it, "criticism has taken the very idea of 'aboutness' away from us. It has taught us that language is tautological, if it is not nonsense, and to the extent that it is about anything it is about itself. Mathematics is about mathematics, poetry is about poetry, and criticism is about the impossibility of its own existence." In an essay on "Reading Criticism," in *PMLA*, Cary Nelson refines this theory: "The value of identifying the critic in his criticism," Nelson writes, "is much greater than the value of deciding which theories of literary history are correct and which are not. Part of the pleasure of reading criticism is experiencing the subtle ways in which the biases, hopes, and frustrations of the critic are woven into the texture of his language and even into the language of the texts he examines. This dialectic between self and other, embedded in the critic's language and method, is really what criticism is 'about.'"[54] Note that Nelson is not saying merely that critics, like most people, are governed by "biases, hopes, and frustrations," so that a greater degree of awareness of these motivational underpinnings would advance their work. Not content with so unexceptionable an assertion, Nelson argues that it is these motivational underpinnings, "the dialectic between self and other," that criticism is really "about." To be sure, his phrase "dialectic between self and other" leaves a small opening for "other" things such as literary history, but these things are lacking in interest and value. The *real* value of criticism lies in what it tells us about the critic.

That readers misinterpret literature has probably been recognized as long as literature has existed. But only recently has this human deficiency been turned into a law. And from a law it has become a recommendation—and a means of liberating oneself from humanistic bad conscience. Thus in some instances the attack on objective interpretation has been given a quasi-Marxian

twist, with the suggestion that the concept of textual determinacy
is an extension of the system of private property. This strategy
exploits a number of analogies: between literary and economic
"currency," linguistic and legal "contracts," authorial control
over meaning and paternalistic domination of the family. By
freeing literary texts from their authors' intended meanings,
stripping them of authority, treating them as "multivalent,"
plural, and open to the free play of interpretation, criticism, it is
implied, transgresses the patriarchal system of ownership:

> A multivalent text [Barthes writes] can carry out its basic
> duplicity only if it subverts the opposition between the true and
> the false, if it fails to attribute quotations (even when seeking
> to discredit them) to explicit authorities, if it flouts all respect
> for origin, paternity, propriety, if it destroys the voice which
> could give the text its ("organic") unity, in short, if it coldly
> and fraudulently abolishes quotation marks which must, as we
> say, in all *honesty*, enclose a quotation and juridically distribute
> the ownership of the sentences to their respective proprietors,
> like subdivisions of a field. For multivalence (contradicted by
> irony) is a transgression of ownership. [55]

In his reading of Balzac's "Sarrasine," Barthes does not go so far
as to refuse to attribute quotations to the author, as he here
advises. But his reading of this work with no concern for Balzac's
apparent intention is presumably a blow aimed at bourgeois
"propriety" (paralleled by bourgeois "paternity"), not merely the
external propriety of social and literary decorum but the structures of (masculine) possession and control this decorum supposedly rationalizes. At the very least, this kind of reading
undermines the ideology of professional literary study.

The attempt to divest criticism of solemn academicism has
stimulated a new species of "playful" academicism, which
appears to derive about equally from Karl and Groucho Marx. Its
rationale is stated by Verena Conley in *Diacritics,* the journal that
has taken the lead in promoting the new "textual politics."
Conley is comparing her subject, Hélène Cixous, to the boxer,
Muhammad Ali:

Like the pugilist she eludes the everlasting constriction of
formulaic writing by forcing her opponent—-and here is the
brilliance of her textual politics—to make his heavyhanded
move, to hit below the belt, to respond to her voluble and
prancing words with either monolithic criticism, anathema or a
facile emulation.

This indeed is part of the histeric, histheoric misstery in its
urgent call for missexual writing. If any introductive name can
be assigned to it, at this point the best etiquette since *La Jeune
Née* might be found in the great reach of her millimetric
M-même. The work will doubtless, from the vantage of another,
give, and in giving, finally open a breech in American writing.[56]

Critics who see the need to liberate the reader from the determinacy of the text almost always write as if the only alternative to
such strategies were "monolithic criticism," a kind of critical
Final Solution that shuts off potential disagreement out of a
neurotic fear of uncertainty. Thus Barthes dismisses the problem
of interpretive truth by asserting that "the language each critic
chooses does not come down to him from heaven,"[57] as if the
objectivist interpreter necessarily assumes that it does. The
implication is clear: if you are looking for some kind of objective
validity in your interpretations, you are probably longing nostal-
gically for a theocratic authority to relieve you of the anxiety of
choice. Start believing in the existence of an objective world or a
determinate textual meaning and the next thing you know you
may be calling out the ideological police—suppressing disagreement and perhaps even demanding censorship.

This reduction of the issue to a clear-cut moral polarity of
authenticity vs. bad faith is seen in a much-quoted statement by
Derrida:

There are thus two interpretations of interpretation, of structure, of sign, of freeplay. The one seeks to decipher, dreams of
deciphering, a truth or an origin which is free from freeplay or
from the order of the sign, and lives like an exile the necessity
of interpretation. The other, which is no longer turned toward
the origin, affirms freeplay and tries to pass beyond man and
humanism, the name of man being the name of that being who,

throughout the history of metaphysics or of ontotheology—in other words, through the history of all of his history—has dreamed of full presence, the reassuring foundation, the origin and the end of the game.[58]

Quoting this passage, Frank Kermode characterizes the contrast between the two types of interpretation as one between "the old, Puritan, strict, limited, theocratic, radiating certainty about emblems and types"; and "the new, which depends on the activity of the individual creative mind, on the light of imagination. . . ."[59] And Richard Howard, in his introduction to a translation of *The Pleasure of the Text*, says Barthes's book instances "our ecstasy, our bliss in the text against the prudery of ideological analysis."* The choice having been reduced to one between defensive Puritanism and open-minded creativity, not much remains to be argued about.

Beyond High Culture

The distinction between high and low culture, like that between literary realism and objective criticism, is attacked as a symptom of elitist ideology. This "elitist" stigma is sometimes applied to virtually any critical reservations about mass culture. Leslie Fiedler, for example, equates high culture with "the finicky canons of the genteel tradition."[60] Against this genteel tradition Fiedler poses an insurgent, anti-hierarchical, irreverent popular culture, and a postmodern art and criticism impatient with the old boundaries and determined to "cross the border, close the gap." "What the final intrusion of pop into the citadels of high art provides, therefore, for the critic," Fiedler declares, "is the exhilarating new possibility of making judgments about the 'goodness' and 'badness' of art quite separated from distinctions between 'high' and 'low' with their concealed class bias."[61]

Richard Wasson expresses a similar exhilaration. The merging

*Richard Howard, in "A Note on the Text," introduction to Roland Barthes, *The Pleasure of the Text,* trans. Richard Miller (New York: Hill and Wang, 1975), vii. Barthes, in *The Pleasure of the Text*, shows us how we can regard a literary text as "a body of bliss consisting solely of erotic relations" (16).

of high and mass culture in the sixties, Wasson believes, signalled
the end of the dichotomy of action and contemplation that had
long kept the intellectual in a position of sterile isolation. The
sixties, he writes, "give us a series of metaphors of culture which
we might categorize as incarnational: culture leaves its sacred
cloister and goes into the world to participate in the joys and
sorrows of the human community and to work for its redemp-
tion."[62] One of Wasson's examples of this "incarnational"
overcoming of distinctions is Northrop Frye's system of archetypes, which "demystify the discipline of English studies" by
enabling us to recognize that the same mythic and generic structures pervade high and low forms alike. "That is why the
standard criticism of Frye—that one can find archetypes everywhere—is so absurd; it's precisely because they are omnipresent
that the literary critic can speak to the problems of civilization,
can use his special competence to participate in the efforts of
mankind to shape the world."[63] And again: "for Frye, the job of
the man of culture is not to defend highbrow culture but to
demystify forms of communication by revealing their connections."[64] In Frye as in Marcuse and Norman O. Brown, Wasson
concludes, "imaginative culture" transcends traditional distinctions; it "furthers the cause of Eros, of freedom, of liberation; it is
not a spiritual discipline, an inner check, a hostile force opposed
to the mass and popular arts, but a vehicle of liberation."[65]

The logic of this argument leads Wasson to congratulate Frye
for declining to "consider advertising as 'bad' or 'false' or a mass
media to be opposed by highbrow taste." He refers specifically to
a statement by Frye that "to protect ourselves in a world such as
ours" we have to look at advertising ironically, so that instead of
rejecting it we "choose what we want out of what's offered to us
and let the rest go." Here, Wasson comments, "advertising is
appropriated into the total form of literature, into the world of
archetypes. We react to advertising in the context of our understanding of verbal statements, of the visions of the world that
literature gives, and in that context we accept or reject the vision.
Literature, literary criticism, and literary education play then a
decisive role in shaping the civilization we have and the civilization we want."[66]

This argument is elusive. One can certainly go along with Wasson's desire to demystify literary studies by applying literary methods of analysis to popular culture. But in his argument, this project has got tied up with the liquidation of high cultural perspectives. One can see how this happened. Since "popular" culture, as its name indicates, is the culture enjoyed by the masses, it seems to follow that popular culture is *democratic*—as if it were the masses who determined the content of this culture independently of businessmen and managers. Therefore, any criticism of popular culture from the point of view of high culture must necessarily spring from the snobbery of the elitist few. It is only a short step from this position to the idea that social criticism itself is elitist.

But Wasson would like literary studies to function as social criticism. Having discarded high culture as a possible source of critical perspectives, Wasson leaves unclear where these perspectives shall come from. Take his discussion of advertising. If, as Wasson suggests, advertising is something from which we need to protect ourselves by means of irony, then where is this irony to come from if not from some external perspective superior to that of advertising? But how can one adopt a perspective superior to advertising without becoming an elitist? Wasson's dilemma (which is related to that of formalist literary critics) is typical: he wants us to hold onto a critical view of society, yet his tendency to confuse all criticism and highbrow taste with snobbery encourages the elimination of critical distance. Wasson implies that mass culture may fail to correspond to "the civilization we want"; but how do we know "what we want" unless we examine our desires critically and objectively? Critical principles seem to be required somewhere, yet such principles must be suspect in a culture defined as an expression of the joys of Eros and of "incarnational" unity of being. If detached criticism is elitist, then the very resistance of intellectuals to society comes to seem anti-egalitarian.

Radical Self-Nullification

Here we can begin to see how the typical equations, identifications, and oppositions of radical esthetics open it to the kind of difficulties already sketched in my previous chapter. By associating imagination, Eros, and the pleasure principle with liberation, and conceptual rationality with repression and elitism, radical esthetics accedes to the kind of technological dissociation of sensibility that it aims to oppose. Though this esthetics protests against positivistic and philistine reductions of art to the status of mere fantasy and myth, it reinstates these reductions in its own definition of art as an expression of "the return of the repressed." Radical esthetics may claim to "reconcile" art and rationality, but the reconciliation is prevented by the repudiation of mimetic theories and by the antinomy of theoretical and imaginative truth. Having decided that rationality as such equals functional rationality, radical esthetics is forced to attempt to make creative imagination, the senses, the unconscious, Eros, and so on do the critical work that only the reasoning intellect can do.

This quixotic effort implants a familiar contradiction into radical culture. In exposing objective reason as a mere ideology, cultural radicalism leaves itself no means of legitimizing its own critique of exploitation and injustice. If objectivity is a bourgeois mystification, then the rationale of tyranny is undermined, but so is the rationale of principled resistance to tyranny. Radicals who triumphantly declare that, because all thinking is historically "situated," it is therefore compromised seem not to notice that they discredit their own analyses and protests in the process.

One sees this contradiction vividly in the reasoning of the existentialist left. As Eldridge Cleaver says, "There is no more neutrality in the world. You either have to be a part of the solution, or you're going to be part of the problem. There ain't no middle ground."[67] In reducing everything to partisanship, the exponents of this view fail to notice they have undermined the grounds of partisanship. There are no longer such things as good reasons, resting on disinterested application of principles, motivating commitments. Concepts like truth, justice, and fairness become mere party slogans and rationalizations. Of course it is true that such concepts are often used as slogans and rationalizations, but it has been thought that they do not *have* to be used in this way, that disinterestedness is at least possible, and is thus an

ideal to be preserved rather than scorned. Insofar as we discard
this ideal, we resign ourselves to a view of politics as a swindle in
which words like "justice" have no meaning. This cynical posture
then contributes to politics *becoming* just such a swindle.

Cleaver's statement may stand for the crude version of the
left-wing attack on objectivity and neutrality. The sophisticated
version is summarized by a recent historian of "existential
Marxism," Mark Poster. Poster sums up the existential Marxist's
critique of traditional social science: "The error of the social
scientists lay in their methodology and theory of knowledge. Their
idealism situated the knower outside the field of knowledge,
outside history. Merleau-Ponty complained that 'Durkheim
treats the social as a reality external to the individual and entrusts
it with explaining everything that is presented to the individual as
what he has to become.'"[68] And again: "Sartre insisted that the
observer had to implicate himself in the act of comprehension. All
forms of 'de-situated' knowledge (value-free sociology, objective
science, etc.) were ruled out.... The social scientist could not
remain a remote, disinterested observer."[69]

The trouble is, it is difficult to conceive of any knowledge that
does not in some sense "situate the knower outside the field of
knowledge, outside history." One no sooner makes assertions like
Poster's about the situated nature of the knower and his historicity than one has oneself assumed a position outside the context
one is talking about, if only at a stage prior to responding to this
context. We all become value-free objectivists to some extent
when we attempt to make sure our value judgments rest on an
unbiased understanding of the object. In other words, value-free
objectivity is a necessary first stage of making value judgments—
the descriptive, disinterested determination of what it is that is to
be judged. The technique of what might be called methodological
neutrality, of "getting the facts right" before leaping in with our
value judgments, is one of the progressive achievements of
civilization. It is true that nobody can be *totally* neutral, and it is
true that nineteenth-century scientific objectivists and historical
reconstructionists believed in the self-effacement of the observer
in a naive way. Yet we do not have to repeat this naiveté to
recognize that observational neutrality is relatively approachable

as an ideal, and that the technique of methodological detachment
is something that can be acquired and improved by training. The
fact that we do not, phenomenologically or psychologically,
perceive objects as wholly distinct from our colorations of value
does not mean that we are incapable of distinguishing between
descriptions and evaluations. Description is *logically* prior to
evaluation, even if the two must be experienced as a unity. When
we introduce evaluations prematurely, without a properly disinterested understanding of what it is we are evaluating, we
muddle inquiry and make discussion almost impossible. The
truth of this has been brought home to anybody who has suffered
through an argument over values in which the participants have
not first sought to determine whether they agree on *what*, de-
scriptively, it is they are arguing about.

The real error of the positivist sociology against which the
existential Marxists react is not the assumption that descriptions
can be value-free, but the assumption that we cannot move
logically from value-free descriptions to value judgments themselves. Whereas the positivists separated descriptive understanding from evaluation, the existential Marxists (and other phenomenologists) bridge this separation by confusing the two, through a
murky concept of "fusion" of subjective and objective horizons
that compromises the authority of knowledge. These adversaries
resemble one another in a common failure to recognize any
logical connection between understanding and evaluation. The
way to overcome the positivistic neutralization of understanding
is not to try to discredit the claims of objectivity by proving that
objectivity is really shot through with subjective value but rather
to assert that value itself is objective in that it rests on prior
objective understanding. Insofar as we "humanize" knowledge by
denying its objective basis, we merely emasculate the language of
morality and politics.

The rejection of objectivity in the name of "situated" knowledge is the epistemological equivalent of anti-mimetic esthetics.
The first severs the knower, the second the work of art, from the
possibility of understanding the world. It is this chronic epistemological weakness that makes the anti-mimetic position self-
defeating when used as an esthetic of radical intransigence.

Though in one of its phases this anti-mimetic position opposes art to reality, in another it confuses art with reality. One cannot always tell whether this position is contrasting art and life or annexing "life" to the domain of art. A radical formalist like Poirier, for instance, is capable of having things both ways. Having, along with Gilman, condemned the "confusion of realms," Poirier can write in this vein:

> . . . while all expressed forms of life, reality, and history have a status different from fiction as it exists in novels, poems, or plays, they are all fictions nonetheless and they can be measured on the same scale. To talk or to write is to fictionalize. . . .
>
> Insofar as they are available for discussion, life, reality, and history exist only as discourse, and no form of discourse, as Santayana insisted, can *be* what it expresses; no form of discourse can *be* life, reality, or history. Where is the Civil War and how do we know it? Where is the President and how does anyone know him? Is he a history book, an epic poem, or a cartoon by David Levine?[70]

The "confusion of realms" could hardly be more beautifully exemplified. On the one hand, creative imagination withdraws from history and politics into its own "world elsewhere." On the other hand, the imagination gets its revenge on history and politics by absorbing them into its own fictive structures, transforming history and politics into shadowy manifestations of the ego. The literary imagination reacts against the theatrical contamination of public reality by universalizing theatricality and myth and abolishing reality itself. In the process, the imagination's critical power is undermined.

The radical critics' quarrel with the classical, mimetic view of language is twofold: this view ties language (1) to a predetermined order of reality and (2) to a predetermined set of agreements about the nature of this reality. The two great ideological supports of unfreedom, then, are the belief that there is a *correspondence* between language and external reality and the belief that this correspondence is or can be enshrined in agreed-upon conventions of speaking. The first belief binds men to the way things are, the second binds them to the orthodoxies of

others. It follows then that any time we acknowledge that an
external reality exists and can be shared through common forms
of language, whether we know it or not we are encouraging
passive *adjustment* to the status quo. To attack literary mimesis is
to attack both the ideology of correspondence of word and object
and the ideology of common agreement.

The confusion in this radical argument seems to lie in its failure
to distinguish between specific historical manifestations of a thing
and the thing as it might be in other circumstances. This tossing
out of the baby with the bathwater is seen in Barthes's categorical
repudiation of "thinking in essences" (which is always a "bourgeois mythology"), of "Order" (which always "indicates repression"), and "socialized discourse" (which is always a "security
system" for the ruling class). It is true that the idea of a "natural
correspondence" between language and reality has often been
used to justify the view of reality held by those wielding political
power. But one can reject the ideological bias of such a justification without rejecting the principle of correspondence itself.
Indeed, one can argue that the established ideology fails to
correspond to reality, and go on to present an alternative view
which corresponds more closely. In a similar way, the fact that
our shared linguistic contracts often conceal ideological mystifications favorable to the interests of the ruling class is an
argument for exposing these particular linguistic formulations,
not for attacking the very concept of shared formulations. We
attack conventional formulations in the hope of persuading
people to agree on other formulations, not to do away with
agreement, which would be self-defeating.

To argue that there is something intrinsically ideological and
coercive about shared (or sharable) linguistic contracts, as distinct from specific instances of such contracts, is simply to attack
political discourse itself. Such discourse depends on the possibility of giving uniform meaning to terms such as "justice,"
"equality," "exploitation," "oppressor," and "oppressed."
These terms may be perverted in systematic ways by ruling-class
propaganda, but then the task of demystifying the perversions
must be to rescue these concepts from the debased common usage
by reasserting a normative usage. This appeal to a normative

usage depends in turn, however, on the appeal to a real world of things, relations, and processes outside language. In other words, the project of political demystification is to free terms from misuse by attaching them to the appropriate referents, not to dissolve the very notion that language can have referents. But this is merely a rather cumbersome way of saying that to attack the political mystifications of language we have to "call things by their right names."

Our ability to identify a perverse use of terms *as* perverse depends on the assumption that there is such a thing as calling things by their right names, and this in turn depends on the assumption that there is a common world and that language's relation to it is not wholly arbitrary. By mistaking shared reality and shared language with adjustment, conformity, and oppression, critics like Barthes end up attacking no particular society but rather the process of socialization. Their arguments rest finally on a definition of freedom as the refusal of community—a bourgeois definition of freedom if there ever was one.

The Power of Powerlessness

A radical esthetic based on formalist perceptual defamiliarization encounters other problems besides those discussed above. By breaking with the concept of a common language, such an esthetic deepens the division between art and society and perpetuates the spiral of artistic impotence and alienation. The more violently the arts overturn objective consciousness, the representational view of art, and the common language, the more surely do they guarantee their marginality and harmlessness—a condition which, in turn, inspires renewed artistic attempts to overturn objective consciousness, representation, and common language. Aiming at intransigence, art ends up collaborating with its scientific, commercial, and utilitarian adversaries to ensure its unimportance. Redefining its alienation from society as a model of liberation, art boasts of its "secularization" as if this were a consciously chosen position rather than a consequence of antagonistic conditions. The vehement refusal of obedience to

social demands on art permits the artist to ignore the fact that
society has stopped making such demands.

The formalist strategy (and I include here those aggressive
formalisms that do not retreat from life but absorb it through the
projection of myth) entails large elements of renunciation and
adaptation. It exploits the incidental benefits of the homelessness, impotence, and marginality which capitalism thrusts on the
artistic intellectual. Recent celebrations of the esthetics of
"play," of the uninhibited exploration of the frontiers of consciousness, ignore the severely restricted boundaries within which
this play and this exploration take place. Such celebrations take it
for granted that the artist has been dispossessed irrevocably of
an interpretation that would permit him to master social experience. Separation from society and the loss of the perspective
by which this separation might be understood cease to be merely
the unfortunate condition of art under a certain form of society,
and become part of the very *definition* of art.

But the self-induced separatism of art represents only one side
of a contradictory state of affairs. As the arts have willfully separated from society, they have, in certain new and paradoxical
ways, become reunited with it. The estrangement of art from
society has coincided with the estrangement of society, or of great
segments of society, from itself. As the middle class has become
disillusioned with science, commerce, affluence, and consumption and skeptical toward traditional bourgeois certainties, the
separatism of the arts has actually drawn art and society into
closer relation. Advanced art is, after all, not socially marginal;
or, rather, its very marginality makes it central in a society where
displacement from the center (or the suspicion that there is no
center) has become the common fate.

If art, like the family and the church, has begun to be seen as a
"haven in a heartless world," in Christopher Lasch's term, a
refuge of "humanness" that offers itself as a sort of vacation from
the menacing world of work and competition, this fact only
establishes its common ground with the community.* Insofar as

*Christopher Lasch, *Haven in a Heartless World: The Family Besieged*
(New York: Basic Books, 1977). Lasch's argument in this book is that the

formalist gestures provide a way of living with alienation, this fact ties them to society rather than draws them apart from it. In its ability to redescribe displacement from centrality as a revolutionary form of freedom and potency, advanced culture furnishes a model by which social powerlessness can be experienced as gratification. In this sense, those (largely on the left) who think that intellectuals like themselves have no power and those (largely on the right) who think that such intellectuals have too much power are both right. In the cultural world today, powerlessness (and the command of its intellectual paradigms) confers power.

The terms in which it defines revolution and liberation make radical esthetics congenial to many elements of consumer society, for liberation from traditional constraints is an essential condition of the expansion of consumption. Consumer society, in its destruction of continuity through the exploitation of fashion, ephemeral novelty, and planned obsolescence, effects a "systematic derangement of the senses" that makes the disruptions and defamiliarizations of vanguard culture look puny by comparison. The juxtaposition of terror and triviality, consequence and irrelevance, in an average newspaper front-page or news broadcast does more to assault hierarchically ordered thinking than the most uncompromising example of anti-object art. The superannuation of the past, the fluidity of personal relations, the malleability of the physical environment before technology and of the spiritual environment before the myth-making of advertising, journalism, entertainment, and political propaganda combine not only to erode our assurance of reality but our ability to recognize the erosion and see it as harmful. Alienation from work, from the possibility of community, from belief in the possible intelligibility of experience have increasingly become the shared ground of middle-class life. As this occurs, adversary epistemologies challenging the "logocentric" correspondence of mind (or language) with things not only lose their oppositional force but harmonize with the prevailing tune. In demanding that

---

idea of the family as "haven" is a myth, for the same industrial forces that have caused the family to be conceived in these defensive terms have penetrated the defenses themselves. Thus the parallel with literature is complete.

words be liberated from the significations, fixed in advance, of socialized discourse, Barthes and other vanguard critics ignore the extent to which advertising and mass culture have already accomplished this end. The critics' exposure of the inherently ideological nature of thought finds an echo in the popular cynicism that regards all judgments as "matters of opinion" and asks —without staying for an answer—"who is to say" what is real and what is not.

Consumer society not only generates feelings of social uselessness, it helps shape the diagnoses of these feelings and the proposed remedies. Hence the emergence of new industries for the profitable dissemination of advanced theories of alienation and liberation. The politics of the self, which reduces history to the psychodrama of the autonomous imagination contending against a repressive superego, spreads from the esoteric discussions of intellectuals into everyday social and even commercial life. But again, commerce, advertising, and popular entertainment surpass the power of the most visionary art to offer a prospective escape from the limitations of ordinary human existence, by way of a life of infinitely multiplying personalities and "life styles" against a background of "total environments."* Through commodities symbolic of the open and liberated life, personal autonomy is consumed as a compensation for the superfluousness of

---

*"Counterculture may be described as the tribalized, ritualized mirror of national culture. Both rely on economic security, technology, and corporate forms of behavior; both reject the literary, philosophical and moral assumptions on which culture has traditionally been based; both are permissive, antipolitical, pleasure oriented, media directed, and ahistorical; both are affected by the same combinations of dependence on technique and concern with subjective emotions; both treat experience in a reductive way. More particularly, counterculture is the area of behavior in which the national culture is defined pleasurably. Far from a threat to culture, it sustains national culture by showing how the recent cultural alterations can confer gratification. . . . [The young's] behavior is the subject for endless adult analysis and discussion precisely because they have been implicitly assigned the social task of testing behavior which, when it works, will be incorporated into adult mores, and when it fails, be condemned" (Jay Martin, "A Watertight Watergate Future: Americans in a Post-American Age," *The Antioch Review*, 33, no. 2 [Summer 1975], 20).

the consumer. Recapitulating the fate of romantic art, the individual achieves autonomy at the very moment his contribution ceases to matter. Just as the autonomous artistic imagination is placed beyond criticism, the modern self is consoled for its dispossession of history, community, and reality by having its "needs" placed beyond criticism. The "triumph of the therapeutic" closes the gap between sophisticated and lay cultures. No great distance separates the literary intellectual who strives to kill "the prudery of ideological analysis" in himself so he can appreciate a text as "a body of bliss consisting solely of erotic relations" from the encounter-group participant struggling to "get in touch with his body."

The "adversary culture," with its stylish powerlessness redefined as a form of erotic potency, thus becomes indistinguishable from the "adversary." Though advanced art is not necessarily popular or commercially successful, neither unpopularity nor commercial failure can any longer be plausibly attributed to the public's intolerance of innovation. The antinomian disparagement of "bourgeois values" is celebrated by the agencies of publicity, exploited by the manipulators of cultural fashion, and emulated in personal conduct—an additional reason why the ante of provocation and radical experiment must continually be raised if a work is to earn its vanguard credentials. Not even by refusing to assume material existence at all can art succeed in disappointing—as we can see from the benign public acceptance of Conceptual Art. It is impossible to say whether the artistic "vanguard" is leading society or struggling to keep up with it.*

*In some respects, this argument resembles that of Daniel Bell in *The Cultural Contradictions of Capitalism* (New York: Basic Books, 1976). Bell too is concerned with the diffusion of modernist ideology into mass culture, a phenomenon he attempts to situate within a larger theory of postindustrial society. According to Bell, the "techno-economic" realm of society has come into conflict with "the culture"—the realm of art, values, and personal behavior. The techno-economic realm continues to depend on the traditional values of austerity, Puritanism, postponement of gratification, etc., whereas the cultural sphere—which has been overtaken by the modernist heritage—is dedicated to the values of hedonism, experimentalism, and immediate experience. As Richard Wollheim has pointed out, however, there may be less of a "contradiction" here than

In short, cultural radicalism ignores the disappearance of the
paternalistic repressions it seeks to dissolve. Though "conserva-
tives" may here and there protest the triumph of godlessness and
immorality, no conservatism opposes the necessary expansion of
consumer markets. Whereas the ruling class once required the
appearance of sanction by the spiritual ideas of high culture, it
now finds it possible to do without such sanctions, to exploit a
culture of radical pluralism and ideological dissonance. Far from
representing tradition and "elitism," the contemporary corporation is hostile to the fixity of traditional standards, which stand in
the way of progress. As J. H. Plumb observes in *The Death of the
Past*, "industrial society does not need the past. Its intellectual
orientation is toward change rather than conservation, toward
exploitation and consumption. The new methods, new procedures, new forms of living of scientific and industrial society have
no sanction in the past and no roots in it. The past becomes,
therefore, a matter of curiosity, of nostalgia, a sentimentality."[71]
Hence the welcome extended by corporate society to the kind of
culture that crosses all the borders and closes all the gaps. Attacks on the vestiges of high cultural standards and realistic
sensibility only further the transformation of culture into an
appendage of the fashion industries and the subjection of art,
ideas, and persons to the law of planned obsolescence. The blur-
ring of cultural levels celebrated by critics such as Fiedler and
Wasson as an overcoming of "concealed class bias" only be-
speaks the irrelevance of traditional discriminations of taste to
the goals of managers and publicists. Insofar as radical criticism
makes the extirpation of high cultural snobbery the central objective, it encourages the illusion that mass culture is the democratic expression of the people, as if mass culture were not owned
and operated to suit private interests.

Marx showed that bourgeois capitalism could not develop until
the institutions and beliefs of feudal society had so weakened that

---

Bell thinks: "what more natural cultural counterpart could there be to
an economy geared to the voracious consumption of goods and services
than the unfocused, self-generating kind of hedonism in which, according to our author, 'the society' is currently engulfed?" ("Trouble in
Freedonia," *New York Review of Books*, 23, no. 11 [June 24, 1976], 35).

a critical mass of "free laborers," ready to sell their services on the open market, could come into being. By an extension of this view, it can be argued that our present consumer-oriented capitalism could not develop until bourgeois moral and psychological restraints had been dissolved. "Radical" culture seems to have served this function well. Its experimentalism, relativism, energy-worship, and glorification of "process" and "experience" lend themselves to what Lasch terms "the propaganda of commodities."[72] Without "radicalism," we should be far less ready consumers than we are today. This is not to argue that any radicalism is necessarily doomed to serve as an instrument of consumerism. It is to argue for a closer examination of the real social content of the culture we decide to call "radical."

The New Academic Professionalism

The situation in the university departments of literature and the humanities mirrors that of the social macrocosm. Just as the esthetics of radical defamiliarization blends with the dynamics of consumer society, attacks on the traditional modes of academic criticism and interpretation do not really conflict with the spirit of academic professionalism. The departments of the humanities some time ago became principal patrons and expounders of esthetic innovation. There is no visible reason why they should not encourage radical innovation in criticism. The antithesis of "academic" and "avant-garde" is as obsolete as the antithesis of "bourgeois" and "bohemian."

A new professionalism has emerged in humanistic studies which has no more attachment to traditional values than does the contemporary corporation. It is true, of course, that the ritualistic forms of genteel decorum—in taste in clothing, food, wines, music, theater, and so on—are still often assiduously maintained in common rooms and faculty clubs. Such quaint survivals should not disguise the fact that the new professionalism is indifferent to whether high cultural values prevail or not. Indeed, just as a postscarcity economy may require the liquidation of traditional

moral restraints, academic professionalism may require radical
critical innovation as a condition of its expansion.

Where quantitative "production" of scholarship and criticism
is a chief measure of professional achievement, narrow canons of
proof, evidence, logical consistency, and clarity of expression
have to go. To insist on them imposes a drag upon progress.
Indeed, to apply strict canons of objectivity and evidence in
academic publishing today would be comparable to the American
economy's returning to the gold standard: the effect would be the
immediate collapse of the system. The new wave of paracritical
and metacritical improvisation in criticism, sometimes to the
point of transforming interpretation into prose poetry, may be a
necessary spur to industrial growth at a time when the conventional modes of professional publication have worn thin.

Pleas for critical innovation invariably present themselves as
challenges to professional vested interests, and, in the world of
scholarship, the General Motors of the vested interests is of
course the historical method. Paul de Man, for example, says that
"the vested interest that academics have in the value of history
makes it difficult to put the term seriously into question."[73] De
Man speaks as if academics did not have an even greater vested
interest in liquidating historical method, for this method obliges
the scholarly writer at least to produce some facts about the
author and his time, whereas "putting history in question" requires him only to master certain forms of verbalization. Ever
since the New Critical discovery that almost any work of literature
could be read as a complex of paradoxes and ironies, critical
"methodology," whatever other purposes it has served, has been
an instrument for generating new "readings"—and thus new
publications. The recent discovery that every text can be reinter-
preted as a commentary on its own textual problematics or as a
self-consuming artifact ensures that the production of new
readings will not cease even though explication of many authors
and works seems to have reached the point of saturation.

Repressive Desublimation

Cultural radicals have not necessarily ignored the social changes I
have been describing here. For some of them, the new accommo-
dation of established society and the university to vanguard art
and ideas is merely conclusive evidence that the revolution is
already taking place. For those more pessimistic, this accom-
modation threatens the success of the cultural revolution—
though it by no means discredits its essential outlook. For Marcuse, the new popularity of vanguard cultural attitudes is a
manifestation of "repressive desublimation"—the dominant
society's repression of culturally revolutionary ideas by assimilating them in harmless forms. Marcuse observes acutely that
high bourgeois culture, with its idealism, its love of beauty,
renunciation, and sublimation, "has ceased to be the dominant
culture." Therefore, a new question arises:

> . . . if today we are witnessing a disintegration of bourgeois
> culture which is the work of the internal dynamic of contem-
> porary capitalism and the adjustment of culture to the require-
> ments of contemporary capitalism, is not the cultural revolu-
> tion then, inasmuch as it aims at the destruction of bourgeois
> culture, falling in line with the capitalist adjustment and re-
> definition of culture? Is it not thus defeating its own purpose,
> namely, to prepare the soil for a qualitatively different, a rad-
> ically anticapitalist culture? Is there not a dangerous diver-
> gence, if not contradiction, between the political goals of the
> rebellion and its cultural theory and praxis? And must not the
> rebellion change its cultural "strategy" in order to resolve this
> contradiction?[74]

In the fifty pages following this passage in *Counterrevolution and
Revolt*, I find no statement which addresses these extremely
pertinent questions. Marcuse concedes that there is an "unre-
solved contradiction" blocking the revolutionary program, that
this program has been all too easy to vulgarize and divert into
frivolity and self-deception. But this fact is not permitted to call
into question the program itself. Marcuse is content to reaffirm
his faith that "the cultural revolution remains a radically progressive force."[75]

In other words, Marcuse declines to draw the logical conclusion
to which his own social theory leads: that the new sensibility in art
and culture does not so much negate "one-dimensional society"
as mirror it. In the same way, Marcuse's formalist esthetic mirrors the self-validating autonomy which he and other social critics
have discovered in the technological, bureaucratic, and economic
processes of advanced society. In *One-Dimensional Man*, Marcuse says that the language of one-dimensional society "controls
by reducing the linguistic forms and symbols of reflection, abstraction, development, contradiction; by substituting images for
concepts. It denies or absorbs the transcendent vocabulary."[76]
Here Marcuse perceives—correctly, I think—that an art which
"substitutes images for concepts" apes the "one-dimensional"
perspectives of technocratic society. Yet substituting images for
concepts, in Marcuse's neo-Kantian esthetic theory, is the very essence of the artistic activity. Marcuse's esthetic theory stands
condemned by his social theory for voiding art's critical power.

This example typifies the difficulty with the subversive claims
made for the disorienting and "model-making" powers of art,
whether these claims are advanced specifically for fantasy genres
such as science fiction or for art in general. Suppose we grant that
a particular work of art serves to "destroy old assumptions and
suggest a new, more visionary reality." It does not follow that
such a work induces its audience to see things more critically. The
"radical disorientation" of perception and the "cognitive estrangement" discovered by recent critics in the conventions of
science fiction may result in a dulling of the audience's sense of
reality, in shell-shocked acceptance rather than critical intransigence. The "models for the future" celebrated by Scholes and
other critics of science fiction may stimulate escapist fantasies
rather than critical thinking—all the more probably if these
models are inserted into an already uncritical, fad-worshiping
mass culture. In other words, there is no way of determining the
critical character of a literary work unless we know its disposition
toward reality. If esthetic disruption and projection are not regu-
lated by a rational respect for reality—that is, by a controlling
realism—their critical value cannot be taken for granted. Radical
esthetics, determined to liberate fantasy from "the problem of

correspondence or noncorrespondence with some present actuality or some previously experienced past," has no way of justifying
its claims for the critical power of fantasy. James Stupple points
to this problem with science fiction itself: "rather than encouraging analysis," Stupple writes, the use of disorienting conventions in this genre "actually impedes it, putting an end to critical
thought."[77] Whether fantasy makes us more critical or merely
more solipsistic and self-indulgent depends finally on whether it is
accountable to something that is not fantasy. But it is just such
accountability that radical esthetics confuses with acquiescence.

That a great deal of putatively radical art has become an aspect
of the confusion it rebels against is, as we have already seen, the
very criticism Marcuse himself levels at the irrationalistic impulse
in contemporary art and in the counterculture. In merging art
with life, Marcuse observes, the new sensibility often "loses the
transcendence which opposes art to the established order."[78] But
this same criticism logically applies to Marcuse's own conception
of art. Since he puts art under no obligation to reflect conceptual
reality, Marcuse has no way of explaining why art should "transcend" established reality in a critical rather than a solipsistic or
escapist fashion. His theory deprives itself of the critical principle
that is needed if we want to distinguish between substantial and
trivial forms of artistic imagination. Marcuse sees art as "another
reality, another order repelled by the existing one." But can a
work of art be "repelled" by existing reality unless it has the
power to understand what that reality is? Art must be granted the
power to conceptualize the existing reality, to see it *as* distorted,
before it can effectively negate it.

Marcuse and other cultural radicals do not follow the logic of
their position to its natural conclusions. If they were to do so they
would have to abandon their belief in the parallelism of cultural
and political revolution. They would have to acknowledge that the
esthetic of defamiliarization and projection, of formalist assault
on the reality principle, falls in line with "the capitalist adjustment and redefinition of culture." This, in turn, would call into
question the larger assumption that the liberation of Eros and the
pleasure principle is a necessary counterpart of the revolt against
injustice. And then, one might ask, must we have a new cultural

sensibility, a "new sensorium," a reorientation of perception, an "a-logical" celebration of being, a release of "will and joy" and Eros, a flight beyond humanism and the logocentric idea of man, if we seek to bring about greater truth and justice? Or has the goal of relieving boredom replaced truth and justice as the purpose of politics? But to think these thoughts is to question the very foundation of cultural leftism. That the cultural revolution is regrettably vulnerable to "co-optation"—this can be conceded. But that the cultural revolution in itself, not merely in its vulgarized forms, is misconceived—this is unthinkable.

At the very moment when radical culture began to focus its attack on the authoritarian ideology undergirding advanced society, this society had already undermined the social basis of that ideology. This last point cannot be emphasized too strongly, for it is central to understanding our current taste for self-nullifying argument in all areas of culture. A great deal of our thinking about culture expresses a defensive recoiling from the nightmare of modern history—from war, totalitarianism, and exploitation. In order to escape complicity, art has had to repudiate rationality and representation—perhaps even meaning itself—and criticism has had to repudiate objective methods of analysis and firm standards of taste. It is by these routes that humanistic culture has so often deprived itself of the critical perspective it might well contribute to the larger society.

The understanding of advanced society needed to correct such misconceived reactions is already present or latent in much of the thinking of our radical culture. But this understanding remains strangely isolated and set apart when we come to determining what constitutes a radical strategy in art and culture. And the old understanding, the myth that we live in a "repressive" society and that patriarchy, authoritarianism, and elitism are our main enemies, dies hard. Thus our radicalism is diverted from legitimate targets—injustice, poverty, triviality, vulgarity, and social loneliness—to a spurious quest after psychic liberation.

Four

English in America

Richard Ohmann's *English in America: A Radical View of the Profession* makes a brave attempt to disturb the quiet that has descended on the universities in the wake of the political upheavals of the sixties. The book revives neglected questions about the place of language and literature in our society, and it makes some tough charges about the way the teaching of these subjects has affected our politics. Much of it is hard to disagree with, particularly its suggestion that the university literature departments are in deeper trouble than they recognize—not only financial but moral and philosophical trouble. But in its diagnosis of the trouble and the hints it gives toward possible cures, Ohmann's book illustrates the weaknesses of contemporary radical approaches to the crisis of higher education.

As a "cultural revolutionary" Ohmann is saner, less irrationalistic, than the critics I discussed in the previous chapter. There is, it is true, a hint of the current avant-garde in his frequent use of the all-purpose term "liberation," and in his view that literature "disrupts the routine perceptions of everyday, and makes us see the world with new vision."[1] And when Ohmann complains that English courses ask the student "to depersonalize, to deny his *own* selfhood,"[2] he promotes the common non sequitur that to personalize literary experience is somehow to radicalize it. But Ohmann's approach contains little of the appeal to Eros, desire, and desublimation that we find, say, in the neo-Freudian left. His thinking is more hardheadedly political than psychological, and owes more to the New Left than the New Sensibility. One of the chapters in *English in America* was published in the New Left anthology *The Politics of Literature* (1972), edited by Louis Kampf and Paul Lauter, and Ohmann's assumptions echo the outlook of that manifesto. That outlook, broadly summarized by the editors in their introduction, held that "high culture propagates the values of those who rule and therefore helps to maintain current social arrangements."[3] Ohmann makes much the same point in these words: "I used to wonder why it is that society pays English teachers so much money to do what by and large is fun: teaching fine literature. I now think that our function is extremely valuable: namely, to ensure the harmlessness of all culture; to make it serve and preserve the status quo."[4]

The Indoctrination Theory of English

In short, Ohmann goes by what might be called the indoctrination theory of English. This theory holds that English operates as an instrument of "acculturation" into ruling-class values. This indoctrination theory should not be confused with a conspiracy theory: the indoctrination comes about through the natural operations of the system as such and does not depend on the conscious intent of those operating the system. But the indoctrination is there and it works. Most especially is this true of English composition, which Ohmann in one chapter dissects as a form of "administered thought." Composition teachers, Ohmann says, "teach the style, broadly defined, of the managerial and professional classes. Style of thinking, style of work, style of planning and organizing, style of language."[5] In a chapter on English placement examinations, Ohmann finds that these tests steer the astute pupil toward "those ideas that will be safe for him."[6] Another chapter shows that English rhetoric textbooks divorce writing about "problems" from the social contexts in which the student might experience such problems. These texts see the student "as newborn, unformed, without social origins and without the needs that would spring from his origins. He has no history."[7] "Argument" presented this way, "divorced from power, money, social conflict, class, and consciousness," is "pseudo-argument." But then "pseudo-argument is good training for entry into a society with a pseudo-politics"—that is, where major decisions are made through processes imperceptible to the citizen and where the real issues are obscured by mystification.[8] Another chapter analyzes the meretricious language of Pentagon

war-managers and futurological social theorists. The implication
is that freshman English implants or intensifies the amoral
"problem-solving" mentality of management and bureaucracy:
"Both the skills (fluency, organization, analysis) and the attitudes
(caution, detachment, cooperation) that we encourage in the
young are essential to the technostructure and to the smooth
functioning of liberal (not liberated) society."[9] As Ohmann presents it, composition bears approximately the same relation to the
student body which Methodism bore to the nineteenth-century
industrial proletariat.

It is not always clear what Ohmann thinks should be done
about the situation he deplores. It is evident that he does not
belong to the let-it-all-hang-out school of composition theory,
which supposes that the discarding of discipline is revolutionary
or liberating. And he seems more intent on extracting the critical
potential of traditional disciplines than on getting rid of them. At
times, however, Ohmann seems to suggest that orthodox discipline is itself intrinsically reactionary:

> Is the myth of our usefulness to the rest of the university and
> to society, then, totally unfounded? I think not. Recall. . .some
> of the things we have traditionally attempted to teach: organ-
> izing information, drawing conclusions from it, making re-
> ports, using Standard English (i.e., the language of the bour-
> geois elites), solving problems (assignments), keeping one's
> audience in mind, seeking objectivity and detachment, con-
> ducting persuasive arguments, reading either quickly or
> closely, as circumstances demand, producing work on request
> and under pressure, valuing the intellect and its achievements.
> These are all abilities that are clearly useful to the new indus-
> trial state, and, to the extent that English departments nourish
> them—even if only through the agency of graduate assistants—
> they are giving value for society's money.[10]

It is difficult to know how to take this passage. It seems unlikely
that Ohmann would seriously maintain that conventions such as
keeping one's audience in mind, seeking objectivity and detachment, and valuing the intellect and its achievements are inherently repressive or elitist. Yet by associating these conventions
with the fetishism of Standard English and the mechanical carry-

ing out of assignments, Ohmann invites his reader to draw just such a conclusion.* The paradigms of radical polemic, if not Ohmann's own thinking, force him into apparent anti-intellectualism: conventional methods of writing have been used to reinforce privilege; therefore, if we dismantle these conventional methods, we help undermine the ruling class. By the logic of this argument, *competence* as such becomes reactionary when it exists within an unjust system.

The problem is that some techniques which may be "essential to the technostructure" may also happen to be essential to thinking and expression as such, including thinking and expression that challenge the technostructure. The fact that, at present, these techniques feed the corporate vocational system—and since there is no other system, it is hard to see how they could not—is not a point against the techniques but against the way they are used. Rather than attack the techniques themselves, a more useful strategy might be to demand that they be put to a more critical use—at least in the classroom, the only area within the English teacher's sphere of control. To some extent, this is precisely what Ohmann recommends. But he persistently confounds the ideological misuse of standard conventions with the conventions themselves. Thus Ohmann's book lends some encouragement to those who would go a good deal farther than he and would argue that teaching the conventions of logical exposition violates the student's authenticity, or his "right to his own language."

*Other critics of standard composition practices leave even less to the reader's imagination. Donald C. Stewart, in *College English,* writes of the "rhetorical malnutrition" in the standard "organizational paradigms" of scholarly writing: "For the most part, . . .the articles I read repeated, with mind numbing consistency, a pattern of organization which varies only when some of these components are omitted or slightly rearranged: (1) statement of the problem; (2) review of the relevant scholarship; (3) statement of method in discussing the problem; (4) analysis of evidence to support generalizations; (5) conclusion. . . ." ("Rhetorical Malnutrition in Prelim Questions and Literary Criticism," *College English,* 39, no. 2 [October 1977], 162-63). Stewart's list of "offenses" bears comparison with Ohmann's.

How persuasive is the claim that the type of writing competence aimed at in the composition course is vital to the managerial system? Is there really a sympathetic connection between the ideology of freshman English and the ideology of the Pentagon or the corporation? How far is verbal competence a condition of success in America? These are difficult and important questions and one cannot dismiss Ohmann's charges lightly. It is hard to deny that verbal competence plays a role in social stratification, that college English, as Ohmann says, functions as part of a "sorting-out system" that disqualifies underclass groups from prosperity and status. The fact that ability to use certain verbal formulas will get a student into the university (if his parents can afford to send him) and thus open up opportunities denied to others shows that verbal skill is indeed bound up with class structure. But does it then follow from this fact that the type of expression encouraged in college English courses is "essential to the technostructure" or that English as a whole instills a conservative ideology? Might there not be something anachronistic in Ohmann's analysis, as Ohmann comes close to conceding at several points?

For instance, Ohmann admits that even though freshman English teaches skills and attitudes supposedly essential to technocratic society, it usually teaches them badly. He concedes that composition courses are "notoriously ineffective." The question then arises, why, if the technostructure thinks these skills and attitudes are so essential, does it tolerate such ineffectiveness in imparting them? We have seen that Ohmann believes freshman composition teaches "the style, broadly defined, of the managerial and professional classes." Yet he also observes that English teachers "often show esthetic contempt for the language of businessmen, bureaucrats, advertisers"—the very language, we have been told, which it is their business to teach.[11] At another point, Ohmann all but abandons his argument that composition courses transmit the style of an elite class: he observes that English teachers have recently "become more sophisticated" and given up the "myth" that "one usage or dialect is absolutely correct."[12] But Ohmann declines to draw from his own perceptions the seemingly plausible conclusion that both society and English teaching have changed in some important way, that the indoctrination theory, as he has stated it at any rate, will no longer do.

When Ohmann moves from the teaching of composition to the teaching of literature, his analysis becomes both more consistent and more subtle. In an essay on the American New Critics that avoids the common tendency to caricature them as mere "formalists" or literary technicians, Ohmann shows how this and other critical schools in the post-World War II period conferred on literature and literary study an illusion of independence from the social and political world. "All the schools of criticism agree," Ohmann writes, "that literature is a very special and separate thing, whose privileged cultural position needs defending—against science, against politics, against commercialization, against vulgarity, against nearly the whole social process."[13] Now as I suggested earlier, the literary separatism Ohmann describes here is only one motif in modern critical thinking. It is complemented by another—seen in visionary theorists from Blake to Frye and others—which exalts literature as the political conscience of society. Still, Ohmann's argument is persuasive because he does not ignore the important cultural and humanistic aims that have accompanied the modern critical separation of literature from external contexts.

In two extensive chapters on "What English Departments Do" and "Why They Do It," Ohmann traces the rise of departmentalism and professionalism in English since their beginnings in the 1880s, and he shows how these trends have subverted many of the declared purposes of humanistic education. Since a department's prestige is proportional to the eminence of its research scholars and critics, the curriculum tends to be determined, whether anybody wants it that way or not, by the range of specializations in the faculty rather than by educational philosophy. The resulting incoherence of the curriculum is then rationalized as a triumph of pluralism. Ohmann cites Thomas Wilcox's finding that the English major "is amorphous, without evident principles to justify its substance or sequence. Apparently the concept 'English major' is a necessary but empty one."[14] This is just the kind

of insight that undermines rather than supports the indoctrination theory of English: a system that is intellectually amorphous
and without principles is not likely to be effective in indoctrinat-
ing anybody, at least not in the conventional fashion. If one wants
to argue the contrary, one will need a different conception of
indoctrination and a different conception of ideology than those
implied by Ohmann. Ohmann on the teaching of literature,
though superior to Ohmann on composition, is again hindered by
the liabilities of his radical theory.

These liabilities emerge when Ohmann discusses the growing
disparity between the kind of work the profession most values and
rewards and the work for which it is valued and subsidized by
society. The composition teachers constitute a proletariat which
supports the leisure of the professorial aristocracy. Poorly paid
teaching assistants in English 101 handle the bulk of the students, whose tuition money underwrites high-salaried research
professors pursuing their esoteric projects in the serenity of the
graduate seminar. "Hence, the familiar paradox," Ohmann
writes, "that the part of our job that justifies us to others within
and outside the university is the part we hold in least regard and
delegate to the least prestigious members of the profession."[15]
The argument is hard to challenge, but it is not quite as good as it
looks on all points. Again, I think Ohmann has permitted traditional radical categories to do his thinking for him, the result
being that he views the English department of today in terms that
would have been more appropriate three decades ago. The image
of the humanities professor as a superspecialized expert whose
work is irrelevant or incomprehensible to the majority of students
and to society in general still has some basis in reality, but it leaves
out of account the increasing popularity of modern literature and
modern literary ideas both in and outside the university. In his assurance that composition is still "the part of our job that justifies
us to others within and outside the university," Ohmann neglects
to consider that transmission of modernist sensibility and "life-
styles" may have become as important as the transmission of
good grammar. And his analysis of the conservative ideology of
freshman English and the ivory-tower mandarinism of the profes-

sors ignores the degree to which both freshman English and the professors may have been transformed by the influence of the adversary culture of modernism.

English as Consumption

Had Ohmann pursued the implications of his own point that English teachers "often show esthetic contempt for the language of businessmen, bureaucrats, advertisers," he might have noted that the origins of this contempt are now different from what they used to be. Such contempt now derives less from genteel snobbery than from a more modish rebellion against bourgeois culture. Who, after all, if not the literati, have popularized the term "bourgeois" as an accepted expression of derision? And among whom did they popularize this derision if not the bourgeoisie? In 1846, Baudelaire observed that "there are no more bourgeois, now that the bourgeois himself uses this insulting epithet—a fact that shows his willingness to become art-minded and listen to what the columnists have to say."[16] Ohmann does make passing mention of Lionel Trilling's (and others') thesis that the adversary culture has been largely assimilated, domesticated, and trivialized by mass education and the media.[17] But this thesis is not integrated into Ohmann's analysis—and it could not be integrated without undermining many of his presuppositions. Ohmann's indoctrination theory confuses two distinct cultural phases of advanced industrial society: it attacks "bourgeois" culture and "technocracy" in the same breath, as if technocracy were not profoundly destructive of bourgeois traditions. This tempts him to imply that avant-garde dismantling of traditions ought to be politically subversive—a conclusion he himself senses to be untrue.

One might reply to Ohmann that if English has an ideology today, it is the anti-bourgeois ideology of literary and cultural modernism. This is an ideology of "alienation," cultivation of the self, elevation of private over public experience (even when the privacy is communal), and "liberation." In this sense, English does impart the ideology of society but of a society which has to a large degree become disaffected from society, or at least from its

traditional bourgeois institutions and pieties. It is difficult to say
to what precise extent the teaching of composition and literature
has been transformed by therapeutic goals such as the quest for
personhood and realization of the inner self. The degree varies,
depending on the institution and its location. But it seems fair to
say that such aims have diluted the older aims of training for
citizenship, vocation, and good manners, if they have not done
away with these aims entirely. And it seems fair to predict that
this will be the direction of things to come—"back to basics" or
no.

Some support for this prediction can be found in current trends
in composition theory exemplified by writers who do not claim to
be radical but whose thinking reflects the influence of liberal-
radical paradigms. A case in point is the reorientation of attention from writing as *product* to writing as *process*. As John
McNamara says, "more and more teachers and researchers are
insisting that we concentrate on the process of writing itself,
a process that our traditional approaches have not directly
treated."[18] Such a reorientation is not itself undesirable—especially when one considers the failure of earlier approaches which,
as McNamara notes, concentrated exclusively on "the principles
of rhetoric and the rules of grammar as matters the student must
master before actually writing" or on "exemplary models in an-
thologies that the student is supposed to emulate in his own
writing."[19] Moreover, this reorientation is based on two legitimate insights: (1) that, as James M. McCrimmon says, "a writer
learns about his subject by writing about it,"[20] and (2) that good
writers manage to incorporate the movement and excitement of
discovery in the form of their compositions. These legitimate
insights, however, are frequently used to justify contempt for
logic, consistency, and organized thought.

Thus in an article on "rhetorical malnutrition" as a feature of
academic writing, Donald C. Stewart proposes the process-over-
product thesis as a cure—celebrating its advent with the comment
that "those of us who attempt to keep up with the leading edge
[sic] of composition research and theory are now aware that we
are poised on the edge of a frontier which opens out into a
compositional territory that is vast and unexplored."[21] Stewart

recommends Richard Poirier's concept of writing as "performance" as a promising model for composition, a concept which,
as we saw in earlier chapters, glorifies "energy" over "repressive
analysis."[22] Stewart also cites Francis Christensen's advocacy of
the cumulative sentence, which, in Christensen's words, "does
not represent the idea as conceived, pondered over, reshaped,
packaged, and delivered cold."[23] This packaging of thought, in
Christensen's view, is a legacy of "Cartesian reason or intellect,"
which in the seventeenth century displaced " 'the direct sensuous
apprehension of thought' (T. S. Eliot's words)."[24] In short, these
applications of the process-product distinction express the
most hackneyed dualisms of romantic and postromantic literary
propaganda, the implication of which is that analysis and logic
are hostile to unified sensibility and that insofar as a writer is
preoccupied with the mere conclusions to which his discourse is
directed—"the idea as conceived, pondered over, reshaped"—he
is furthering a rhetorical complement of capitalism, wherein
ideas are "packaged, and delivered cold."

Along similar lines, David H. Hill diagnoses the ills of college
composition as a consequence of our society's overemphasis on
"self-extinguishing, false objectivity" at the expense of emotional
response, "continuing, co-operative dialogue," and "ongoing
interaction"—again as if such an analysis had not long ago
become a commonplace of modernism and, more recently, of the
therapeutic culture.[25] "While I'm not saying we ought to think of
ourselves as howling Athenian mobs," Hill writes, "neither
should we always regard ourselves as disinterested consumers and
producers of coolly logical, perfectly packaged intellectual
products."[26] Even more explicitly than Stewart and Christensen,
Hill brings us through a series of equations from a particular
technique of writing (or of teaching writing) to capitulation to
capitalist dehumanization. "Cool" logic=disinterestedness=
packaging=consumption=dead products. What is the remedy?
"Maybe we need—not only in the English classroom but also
in the society which, after all, that classroom inevitably reflects—
to get 'back to the basics' in the sense of thinking a little more
systematically about the processes people go through as writers
and a little less exclusively about the products which they present

at the end of the process."[27] Again, a reasonable enough attempt
to shift the focus of composition to the process of writing has got
mixed up with a modernist ideology that confuses objective and
logical methods with technocratic conformity and loss of self. And
again we see a determination to remedy this surfeit of objectivity
and logic by glorifying the "performances" of consciousness, as if
the quality of a performance had no relation to its substance.
Though in theory these commentators insist on the personal and
creative nature of writing, the predictability of their own rhetoric
makes one feel it is not a person speaking so much as the radical-
liberal-therapeutic paradigm itself.

But the invocation of writing-as-a-performance as an antidote
for excessive emphasis on substance reaches a culmination in
another work, *Style: An Anti-Textbook*, by Richard A. Lanham.
In this book, the transfer of concepts from modernist formalism
to composition theory, hinted at in the other writers I have
mentioned, is complete. Lanham's basic argument is that "the
scientific attitude," with its strict emphasis on conceptual communication and its view of style as ideally transparent and self-
effacing, has corrupted American attitudes toward writing.
Americans, he says, have been conditioned to look at writing
almost solely for the payload of concepts that can be got out of it
and not at all for the self-conscious verbal play that can be
enjoyed for its own sake: "American pragmatism insists that
words are for use not enjoyment; American puritanism insists
that expression is a duty not a pleasure."[28] "Surely we ought to
move in the opposite direction from such moral earnestness,
stressing not words as duty but words as play."[29] Having
overemphasized "the sacred-scientific-duty-to-express-concepts
clearly," Lanham says, we have neglected the "dramatization of
character" and "the presentation of the writer's self"—as if the
expression of concepts and the presentation of self were necessarily antithetical.[30] What is new here, as Patrick Story observed in
his review of the book, is the transfer of "postwar Modernist-
formalist aesthetic assumptions which blur or deny our knowledge of objective reality...not only in poetry and fiction, as in
the postwar era, but *in discursive writing itself.*"[31] Lanham does
away with the old formalist opposition between poetry and exposi-

tory prose not because he values the prose function of poetry but because he regards expository prose as itself, ideally, something that functions for its own sake.

Though Lanham is consistently derisive toward scientists and the scientific attitude, he concedes generous amounts of territory to them. Indeed, Lanham consigns virtually all "conceptual" uses of language to science, a division of labor that narrows all writing that is not purely scientific to "eloquence," "style," and "the play attitude toward style."[32] There are occasional hints of a politics motivating this division of territory, a politics we have earlier seen exemplified in literary-critical repudiations of mimesis and realism. Lanham's antithesis between conceptual communication and style is made to correspond at one point with the opposition between the bureaucratic world, associated with "the remote inhumanity, the impersonality of journalistic reporting, of mumblespeak, of the preposterous drivel that politicians talk," and the beleaguered modern individual's struggle to fight free of this depersonalization.[33] At another point, Lanham says that "just as our scientific attempts to 'conquer' nature end by destroying and dehumanizing it, our efforts to Do our Duty as Effective Communicators end up holding language at arm's length."[34] And finally, Lanham says that we tend "to degrade all verbal pleasure into utility, just as we degrade all human motive into the cash nexus."[35] In these examples the conceptual functions of writing and speaking are associated successively with (1) inhuman bureaucracy and politics, (2) the technocratic rape of nature, and (3) the reduction of human qualities to the level of commodities. That somebody might want to combat bureaucratic power, technocracy, and commerce by contesting rather than conceding their monopoly over the conceptual functions of communication is an idea that never arises.

But Lanham makes no effort to conceal the concessive direction of his argument. As modern technology takes over more and more of the practical functions of everyday life, he notes, most of us have less and less need to communicate practical messages anyway. Making a virtue of necessity, writing and speaking can now take advantage of their uselessness:

Don't the signs now suggest an aristocratic stage beyond the utilitarian one? We certainly possess the only begetter of aristocratic taste, moneyed leisure. In the future that Alvin Toffler has conjured up in *Future Shock,* utilitarian pressure will evaporate entirely. We won't have to do anything. Everything will be done for pleasure. The proud slogans of the Renaissance will become literally true. Man will remake himself in whatever form or style he chooses. We shall have to develop both acute self-consciousness and an equally acute sense of style. Electronic intelligence may entirely appropriate prose's obligation to communicate concepts. Such a world speaks and writes entirely for pleasure, entirely for style.[36]

No doubt a shrewd critic of futurological rhetoric like Ohmann would ask who is this "we" who, in Lanham's utopian calculation, will have the moneyed leisure to do nothing except remake himself in whichever form or style he chooses at the moment. Ohmann would point out, rightly, that this abstract "we" obscures the distinction between those in control and those being controlled, however much the latter may be compensated for their servitude by the joy of style. Yet without at all accepting Lanham's benign view, we can see that his statement reflects more of the actual social pressures shaping thinking about language and composition in a consumer society than do the diagnoses of Ohmann and his colleagues on the left. The real import of Lanham's celebration of style divorced from utility is that freedom to enjoy the self in all its possibilities has become a compensation for dispossession from power. What the radicals ignore—or fail to take seriously enough when they do not ignore it—is that the pressure to domesticate writing to traditional puritanical, scientific, and utilitarian demands has been met by a counterpressure to mobilize writing in the campaign for compensatory self-consumption.

The Fluid Status Quo

In advancing its view of the way English does the work of society, the standard left-wing critique assumes that English is tied to the mechanism of production and administration, that it serves either as training for work or attitudes congenial to work. But it may be that English—and the humanities—today teach not the ethos of work so much as a new ethos of leisure and consumption. Increasingly, English education acts not as socialization in the Protestant or the managerial ethic but as the kind of accredited de-socialization (or re-socialization) required by an economy of planned obsolescence, where one's function as a consumer may be more important than the work one does to earn the where-withal for consumption. Courses in vanguard topics, which draw big enrollments, help implant those types of alienation which are politically harmless and shape consumption attitudes. The atmosphere of the campus is less and less distinguishable from that of the supermarket, the shopping center, and the "funky" boutique; students are trained to shop for humanities courses and to evaluate them by consumer criteria. In this atmosphere, the vanguard professor-intellectual becomes a new kind of celebrity—his notoriety often extends far beyond the limits of the campus.

With the trivialization of work and the emptiness of a life centered more and more on consumption, large numbers of people now feel their experience lacks meaning. The vanguard professor-intellectual, a kind of expert in "existential encounters," engaging in allegedly risky adventures on "the frontiers of consciousness," provides consolations, explanations, and solutions. Though he may operate on the loftiest level and may even call himself a revolutionary, the vanguard professor-intellectual fits in: he hands on the "alternative" ideas and "life-styles"—that is to say, the consumer tastes—which mark the approved modes of social estrangement. He enacts an exemplary drama of powerlessness which gives him considerable power in the cultural sphere—power to shape the styles of powerlessness.

This is not to say that the vanguard literati are the only kind of professors who are influential, or that their ideology has extinguished all its rivals. In today's university, as Ohmann recognizes, incompatible and incommensurable viewpoints coexist peacefully—things being arranged to ensure that these viewpoints rarely come into contact. Here again is why the thesis of Kampf and Lauter that "high culture propagates the values of those who rule" will no longer wash. This thesis credits high culture and those who rule with a coherence of outlook neither any longer possesses. When the modernist revolution made Matthew Arnold's concept of culture seem outmoded, high culture lost what relative unity it may have had. A high culture which includes both Arnold and Artaud, Samuel Johnson and Samuel Beckett, has no ideological unity. As for those who rule, it is self-flattering but mistaken to think that these flexible pragmatists require high culture as a means of justifying or consolidating their power.

The modern corporation has disencumbered itself from any "values" except the long-range maximization of profit, and profit will appropriate any type of values and any type of culture. The corporate spirit, far from being rigid or absolutist, is cool, opportunistic, unsentimental; it adapts to "rapidly changing times" and encourages innovation. It understands the impracticality of having any particular ideology. That is why corporations entrust the job of formulating their "images" to outside public-relations and advertising specialists whose business it is to be in tune with the most advanced ideas. If thus being in tune means affecting the accents of the adversary culture, that is not necessarily bad for business.

The ability of capitalism to do without a fixed ideology was well perceived by Tocqueville as early as the 1830s. "The wealthy members of democracies," he writes in *Democracy in America,* "never form a body which has manners and regulations of its own; the opinions peculiar to their class do not restrain them" from the pursuit of commercial profit. "To tell the truth," Tocqueville continues, "though there are rich men, the class of rich men does not exist; for these rich individuals have no feelings or purposes, no traditions or hopes, in common; there are individuals, therefore, but no definite class."[37] Tocqueville anticipates Marx's recognition that, though the manufacturers form a "class" as defined by their common interests, these very interests discourage any permanent set of manners and beliefs peculiar to this class.

Indeed, by the end of the nineteenth century, the self-confidence of the ruling class had lost its economic basis. As early as 1878, Engels saw the transition to corporate forms of capitalism turning the capitalist himself into a superfluous person:

> If the crises revealed the incapacity of the bourgeoisie any longer to control the modern productive forces, the conversion of the great organisations for production and communication into joint-stock companies and state property shows that for this purpose the bourgeoisie can be dispensed with. All the social functions of the capitalists are now carried out by salaried employees. The capitalist has no longer any social activity save the pocketing of revenues, the clipping of coupons and gambling on the Stock Exchange, where the different capitalists fleece each other of their capital. Just as at first the capitalist mode of production displaced the workers, so now it displaces the capitalists, relegating them, just as it did the workers, to the superfluous population, even if in the first instance not to the industrial reserve army.[38]

The habit of conceptualizing the ruling class through metaphors of "establishment" or "status quo" encourages the delusion that contemporary commercial culture is confident, stolid, and immovable. From this misperception follows the complementary one that the unsettling of cultural traditions and conventions is politically revolutionary. But as I argued in the previous chapter, the traditions which serve as targets of radical demystification were long ago dissolved or rendered innocuous by capitalism itself.

Marx's best known contribution to the theory of ideology was of course his view that class societies develop beliefs that reflect the material interests of the dominant class. Less widely noted is Marx's more subtle perception that the capitalist form of society is so fundamentally volatile and irreverent that it weakens the authority of all ideologies. As Marx and Engels noted, capitalism brings about an "uninterrupted disturbance of all social conditions, everlasting uncertainty and agitation. All fixed, fast-frozen relations, with their train of ancient and venerable prejudices and opinions, are swept away, all new-formed ones become antiquated before they can ossify. All that is solid melts in air, all that is holy is profaned. . . . "[39] Marx here anticipates the fact that, in a capitalist society, the idea of *tradition* gives way to the idea of *fashion,* and revolt against tradition becomes profitable.

At the root of this disruption of tradition is the commodity, the unit of capitalist production and consumption. According to Marx in *Capital,* the commodity is "a born leveller and a cynic, . . . ready to exchange not only soul, but body, with any and every other commodity."[40] The fact that capitalism levels all relations into the common measure of exchange value is one reason why the culture of capitalism is a culture of perpetual metamorphosis. One could argue that surrealism rather than puritanical bourgeois rationalism is the cultural counterpart of contemporary capitalism. Such a metamorphic culture renders radical attacks on the presumably entrenched past superfluous, just as it turns this kind of radicalism into a commodity.

Ohmann's type of critique does not give capitalist society much credit for subtlety or adaptability. It assumes that the only way in which capitalism can deal with ideological heterodoxy is either to repress it or oppose it with ideological orthodoxy. Such a view presupposes the continued existence of the sort of correlation between power and ideology which had already begun to dissolve in the nineteenth century. The society of consumerism and planned obsolescence turns the traditional correspondence between power and ideology on its head. With the assistance of mass-communications, this kind of society subjects traditions and ideas to the same obsolescence that affects material products, and ruling-class traditions and ideologies are not immune to this process. In this kind of society, values, ideas, artworks, and other products of the spirit are assimilated into the logic of the fashion industries. Revolutions in artistic form, critical approaches, and ideas in general become as ephemeral, as arbitrary, and as insignificant as changes in automotive design or the styling of hair. This new way of appropriating culture, which does not need to "administer" thought when it can patronize it, does not make radical criticism useless. But it calls for concepts and strategies of opposition which are rarely found in the thinking of the cultural left.

Back to Basics

Though we hear complaints that today's college students are less
contaminated by familiarity with conventional modes of writing
than ever before, their disposition to take a critical view of society
does not seem to have correspondingly increased. It might be
argued that freshman English would have more success in encouraging students to think critically and even radically if it were
more "elitist"—that is, if it demanded that students master the
techniques of "organizing information," "drawing conclusions
from it," "seeking objectivity and detachment," and the other
items on Ohmann's list. A student who has learned traditional
logical and rhetorical principles might be more apt to recognize
contradictions in his social environment than the student who has
been exposed to the latest form of radical culture and propaganda. It is true that the traditional techniques of thinking and
writing, like the rest of the cultural heritage, have been used to
further the interests of the elite and the upwardly mobile. But
then the task of educational radicals ought to be not to dismantle
these techniques but to restore them to the groups from which
they have been stolen. The assumption that the traditional heritage is intrinsically corrupted by the uses to which class societies
have put it cannot be found in Marx, Trotsky, Kropotkin, or
Bakunin.

    Recently, in a general reaction against the excesses of the edu-
cational reformation of the sixties, there has arisen a "back to
basics" movement. This has meant bringing back the freshman
writing course, given up by many universities a few years ago in
favor of more immediately stimulating subject matter. In literature, it means the revival of a more old-fashioned curriculum.
One should note that the impetus for the advanced styles of
educational thinking referred to above is grounded not only in the
psychology of the educators and the public but in the economics
of universities, which must make increasingly consumeristic
appeals if they want to hold a competitive position in a tightening
educational market. As cold enrollment statistics increasingly
determine the content of the curriculum, Donne and Pope (if not
Shakespeare) may be hard pressed to hold their own against pop

culture. But even should the return to "basics" succeed in driving out meretricious innovations in the curriculum, there is reason to wonder why the basic approach should be more successful this time around than it was a decade ago, when it was abandoned. What is to prevent the return to discipline, given time and opportunity to fail once again, from inspiring a new wave of efforts at liberation from discipline?

We seem to be caught in an unhappy alternation between a shallowly conceived "traditional" discipline and the shallow radical alternative it provokes. This is not to say that the current return to earth from the psychedelic euphoria of the sixties is a step backward. But the sixties, for all their anti-intellectualism, did pose questions about the social context of education which are not always addressed by the current advocates of retrenchment. The slogan "back to basics" betrays no sign of helpful thought about what *is* basic to a sound education. One senses that its advocates are not inclined to tackle the problem at its root—the fragmentary and disconnected character of the "skills" and information that have characterized American educational programs, whether basic *or* liberated. Even if we were to cut away the mass of frivolous subjects that have cluttered the curriculum since the late sixties, we would be left with a body of materials without an intelligible principle of relation. In this respect, the incoherence of the post-sixties curriculum is really only an extension of the incoherence of the more "basic" pre-sixties curriculum. We now look back on that as a "traditional" education, but it was not very traditional at all, for it dissolved learning into a collection of unrelated subjects without an intellectual unity. Today as before, a tacit pretense is maintained that the goals of a liberal education are understood and shared, and this pretense prevents embarrassing questions of fundamental purpose from being asked. If you do not know what literature is *for*, what are you doing studying it? If you are confused about the aims of liberal education, how can you go on teaching it?

At an earlier time, questions about the goals of education were not raised because most students and teachers understood what these goals were. Now such questions are not raised because nobody knows what these goals are, and the confusion which follows when the questions do break out is too painful to bear. With the deterioration of coherence in the rationale of the humanities, administration rather than ideas and understanding tends to become the unifying "meaning" of the university. But this is not, as the educational radicals claim, because of the ruling class's need to "administer thought," but rather because there has ceased to be any thought to be concerned about. The bureaucratization of the university is tied not to indoctrination but to the disappearance of intellectual content. This de-intellectualization of the university is rationalized by a false pluralism: since no world view or theory is privileged to speak for everybody, the university no longer sees itself as responsible for defining a central body of information or issues. The threat of academic totalitarianism—frequently conjured up as the sole alternative to incoherence—protects the university from having to define its intellectual purposes or even from having to have any. And since there can be no central body of information or issues, the only force capable of binding the fragments of the university into a unity is the machinery of administration, which possesses the advantage of representing no ideas. This is not to say that bureaucracy is intrinsically evil—it is hard to imagine a modern university doing without it—but it appears oppressive when the ends to which it is supposed to be dedicated have so atrophied that it becomes its own end.

Only a student with the rarest powers of synthesis can make sense in a useful way of what passes for a "traditional" program of university courses. In some instances, university education actually makes people stupider—more confused, less able to fit the fragments together. The much invoked "dialogue" does not take place under the present kind of pluralism because there is too little common experience, too little focus. To justify this incoherence on the ground that the modern disciplines, not to mention the modern experience in general, resist systematization and integration, or that the day is long past when any single world view can unify education, is to miss the point. The breakdown of the traditional unity of knowledge is itself part of history and therefore a proper part of the subject matter of a properly integrated education. But instead of making our confusion part of our subject matter and thus helping students to understand it, the university exemplifies the confusion and passes it on. It never ceases to amaze me when radical educational critics accuse the university of handing down an elitist cultural heritage. These critics seem not to have noticed that confusion, not highbrow ideas, has become the cultural heritage.

It is difficult to understand how the university curriculum can become radical, or even how it can begin to promote serious critical thought, until it first becomes coherent. We have seen Ohmann's complaint about the way freshman rhetoric tests, and the courses in which they are used, divorce students from society and history. What is unclear is how the English teacher is to return the student to history when he himself is surrounded by an ahistorical culture that does not equip him with the means to see his own history as part of a coherent process. In order to infuse composition and literary study with a sense of history, to inform them with a sense of their own relation to "power, money, social conflict, class and consciousness," one has to possess some theoretical understanding of history and society. Such understanding, as Ohmann himself implies, is made difficult by the very nature of modern politics and modern society.

One irony of the current situation is that though students study more contemporary literature and culture than they ever did in the past, few of them attain what can seriously be called a minimal comprehension of contemporary literature and culture. Because contemporary material is rarely studied in conjunction with the history against which its identity as "contemporary" is defined, the very concept of the contemporary acquires no meaning. Though "popular culture" is a valid object of study, our isolation of it in its own courses, divorced from history, tends merely to reproduce the experience of discontinuity already sufficiently available in contemporary culture itself. Contemporary culture contains few ideas capable of liberating us from its provincialism. On the contrary, it exudes warnings expressed in the most intimidating of styles, of the absolute futility of attempting to understand it, and the even more absolute futility of trying to resist its charm.

Only a historical view of contemporary subjects can prevent

them from subtracting from understanding. For only a historical view provides a perspective from which to assess the richness and poverty of the contemporary, to see what has been gained from this break with the past and what has been lost—and might be regained. D. S. Carne-Ross has made this point well in defending a traditional literary education that has rarely been tried:

> Literature and the other arts are the purest witness to what has been lost. They reveal, as nothing else can, something that was once presence and is now absence. And could, though in no foreseeable future, be presence again. . . . But for the arts, we would not even know that we are living now without what men have always had. They alone remember and they remind us; everything else encourages us to forget and be content. The arts teach us to be discontent with this "world we live in."[41]

In other words, history is a criticism of the present. It affords the critical perspective on the gains and losses of contemporaneity that contemporaneity fails to provide. Apprehending this criticism in all its complexity and making it accessible is the problem and the challenge.

To make sense of history against the flow of an anti-historical society, yet one that is ahistorical for historically intelligible reasons—this seems to me the most "progressive" function that the university could perform at the moment. It is certainly a condition of any radicalizing of students that would not simply liberate them from intelligence. It is, moreover, the only kind of radical function that has a chance at the moment of securing collective dedication from the diversity of scholars. Unless the returning of the student to his history is to mean no more than inculcating him with the latest radical platitudes, themselves symptomatic of a poverty of historical understanding, we have to suppose that this task can only be accomplished by the university as a whole—that is, by scholars of diverse political inclinations working in common.

In literary studies the rehabilitation of history would require the recovery of the evolutionary concept of literature and culture. In an essay on "The Concept of Evolution in Literary History," René Wellek has shown how this concept fell victim a half century ago to the twin forces of positivistic "factualism" and historicist overschematization.[42] On the one hand, history degenerated into a congeries of disparate facts and documents, into mere "backgrounds" of literary creations instead of their informing principle. It was this degeneration of history into background that set the stage for the rejection of history by the next generation of scholars. When the New Critics rejected the historical approach, or even when they welcomed it, as they more often did, as a necessary adjunct to criticism, it was this debased conception of history as a collection of documents and background facts that they entertained. On the other hand, insofar as a concept of evolutionary history survived, it was often tied to the rigid determinism and naive teleology of vulgar Marxism. Given the reduction of history either to bare particulars or overgeneralized ideas of progress, it was easy for the New Critics to assume that history is something separable from literary structure. From this loss of history as an integrative principle the English curriculum has still not recovered.

To restore his students to history, the English teacher must teach literature as a manifestation not merely of the history of social or economic classes but of history in the totality of its development, or as much of that totality as the teacher and the curriculum can encompass. Such historical teaching requires the collaboration of the English department with the departments of history, sociology, economics, science, philosophy, and other literatures, a collaboration that establishes a common basis of issues—if only to have a focus for disagreement. The fact that scholars do not agree on the nature of history does not defeat such a program, for its purpose would not be to indoctrinate the student with a single theory but to bring him into the debate, to introduce him to the issues, and to equip him with the means to form his judgment of them and see his personal connection with them. The point is not to destroy pluralism but to transform it into a pluralism defined by a community of debate rather than a pluralism of incommensurable positions.

Their ambivalence toward traditional education in composition and literature weakens the critiques of the educational radicals. To be sure, Ohmann does not go so far as programmatic irrationalists like Fiedler and Wasson, who confuse criticism and tradition themselves with elitism. But his persistent implication that the traditional disciplines are contaminated by their abuse in class societies leads in a similar direction. Like more extreme cultural revolutionaries than he, Ohmann chooses to attack bourgeois ideas and traditions which are themselves antithetical to the spirit of contemporary technological society. Nowhere in his analysis do we find a sense of the critical potential latent in traditional humanistic education, could such an education be synthesized out of the fragmentation of the current university.

This chapter only begins to suggest how deeply the modes of thinking that condition our views of literature and the arts enter into our views of education as well. Just as much contemporary literary theory drains literature of its referential substance, much of our educational thinking views content either as an irrelevance or as a repressive threat to the selfhood of the learner. The ideal of the literary work's independence of preestablished reality is echoed in the ideal of the student's independence of preestablished discipline and subject matter. Having lost touch with coherent historical content, contemporary education is often "about" its own process in the same way as contemporary self-reflexive literature and criticism. And like literary theory, educational theory frequently redefines this impoverishment as a progressive advance. Instead of seeking to restore an aggressive ideal of mastery of understanding, educational thought glorifies process and experience for their own sakes and relegates mastery to the rubbish heap of dead ideas.

These generalizations characterize a great deal of radical as well as orthodox liberal educational thought—two versions of the same thing. Both versions have collaborated in combatting the elitism that allegedly inheres in any education that tries to exact "conformity" to preestablished techniques or to what is contemptuously referred to as a "body of knowledge." The very word "mastery" smacks of the "performance principle" that drives competitive society. To be sure, when we look at the pale, dispirited thing that has so often passed itself off as the exemplification of the traditional educational ideal—and that now has begun to reappear under the aegis of "back to basics"—we can easily understand why so many highly intelligent people have reacted against the very concept of traditional education. And when the traditional ideal is represented by rote memorization for its own sake or by an atomized curriculum of "basic" courses without intellectual focus or center, it is not surprising that many people reject the very concept of mastery. Yet our mode of reaction in this instance is as self-defeating as it has proved to be in the literary sphere. We do little to reform a contentless education by turning against content. On the other hand, the recovery of content is no simple matter. It will not come about without collective efforts by scholars to reconstruct our history.

Five

What Was New Criticism?

Not so very many years ago, the New Critics were academic radicals challenging the supremacy of the philologists, the literary and intellectual historians, and the literary biographers. Then, after a period of theoretical polemics and departmental in-fighting, the New Criticism won its battle for academic respectability. But scarcely had it done so than the New Criticism began to suffer attacks from other quarters. Some members of a new generation of teachers and scholars saw in New Criticism the epitome of all that was constricting and deadening about the academic study of literature. The New Critics, they charged, had trivialized literature and literary study by turning critical interpretation into an overintellectualized game whose object was the solution of petty interpretive puzzles. This "formalist" approach to literature, as it was labelled, was charged with ignoring or cancelling the latent moral, political, and personal impact of literary works.

No idea of the New Critics inspired more protests than their assumption of the "objective" nature of the literary text, their view that a poem is an object whose meaning can be analyzed by a detached, ideally disinterested critic. This assumption, which drew heavily from T. S. Eliot's idea of the "impersonality" of poetry, seemed to represent a failure of nerve on the part of the humanists in the face of the prestige of science and technology. The political conservatism of many leading New Critics seemed to reinforce this charge. The New Critics' attempt to emulate the empirical scientists by applying an objective, analytic method to literature was judged as one more symptom of the university's capitulation to the capitalist-military-industrial-technological complex. Today, the political coloration of this attack has faded, but much of the thinking which informed it persists.

The Rape of the Text

We have already seen in chapter 3 that for numerous critics on the cultural left interpretation in the New-Critical style bears roughly the same relation to literature, creative sensibility, and the reader as the urban police bear to oppressed minorities. Susan Sontag's description of interpretation as "the revenge of the intellect upon art,"[1] Richard Poirier's strictures on "repressive analysis,"[2] and the new French criticism's attacks on the ideology of positivism have New Criticism as an obvious target. Bruce Franklin, a more doctrinaire critic, describes New Criticism as a "crude and frankly reactionary formalism." The "essence of New Criticism," Franklin adds, is this: "the ostrich sticks his head in the sand and admires the structural relationships among the grains."[3] Louis Kampf describes New Criticism as the tool of an "educational bureaucracy fathered by advanced industrial capitalism."[4] And Richard Coe says that New Critical "intrinsic" criticism is "so close to a myth of empiricism" as to argue either "influence or a common ancestor." The intrinsic critic, Coe adds, "seeks an absolute basis in scientific empiricism."[5] Whatever the differences in literary and political outlook among these critics, all of them agree that New-Critical style objective interpretation, is an extension of the Western technological mentality with its aggressive need to transform its world into objects.

But an attack on the New Criticism with a similar drift comes from critics grounded in European existentialism. These critics see New Criticism—often along with Russian formalism, French academic historicism, and structuralism—as manifestations of the Cartesian subject-object dualism which plagues the empiricist tradition. As Sarah Lawall says in *Critics of Consciousness*, a study of the Geneva-centered existentialist criticism that includes such figures as Georges Poulet, Jean-Pierre Richard, Jean Starobinski, the early J. Hillis Miller, and Maurice Blanchot, "the historical lines are drawn between 'objective' criticism and a movement that analyzes the consciousness manifest in literature. . . . Any analysis that studies the work as an object, for forms, meanings, varying interpretations, and dictional peculiarities, runs directly counter to this new European attitude in which the work is not an object but an 'act' or 'experience.'" "The work of art as a combination of technical subtleties," Lawall adds, "is not important; its existence is justified because it is the concentrated expression of all humanity."[6] Murray Krieger has pointed out the common ground between this European phenomenological criticism and "our native irrationalist, anti-establishment radicalism," of which Ihab Hassan is his representative. "Despite differences," Krieger says, both groups show "a tendency to deobjectify and repersonalize literature."[7] Though the existentialist revolt against New Criticism need not be formulated in political terms, it too is largely inspired by a reaction against the technological rationality of advanced society. The difference between seeing literature as an "experience" rather than as an "object" corresponds to the difference between treating human beings as *persons* rather than as *things*.

These oppositions are prominent in Richard Palmer's study, *Hermeneutics*, a synopsis of the phenomenological approach to literary interpretation as practiced by Heidegger, Hans-Georg Gadamer, and others. For Palmer and the phenomenologists he expounds, New Critical objective interpretation is symptomatic of "the modern technological way of thinking and the will-to-power that lies at its root."[8] Objective interpretation amounts to "a forcible seizure, a 'rape' of the text."[9] At best this kind of interpretation results in "cold analyses of structure and pattern."[10] For Palmer, the weakness of Anglo-American literary interpretation lies in the fact that it "operates, philosophically speaking, largely in the framework of realism."[11] That is, it presupposes that "the literary work is simply 'out there' in the world, essentially independent of its perceivers. One's perception of the work is considered to be separate from the work itself, and the task of literary interpretation is to speak about the 'work itself.' . . . The preliminary separation of subject and object, so axiomatic in realism, becomes the philosophical foundation and framework of literary interpretation."[12]

In New Criticism, Palmer says, "the text becomes an object and explication a conceptual exercise which works solely within the 'given,' accepting the restrictions of scientific objectivity":[13]

"Science manipulates things and gives up living in them," the
late French phenomenologist Maurice Merleau-Ponty tells us.
This, in one sentence, is what has happened to American
literary interpretation. We have forgotten that the literary
work is not a manipulable object completely at our disposal; it
is a human voice out of the past, a voice which must somehow
be brought to life. Dialogue, not dissection, opens up the world
of a literary work. Disinterested objectivity is not appropriate
to the understanding of a literary work. [14]

Reading a literary work "is not a gaining of conceptual knowledge through observation and reflection; it is an 'experience,' a
breaking down and breaking up of one's old way of seeing." [15]
"Literature, in short, is not conceptual knowledge, but experience." [16] Not only is disinterested objectivity inappropriate to
literature, it is impossible: "There is no privileged access to a
work of literature, no access that stands outside of history and
outside one's own horizon of understanding." [17]

Geoffrey Hartman echoes many of the assumptions described
by Lawall and Palmer in a more recent account of the reaction of
contemporary continentally influenced critics against earlier interpretive orthodoxies such as the New Criticism. According to
Hartman's new philosophical criticism, "the attempt to establish
an objective or scientific hermeneutics is an act of defensive
mastery. It seeks to keep an unruly, changeable language within
the bounds of intelligibility." [18] In less picturesque language,
Hartman echoes Palmer's characterization of objectivity as a
form of rape and subjugation. Like Palmer, Hartman invokes the
authority of Heidegger in suggesting that this attempted mastery
"involves technocratic violence: a will to mastery common to most
theological and scientific explanation. It is precisely this type of
violence which has made us lose contact with things and so with
authentic languaging." [19]

At times, exponents of hermeneutical criticism concede that
the New Criticism was more than a mere literary scientism.
Hartman acknowledges that the New Critics were attempting to
save "the imagination from abstraction." [20] And Palmer says,
with real penetration, that "the philosophical base of New Criticism was always shaky and uncertain, vacillating between realism

and idealism."[21] But whenever Palmer deals with New Critical objective interpretation, he either disregards this vacillation or takes it to be a consequence of philosophical realism. Neither he nor other existentialist-influenced critics question the assumption that New Criticism is rooted in scientific empiricism and its preference for observational neutrality.

New Criticism and Science

The effect of all these indictments is to exaggerate the difference between New Criticism and its antagonists. As the movement's day of prominence recedes into the past, the meaning of the term "New Criticism" seems to become increasingly attenuated. Today the term denotes little more than a "methodology" of interpretation, a technique of "close reading" by which texts are induced —or forced—to give up their ambiguities, ironies, and complexities. This equating of New Criticism with mere methodology has been encouraged by the mechanical imitation of New Critical techniques which quickly arose in the wake of the founders of the movement. The methodology of New Criticism is thus understood apart from the New Critical theory of the nature and function of literature and apart from the larger context of cultural and disciplinary polemics which conditioned the methodology. Isolated from the theory of literature which gave it its rationale, New Critical interpretive method does begin to resemble a more or less trivial preoccupation with technical subtleties aimed apparently at investing literary study with scientific credentials and divesting it of broader humanistic concerns.

New Criticism had many defects, but the scientific reduction of literature to technical subtleties was not one of them. It is odd that the New Critics should be denounced for their arid scientific empiricism, since this was one of the chief cultural ills which the New Critics themselves sought to combat. The New Criticism stands squarely in the romantic tradition of the defense of the humanities as an antidote to science and positivism. The methodology of "close reading" was an attempt not to imitate science but to refute its devaluation of literature: by demonstrating the rich complexity of meaning within even the simplest poem, the New

Critic proved to the "hard-boiled naturalist," as Cleanth Brooks called him, that literature had to be taken seriously as a rival mode of cognitive knowledge.[22] I. A. Richards, one major New Critic who *did* attempt to apply systematic scientific principles to the analysis of literature, subordinated these principles to the larger aim of redeeming culture from the demoralizing effect of the scientific world view. Richards's scientism, like that of Northrop Frye, subserved a romantic esthetic which proposed literature as a compensation for loss of belief.

To see New Criticism as an expression of "the modern technological way of thinking," practicing a kind of "rape" of the literary text, is to have no way of accounting for the persistent condemnations of just this scientific, technological mentality— often couched in similarly vituperative language—running throughout New Criticism from T. S. Eliot to John Crowe Ransom and Brooks. Ransom, one of the most forceful advocates of a scrupulously impersonal and disinterested method of interpretation, also argued that scientific abstractions commit a kind of cold-blooded murder upon the rich, contingent particularity of "the world's body." Ransom's notion of "disinterestedness" in interpretation was aimed precisely at counteracting the practical, *interested* disposition of science. Science, Ransom wrote, is always "committed to a special interest," for the sake of which it abstracts from nature and thus "destroys the image," the concrete particulars of poetry:

> People who are engrossed with their pet "values" become
> habitual killers. Their game is the images, or the things, and
> they acquire the ability to shoot them as far off as they can be
> seen, and do. It is thus that we lose the power of imagination,
> or whatever faculty it is by which we are able to contemplate
> things as they are in their rich, contingent materiality.[23]

Brooks, following Ransom's *God without Thunder*, puts the term "science" into simple antithesis with "love." Science is the reduction of love to lust, the reduction of quality, value, and life to quantity, naturalistic fact, and death. "Love," Brooks writes, "is the aesthetic of sex; lust is the science. Love implies a deferring of the satisfaction of the desire; it implies a certain asceticism and a ritual. Lust drives forward urgently and scientifically to the immediate extirpation of the desire."[24] These statements occur in Brooks's interpretation of *The Waste Land,* a poem whose message for Brooks is that "our contemporary waste land is in large part the result of our scientific attitude—of our complete secularization."[25] The equation Love= Poetry, Predatory Lust= Science reveals a link between the politically conservative Brooks and the cultural revolutionaries discussed in chapter 3.

Instances of such denigrations of science could be almost indefinitely multiplied by further quotations from Ransom, Brooks, Allen Tate, R. P. Blackmur, W. K. Wimsatt, Robert Penn Warren, and Robert B. Heilman. Disinterested objectivity in interpretation was for Ransom and these others an antidote for scientific objectivity, in the same way that literature itself was supposed to be an antidote for utilitarianism: "As science more and more reduces the world to its types and forms," Ransom says, "art, replying, must invest it again with body."[26] Ransom urges the critic to "approach the object as such, and in humility," lest he impose his rational abstractions on it.[27] None of these statements would seem out of place if they showed up in the writings of a phenomenological critic or an exponent of the New Sensibility.

It was not quasi-scientific empiricism that influenced most New Critics to seek impersonality and objectivity so much as the Christian doctrine of Original Sin. Perhaps Original Sin is no more palatable a basis for critical doctrine than scientific empiricism, but it is different. The New Critics saw scientific objectivity as a symptom of that arrogant "humanism" which trusted in the natural goodness of man and the inevitability of progress. The cure for this humanism that was prescribed by writers like T. E. Hulme was a return to "the religious attitude," and in literature and criticism this meant a return to "classicism." Precisely because man was supposed to be fallen and his reason not to be trusted, this classicism was to be entertained as an unconscious attitude in literature rather than as a consciously expounded doctrine. This requirement put writers like Hulme and Eliot in the awkward position of *expounding* a philosophy which by their own account was no good unless it was inherited and felt rather

than expounded. Hence the radically anti-rational character of
this classicism—so unlike the classicism of classical periods—and
hence the curiously didactic quality of New Critical attacks on
literary didacticism.

In short, the New Critics' stress on impersonality and classical
detachment was for them a means of combatting just that ruth-
lessly acquisitive and manipulative will-to-power which today
these critics are reproached for encouraging. As Krieger points
out in his essay, "The Existential Basis of Contextual Criticism,"
the New Critical opposition between poetry and discursive generalization is itself in the spirit of the existentialist contrast between the human world of personal choice and the dead universe
of objective reason.[28] The goal of literature for the New Critics
was that very transcendence of the subject-object model of rationalist epistemology which animates both existentialist criticism
and the apocalyptic anti-rationalism of the New Sensibility. This
goal underlay the New Critical view that literature "fuses" opposites which, to the eye of reason and logic, must remain contradictory, as well as the New Critical preference for the kind of
poetry that asserts that the dancer cannot be separated from the
dance.*

What about Richards, the most aggressively proscientific of the
New Critics? Richards's early theory of poetry as pseudo-statement has led us to think of him as a critic who found poetry
lacking in the kind of truth exemplified by science. But even in
his very earliest works, Richards shows his doubts about the truth
of science itself when it moves from the level of factual observation and becomes a metaphysical hypothesis.[29] Richards con-
cluded that the scientific world view is itself no more than a
pseudo-statement, when tested against its own verifiability criterion of meaning. Though the factual observation-statements of

*Brooks states that the fusion which the creative imagination effects "is
not logical; it apparently violates science and common sense" (Well
Wrought Urn, 18). Allen Tate says, "in poetry, the disparate elements
are not combined in logic, which can join things only. . .under the law of
contradiction; they are combined in poetry rather as experience, and
experience has decided to ignore logic" (The Man of Letters in the
Modern World [New York: Meridian Books, 1955], 335).

science are verifiable, the materialistic metaphysics which li-
censes empiricism itself is as mythical as any poetic belief. Unlike
Arnold, Richards defends poetry as a potential agent of cultural
salvation not because poetry is as true or more true than science
but because it is no less false or nonsensical. Thus he can say that
"if we grant that all is myth"—that is, the scientific as well as the
poetic world-view—then poetry, "as the myth making which most
brings 'the whole soul of man into activity'. . . becomes the necessary channel for the reconstitution of order."[30] Tate, Brooks, and
other New Critics objected to Richards's attempt to ground the
humanistic function of literature in myths irrelevant to the objective world, but their own defense of the truth-claims of literature
was only slightly less equivocal. The New Criticism as a whole was
part of the general revolt against empiricism which characterizes
modern intellectual history—and which today animates those
who believe themselves to be opponents of the New Criticism.

This revolt against empiricism has recently enlisted the philosophy of science itself, a fact which has led some critics to charge
that New Criticism has not so much aped the scientists as lagged
behind their enlightened liberation from the myth of objectivity.
Thus Richard Coe says that contemporary humanists "have yet to
become as humanistic as the scientists whose empiricism we
thought we were imitating."[31] The "humanism" of the scientific
thinkers, seen in such writers as T. S. Kuhn and N. R. Hanson,
consists in emphasizing the creative nature of scientific hypoth-
eses and questioning the correspondence theory of scientific
truth. In the words of one of their opponents, Israel Scheffler,
these thinkers suggest that "reality itself is made by the scientist
rather than discovered by him."[32] For these anti-empiricists,
scientists do not "discover" objective reality but impose their
mental "paradigms" on it. But the New Critics were hardly
strangers to the theorizing that sees truth as a function of our
paradigms rather than of the correspondence of these paradigms
with reality.[33] The New Critical argument that poetry aspires to
"truth of coherence" rather than "truth of correspondence"
strikingly parallels the trend toward coherence theories of truth in
the philosophy of science.

Personality and Impersonality

It is true enough that the New Critics sought to depersonalize literary experience and that their antagonists have sought to repersonalize it. But personalization and depersonalization may be merely different means of registering the same reaction against the industrial ethos. There is a romanticism of self-abnegation as well as a romanticism of self-expression; the impersonality which Eliot, Hulme, and later New Critics identified with classicism was a continuation of the romantic quest to transcend the personal ego—as seen in Keats ("negative capability"), Shelley, Carlyle, Goethe, Hazlitt, and others. This romantic fusion of literary impersonality and anti-rationalistic esthetics is restated by theorists of myth such as C. J. Jung. The artist, according to Jung, "is objective and impersonal—even inhuman—for as an artist he is his work and not a human being." Every great work of art, Jung adds, entails a surrender of the individual to that unconscious "matrix of life in which all men are embedded." It follows that "every great work of art is objective and impersonal, but none the less profoundly moves us each and all."[34] In Jung's usage, the "objectivity" and "impersonality" of literature are not the objectivity and impersonality of science but the necessary remedy for them.

Both New Critical impersonalism and New Sensibility personalism derive from a reaction against objective reason, which is presumably to blame for the "dissociation of sensibility" of modern man. The difference is that the New Critics identified personal self-expression *with* technological reason, with ruthless individualism and secularism and the anarchy of bourgeois democracy, whereas the exponents of New Sensibility see personal self-expression as *subversive* of technological reason, of bourgeois regimentation and sterile order. Eliot's view of poetry as an "escape from personality" and Poirier's celebration of "the performing self" spring from a common revolt against the rationalist mentality assumed to be characteristic of bourgeois society.

The emphasis on impersonality and on seeing the literary work as an "object" represented only one impulse in the New Criticism.

Balancing this impulse was a contrary tendency to see the work as a
dynamic "process," a "dramatic action," an "experience"—these
action words are just as important in New Critical writing as words
that imply a static view of literature like "structure" and "verbal
construct." Poetry, as Brooks put it, *is* "experience rather than any
mere statement about experience or any mere abstraction from
experience."[35] Yeats's "Among School Children" "is a dramatization, not a formula; a controlled experience which has to be
experienced, not a logical process, the conclusion of which is
reached by logical methods and the validity of which can be
checked by logical tests."[36] The talismanic use of the term "experience" and the ritualistic opposition between experience and logical
concepts about experience were perfected by the New Critics long
before existentialist critics, cultural radicals, or deconstructionists
got hold of these formulas. Nearly as much as any later "critic of
consciousness," the New Critics regarded 'literature as expressive
of the drama of the mind in action. New Critical essays such as
R. P. Blackmur's on the later poetry of Yeats or Tate's on the
"angelic imagination" of Poe even anticipate the categories of
French existential criticism by focusing on the subject-object
relation as the pivotal principle of the writer's entire "cogito."[37]
In fact, so insistently did the New Critics maintain that literature
is experience in process and not static propositions *about* experience that it is often difficult to see what distinguishes their
position from radical subjectivism.

   This is not to minimize the differences between the New Criticism and the "criticism of consciousness," which disregards literary form or regards it as a mere transparent envelope through
which the *cogito* of the writer manifests itself. Opposing this
view, the New Critics anticipated structuralism in their insistence
that, as Eliot put it, "the poet has, not a 'personality' to express,
but a medium," and in their tendency to see the operations of this
medium as eternal and ahistorical. If we follow this line of reasoning far enough, we arrive at the view that it is language that
writes the poem, not the poet. This is a frequent motif of New
Criticism, expressed in attacks on "the intentional fallacy." Yet
the New Critics hesitated to do away entirely with the human

subject. Even for Eliot, the poetic medium was a verbal equivalent of states of mind and feeling. When Eliot banished personality, he meant to banish only the *idiosyncratic* personality. The
poem remains an expression of personality, but it is the collective
personality of modern man, or of the "mind of Europe," not the
personality of a unique individual. Similarly, Richards, with
whom Eliot would have agreed on this point, explained that by
the impersonality of poetry he meant merely its bringing into play
a multiplicity of points of view (that is, personalities) rather than
limiting itself to expressing "one particular interest." Thus, "to
say that we are *impersonal* is merely a curious way of saying that
our personality is more *completely* involved."[38] For both critics,
the measure of the value of the work was the amount of *experience* it contained, that experience of dissonant "attitudes" and
"impulses" that the poem dramatized.

This dissonance was supposed to resolve itself in a timeless,
ahistorical unity that somehow transcended the flux of consciousness. But this New Critical attempt to escape the process of
history through the eternal static forms of art was itself evidence
of an almost obsessive sense of history as a "panorama of futility
and anarchy" in which the modern consciousness is lost. This
helps explain why the New Critics repeatedly failed to practice the
objective interpretation they preached but instead read into traditional poets like Donne and Shakespeare their own postromantic
preoccupations with loss of unity and dissociation of sensibility.
Unwittingly, New Criticism conformed to current existential and
hermeneutical injunctions to bring the past work to life by reading it in terms of the historical consciousness of the present.

New Criticism and Its
Contradictions

The New Criticism was pulled in conflicting directions by the
various polemical pressures which surrounded it. On the one
hand, the New Criticism reacted against two approaches to literature—themselves mutually antagonistic—which had lingered on
as legacies of the Victorian and Edwardian periods: hedonistic
impressionism and genteel moralism. On the other hand, the New

Critics also reacted against the reductive consequences they perceived in the literary assumptions held by philologists, literary
and intellectual historians, and biographers as well as by vulgar
Marxists and literary sociologists. As if this battle within the
camp of literary studies were not sufficient, the New Critics also
found themselves defending the humanities against outsiders—
against the condescension of logical positivists and the "hard-
boiled naturalism" the positivists encouraged. Those positivists often regarded literature as a vestige of superstitious magic,
reduced its content to noncognitive pseudo-statements, and re-
fused to grant it any status as genuine knowledge. The method of
close textual analysis was a response on one side to those who
dismissed literature as a frivolity and on the other side to those
who defended it in terms which rendered it frivolous. Close
textual analysis, producing evidence of the richness and complexity of literary works, simultaneously answered the impres-
sionist, who viewed the work as a mere occasion for pleasurable
excitement, the message-hunter or political propagandist, who
reduced the work to mere uplifting propositions, and the positivist, who denied any significance to the work at all. And close
analysis of meaning could also demonstrate to the historians and
biographers that a literary work was more than a datum in the
history of ideas or the life of the author.

The necessity to fight battles on so great a variety of fronts forced
the New Criticism to stretch its concepts till they became ambiguous. Against those who tended to reduce literary meanings to mere
messages restatable without loss in critical language, the New
Critics held that "a poem should not mean but be" and that a paraphrase of a poem should never be confused with the poem's meaning. They argued that a poem had no "meaning" at all in the sense
of a separable conceptual content, that poetic meaning was so
embedded in the organic "being" of the literary structure that it
could not be read as a predication about the external world. The
attack on the didactic and paraphrastic "heresies" proved a useful strategy against those who seemed too eager to confuse poetry
with science, metaphysics, theology, politics, or morals. To speak
of a poem as an "objective" entity in this sense was to see it as a
mute object like a tree or a chair, to emphasize its absolute self-

sufficiency, its irreducibility to nonpoetic terms, its imperviousness to external reference, and even its refusal to refer to the "objective" world.

On the other hand, in combatting a different set of opponents, those who themselves denied poetry any serious cognitive function, these denials of the referential function of poetry would not do. To answer these opponents, it was necessary for the New Critics to suspend for the moment their insistence on the type of poetic "objectivity" which removed the poem from competition with the statements of other intellectual disciplines. In order to reestablish literature's credentials as a serious mode of knowledge, the New Critics emphasized literature's truth to the objective world. To stress the work's "objectivity" in this sense was necessarily to violate the thesis that it was a self-sufficient, nonreferential object. The objectivity of literature now resided in its correspondence with what Cleanth Brooks, following Eliot, called "the facts of experience."[39] But how could one talk of the work's relation to "the facts of experience" if with the same breath one prohibited the critic from going "outside the poem"?[40] And were "the facts of experience" situated out in the external world or were they merely subjective appearances, or some combination of both? In short, the doctrine of the objectivity of literature was ambiguous: it might be invoked in order to close the work off from the objective world or to point the work back toward this world.

Because the New Critics vacillated between arguments designed to refute antithetical positions, they were frequently attacked for contradictory errors. It was not always clear to the opposition whether these critics represented a form of Arnoldian humanism— Alfred Kazin, for instance, attacked them as epigones of the New Humanism of Babbitt and More—or a Paterian estheticism in which literature became "about" nothing but the perfection of its intrinsic form.[41] Critics like Brooks might in one breath warn that poems are autonomous entities with no claim to "truth of correspondence," only in the next to declare that poems yield profound truths about "the complexity of experience." The meanings which the New Critics ascribed to literature in order to refute the demeaning assumptions of one faction had to be suspended when it came time to correct the heavy-handed paraphrasing of another. As I suggested earlier, while New Critical interpretations endowed texts with the most complicated of meanings, New Critical theory frequently seemed to call into question the notion that a literary work could even possess anything so didactic as a meaning.

So the group of critics who did most to perfect the critical method of verbal explication and conceptual paraphrase is also the group which developed the classic arguments against this method—arguments which would in time be turned against the group itself. The assumptions about literature that are presupposed in recent polemics "against interpretation" were the elementary lessons taught by the New Critics: that literature is not conceptual knowledge but experience, that it is a dramatic process not static propositions, that it therefore resists "the heresy of paraphrase." Responding to conflicting polemical pressures, New Critical theory had adopted positions that cut the ground from under New Critical interpretive method.

But it was more than a matter of tactics which set the New Critics at odds with their own procedures and principles. Their contradictions were inherited from a tradition of esthetics which finds it difficult to transcend the antithesis it proposes between experience and ideas about experience. Just as the literary work is doomed to fall short of encompassing the primary reality of experience, the critic's analysis falls short of encompassing the literary work. In relation to nature, the literary work is secondary, but in relation to abstract interpretation, the work assumes the absoluteness, indeterminacy, and opacity of a natural object or force. If one follows the New Critical argument against the heresy of paraphrase to its logical conclusion, one ends with a complete discontinuity between literature and criticism; one may then follow those who reject interpretation as such, or one may turn interpretation into a kind of poetic creativity in itself, a Nietzschean "play" that makes no pretense of corresponding to any text but justifies itself as an existential gesture against an inhuman universe.

Already latent in the New Criticism was an image of the critic as a kind of romantic hero who struggles to create meaning out of a situation he recognizes to be absurd and hopeless. Hazard Adams, a theorist with close affinities to the New Criticism, has characterized this critical anti-hero:

> there is an ineradicable Romantic irony in the enterprise of criticism. Like the quest of the Byronic hero, it is endless and yet at the same time valuable—endless because the terms are finally self-defeating, and valuable because in its own inadequacy it calls attention to the greater adequacy of the poem itself, which manages to say or be more than remarks about it can ever say. For this reason it is possible to characterize criticism as fundamentally negative. It is always denying the adequacy of any critical statement and constantly urging us to look again.[42]

Since nobody would think of denying that a good poem says "more than remarks about it can ever say" or that good criticism constantly invites us to "look again" at the work, this sounds like mere common sense. But romantic irony is not romantic irony if it can be resolved by common sense. Adams actually implies something more skeptical, that critical interpretations are like poetic myths; there is always an existential gulf between them and the objects to which they try to refer. As Edward Said puts it, "the critic is aptly characterized in Lukács' epithet for the novel as being transcendentally homeless."*

The curious wave of self-exhibition which has entered criticism in the aftermath of the New Critics may, then, be less a revision of the New Critical mode than an extension of its logic. If we pursue the argument that the experience of literary meaning is not an experience of conceptual statements, we arrive eventually at the conclusion that criticism cannot deal with literature as long as *it* —criticism—makes conceptual statements. Criticism itself must shed its propositionality and become literature. Thus Harold Bloom, in what must surely be one of the least convincing assertions of recent times, says that "a theory *of* poetry must belong *to* poetry, must *be* poetry, before it can be of any use in interpreting

---

*Edward Said, *Beginnings,* 11. But even the early Lukács of *Theory of the Novel* would probably not go along with Said's conclusion that the "transcendentally homeless" novelist (or critic) cannot represent the objective world.

poems."[43] Of course one wonders whether Bloom himself "means
what he says" here. If he is speaking as a poet in *this* critical
formulation, is he then really *saying* what he is saying at all? If
critics have to become poets in order to make statements about
poetry, do commentators on critics then in turn have to become
poets in order to make statements about critics?

A continuity of assumptions connects the New Criticism with the
more radical skepticisms of recent continentally influenced movements such as the "negative hermeneutics" defended by Hartman
and practiced in different ways by Bloom, de Man, Barthes,
Derrida, J. Hillis Miller, and Hartman himself.[44] Like the New
Criticism, this negative hermeneutics participates in the understandable but misconceived reaction against positivistic certainty
which got under way with the romantic revolt against science.
Hartman says that the new critical "revisionists," as he terms
them, call into question, "by a playful movement, master theories
that claim to have overcome the past, the dead, the false. There is
no Divine or Dialectical Science which can help us purify history
absolutely, to pass in our lifetime a last judgement on it."[45] The
ghost of an authoritarian rationalism is invoked in such a way as to
make irrationalism look like the only alternative. The fact that
there is no "*last* judgment" in criticism is used to make judgment
as such sound suspect.

New deconstruction is in many respects old ambiguity and irony
writ large. In both cases, the basic strategy is one of unmasking, of
dislocating the meaning of the work from the meaning seemingly
intended by the author. For the New Critic, the true meaning is
invariably an ironic inversion of the apparent or explicit meaning.
And the principle of ambiguity guarantees that this true meaning
will be indeterminate. The deconstructionist reading carries both
the irony and the indeterminacy a step farther:

> Much of the criticism of the works of X [so this approach
> runs] has argued that these works revolve around some central
> view of the world. But a closer examination of these works
> reveals that any such thematic idea or ideal center which X's
> language presents as its point of reference or origin is called
> into question and compromised by this very language. Though
> X's works are always suggesting the possibility of some ultimate

reference point for making sense of the world, they no sooner
do so than they defer the presentation of this reference point
or expose its purely fictive and arbitrary nature. X's works
dramatize or put into play a variety of ways of ordering reality,
all of which are seen, finally, as already *written* and therefore
without privileged authority. Ultimately, X's works are commentaries on their own inability to transcend the interpretive
fictions they proffer, and this problem of interpretation is
passed on to the reader. What these works are really "about,"
then, is their unreadability, which is to say, the reader's struggle
to impose his own preferred fiction upon them. Yet by entering
into this game, the reader arrives at an understanding of the
process by which he himself creates his own fictive "reality."

Of course there are some texts for which this approach is suitable,
indeed indispensable. But its applicability is theoretically unlim-
ited. Just as the New Critic knows in advance that all literature
manifests the "language of paradox" and thus can read virtually
any text as an instance of this characteristic, the deconstructionist critic, knowing in advance that all literature is by definition
"about" its own textual problematics, can generate a new reading
of any text whatsoever.[46]

New Criticism and Formalism

To what extent does the term "formalism" fairly characterize the
New Critical view of literature? Enough has been said, perhaps, to
make the answer to this question clear. If the New Critics were
formalists, they were extremely reluctant ones, driven to formalism
against the grain of their own temperaments by their reaction
against the mechanical "mimetic" rationality of industrialism and
positivistic science. In order to equip the literary imagination with
the power to redeem history, society, and nature from their fall into
rationality, it seemed necessary for the New Critics to sever this
imagination from its motivating rational grounds and consider it
as an autonomous law unto itself. There resulted a form of literary
isolationism resembling formalism or "art for art's sake" and
producing the same trivializing effects. Yet this isolationism was
motivated, paradoxically, by the goal of restoring literature's

social, moral, and cultural centrality. The autonomous poem, which "says" nothing and does not represent any reality outside its self-sufficient coherence, somehow embodies a humanistic consciousness that can rescue us from science, dissociated sensibility, and disorder. In order to combat the fragmentation, dissociation, and overspecialization of a presumably hyperrational society, literature is opposed to rational and referential discourse. But this remedy proved to be a form of the disease all over again: stripped of its practical function and defined as an autonomous entity, literature as viewed by the New Critics could only deepen the divisions of modern culture.

The New Critics assigned ambitious cultural functions to literature while defining literature in a way that obstructed its carrying out these functions. This contradiction, inherent, as we have seen already, in romantic theory, presents itself in two of the founding fathers of New Criticism, Eliot and Richards. In his social writings, Eliot laments the fragmentation of modern society, the discontinuity of generations, the disruption of traditions, the specialization of the disciplines, the multiplication of parties and factions unconnected by a shared belief, the negative individualism or pseudo-individualism of Liberalism. In a "negative liberal society," Eliot writes, "religious thought and practice, philosophy and art, all tend to become isolated areas cultivated by groups in no communication with each other. The artistic sensibility is impoverished by its divorce from the religious sensibility, the religious by its separation from the artistic."[47] Yet Eliot's own view of literature makes large concessions to such separations. Side by side with denigrations of "pure poetry" and pronouncements on the importance of belief in literature and the need to create an organic link between literature and its public we find Eliot describing poetry as a self-contained discourse which communicates nothing extrinsic to itself: "*If* poetry is a form of 'communication,'" he writes, "yet that which is to be communicated is the poem itself, and only incidentally the experience and the thought which have gone into it."[48] At best, the meaning serves to keep the reader's "mind diverted and quiet, while the poem does its work upon him: much as the imaginary burglar is always provided with a bit of nice meat for the house-dog."[49] We know what kind of thinking about literature such statements are designed to correct, but this does not excuse the overstatement or lessen its consequences. Reacting to the need to disengage literature from the clichés and didacticism of mass discourse, Eliot in principle divorces it from the public he would win back. His formulations reduce literature to precisely the sort of specialism and separatism that he diagnoses as symptomatic of industrial society.

Richards reveals in his own way the same tendency to minister to a specialized culture by promoting the specialization of literature. Since, for Richards, poetic emotions cannot be grounded in objective beliefs, we have no choice, he says, but to "cut our pseudo-statements [i.e., literary works] free from belief, and yet retain them, in this released state, as the main instruments by which we order our attitudes to one another and to the world."[50] Richards does not explain how poetry is to order our attitudes to one another and to the world without invoking any beliefs or presuppositions about the world. Literature is to serve as the exemplary basis of a new psychic harmony reconciling the psychic and social dissonance of the modern world. It is to be a kind of "League of Nations for the moral ordering of the impulses"[51] and, by extension, of the social factions expressed by these impulses. Yet it is to do all this without making any truth-claims or claiming any understanding of the world. Richards anticipated the now-popular attempt to preserve a humanistic consensus without any shared reality on which this consensus might be based. It is an attempt to defend humanism as a shared mythology—as if the admission that it is a mythology did not destroy our ability to hold it.

We saw in chapter 3 that left-wing cultural critics compromise their attempts to endow literature with radical credentials when they divorce literature from conceptual and theoretical understanding. We can now add that liberal and conservative defenders of humanism such as Eliot, Richards, and the New Critics who follow them compromise their defense by accepting the same divorce. This divorce is forced upon them by their decision to associate conceptual understanding with the ends to which it has been put by industrial society. By a too-convenient analogy, con-

forming to rational procedures of thought is associated with
conforming to the regimentation and determinism of a mechanical society. Taking account of objective reality is identified with
passive adjustment to the status quo, with the mass man's
drugged acceptance of his status as a manipulable object. For the
New Critics, it follows that literature must be defined as a self-
sufficient world, not a mere representation of an already existing
one. Exponents of post–New Critical interpretation accept this
anti-realistic view of literature. But for them it follows also that to
defer to the objective text, as the New Critics sought to do, or to
defer to the author's intention in interpreting the text, is tantamount to submitting to totalitarian social control. The same logic
which caused the New Critics to divorce poetry from conceptual
statements and define it as an autonomous artifact causes current
critics to attack this autonomy as a form of "reification." New
Criticism, phenomenological hermeneutics, and New Sensibility
personalism all combine to oppose rational objectivity to experience and doom themselves to the polarizations they aim to heal.

Six

How Not to Talk
about Fictions

Something has been happening to the concept of "fiction," both in critical discourse and elsewhere. For a long time, this concept operated under commonly understood restrictions. It was used to refer (1) to a certain genre of literature; (2) to a certain aspect of literature in general—the element of plot, action, or fable, including such constituents as character, setting, scene, and so on; (3) to any narrative or story containing a large element of invention. But recently, the concept of "fiction" has undergone an expansion. Though still used to refer to the action or plot of literary works, it has come to be applied to something more: to the ideas, themes, and beliefs that are embodied in the action or plot. It is not only the events in literature that are regarded as fictive but the "message" or "world view" conveyed in the presentation of the events as well. And this is not the end of the matter. Going a step farther, critics now sometimes suggest, by a kind of tautology, that literary meanings are fictions because *all* meanings are fictions, even those of nonliterary language, including the language of criticism. In its most extreme flights, this critical view asserts that "life" and "reality" are themselves fictions.

The Literary Theme
as a Fiction

The critical strategies for neutralizing the truth-claims of thematic statements in literature were fully perfected by the New Criticism: the assumption that literature is "dramatic" or "presentational," rather than propositional; that literary propositions (such as "Beauty is Truth, Truth Beauty") are always utterances of a *persona* and therefore never receivable as assertions; that general propositions in literary works are so qualified by the "pressure of the context" that they surrender their force as assertions;* that when propositions appear in literary works, their *use* (or function) is not to make statements but to "embody attitudes," "experience," and so on; that ideas and philosophies in literary works are present not as assertions to be believed but as pretexts that permit the structural or emotional aspects of the text to unfold.

These deliberate strategies were often complemented by an unintentional one, which was simply to confuse the symbolic or thematic level of literature with the literal level—as if these two levels were one, and as if their fictiveness were of the same order of obviousness. Critics going back to Sidney, Dryden, and Johnson have pointed out that literary actions do not attempt to pass themselves off as literal truth. As Sidney asked, "what child is there that, coming to a play, and seeing Thebes written in great letters upon an old door, doth believe that it is Thebes?"[1] Coleridge had this nonliteral reception of fictions in mind when he made his famous remark about "that willing suspension of disbelief that constitutes poetic faith."[2] But nothing in these critical insights was meant to suggest that literary fictions make no truth-claims whatsoever. The fact that the "Thebes" represented on the stage does not present itself as the *literal* Thebes did not for these critics imply that whatever the play seems to say about human affairs is to be taken as a fiction. If, however, we confuse these levels of statement, we can arrive at just this conclusion. Thus Wellek and Warren, in *Theory of Literature*, move without difficulty from the premise that "the statements in a novel, in a poem, or in a drama are not literally true," to the conclusion that "they are not logical propositions."[3]

Recent theorists who reject much of the New Critical machinery frequently revive these familiar strategies. Here, for example, is

*As Cleanth Brooks says, "poems never contain abstract statements. That is, any 'statement' made in the poem bears the pressure of the context and has its meaning modified by the context. In other words, the statements made—including those which appear to be philosophical generalizations—are to be read as if they were speeches in a drama. Their relevance, their propriety, their rhetorical force, even their meaning, cannot be divorced from the context in which they are imbedded" ("Irony as a Principle of Structure," in *Literary Opinion in America*, rev. ed., Morton D. Zabel, ed. [New York: Harper and Brothers, 1951], 731).

Jonathan Culler on the "thematic conventions" of the novel. The
specific case in point is Flaubert, whose novels "are made possible," Culler says, "by the convention that nothing can resist
irony except complete innocence, which is the residue left by
irony." In reading Flaubert, we know that "the particular forms
of aspiration will be forced through the crucible of irony, which
they cannot survive except as pure form." The question is how
such thematic conventions are to be taken by the reader—how
"seriously" ought he to respond to what they seem to say or imply
about the world?

> We could, of course, speak of such conventions as theories or
> views of the world, as if it were the task of novels to express
> them, but such an approach would do scant justice to the
> novels themselves or to the experience of reading them, for it is
> the nature of such conventions to remain unexpressed since
> they are generally indefensible or at least implausible as ex-
> plicit theories. And we do not read the novels in order to dis-
> cover such theories: they function, rather, as means to other
> ends, which are the novels themselves. It may be more useful to
> speak of myths which are necessary if the novel is to come into
> being or of formal devices which generate the novel than of
> theories which it is the novel's function to express. The former
> naturalizes at the level of the literary system whereas the latter
> naturalizes in terms of a biographical or communicative
> project. [4]

Culler writes of thematic conventions as "myths," but he might as
easily have used the term "fictions."

The first thing to be noted is that this expansion of the concept
of myth or fiction has the effect of reducing the literary theme to
the status of a pretext, something without intrinsic importance.
Flaubert's ironic view of life is translated into a "convention,"
and the tacit assumption is that once any belief has become a
convention, it no longer needs to be treated as a belief. Instead of
conceiving "formal devices" as subordinate means of expressing
the view of life presented in the novel, Culler turns the tables by
conceiving the novel's view of life as itself a kind of formal device
which subserves "other ends." These other ends Culler describes
—not very helpfully, perhaps—as "the novels themselves." When

we read a piece of writing *as* literary, so the argument runs, we contrive to see it not as a "biographical or communicative project" but as a fiction—something that cannot be taken as a genuine statement about the world.

Much the same view is advanced by another recent critic, John Ellis: "when...we treat a piece of language as literature," Ellis writes, "we no longer accept any information offered as something to act upon, nor do we act upon its exhortations and imperatives. We do not generally concern ourselves with whether what it says is true or false, or regard it as relevant to any specific practical purpose."[5] It follows as a corollary for Ellis that we can read the same piece of writing differently, make different uses of it, depending on whether we read it as "information" (Culler's "communicative project") or as literature. For example, when we begin to regard Gibbon's *Decline and Fall of the Roman Empire* as literature, says Ellis, "we characteristically stop worrying about the facts of Roman history; we cease to regard the book primarily as historical information.... Truth or falsity relevant to the specific historical context is no longer the main point, for Gibbon's is no longer the book for that purpose."[6]

As I have already suggested, this reasoning rests on a valid perception: that the truth or falsity of the "information" or the seemingly "factual" content of propositions stated or implied is unimportant when we are reading a literary work. When we read the command, "Call me Ishmael," the fact that there never was any such person as Ishmael makes no difference. And the novel would not be a better novel if there really were such a person. But does it follow that because the pseudo-informational propositions in literary works make no truth-claims, there are no truth-claims in literature at all? Obviously it makes a good deal of difference what kind of utterance you choose as your paradigm of literary language. If you choose sentences like "Call me Ishmael" or "Slowly wading through the meadows of brit, the Pequod still held on her way north-eastward towards the island of Java," you will end up deciding that literary propositions are merely fictive imitations of genuine statements.[7] But *Moby-Dick* also includes sentences like this: "For as this appalling ocean surrounds the verdant land, so in the soul of man there lies one insular Tahiti, full of peace and joy, but encompassed by all the horrors of the half known life."[8] If you take this kind of example into your reckoning, you may have to reopen the question.

These strategies for neutralizing literary statements are echoed in some of the recent literary-critical adaptations of speech-act theory. Critics like Richard Ohmann and Barbara Herrnstein Smith argue that literary works are composed of imitation or make-believe speech-acts.[9] Smith, for example, says that "what is central to the concept of the poem as a fictive utterance is not that the speaker is a 'character' distinct from the poet, or that the audience purportedly addressed, the emotions expressed, and the events alluded to are fictional, but that *the speaking, addressing, expressing, and alluding are themselves fictive verbal acts.*"[10]

Smith concedes that "the statements in a poem may, of course, resemble quite closely statements that the poet might have truly and truthfully uttered as an historical creature in the historical world. Nevertheless, insofar as they are offered and recognized as statements in a poem, they are fictive."[11] How does Smith know that all this is the case? Like Culler and Ellis, she appeals to *convention*: "We may choose to regard the composition not as a poem but as an historical utterance, but then the conventions by virtue of which its fictiveness is understood and has its appropriate effects are no longer in operation."[12] But Smith never explains how she has determined that the proper convention for dealing with literary works is to regard their utterances as fictive verbal acts. One gathers she has simply assumed it as an a priori axiom requiring no argument.

By reducing thematic statements in literature to the status of fictions, the critics have set the stage for their next move: the conclusion that the reader's disengagement of thematic statements from their ostensible truth-claims is the definitive step in experiencing a piece of writing *as* literature. Innocence of truth-claims, in other words, becomes not merely a convention of literary works but a *defining* convention—a necessary condition of "literariness," or of "producing" a text as literature rather than as a "communicative project." If you can read the view of life offered in work X as a fiction (and who is to stop you?), then you are treating X as literature.

Literature as Propositions

Let us return to the passage of Jonathan Culler quoted above, the one that says that we read thematic ideas in novels not as "theories or views of the world," but as "myths" which make possible "the novels themselves." Culler does not deny that novels (and presumably other literary works) can *have* themes, that the reader can appropriately make sense of novels by locating propositions that organize the actions and scenes. Throughout *Structuralist Poetics*, Culler suggests that intuiting thematic propositions is one of the chief means by which readers "naturalize" (or "recuperate" or make "vraisemblable") literary texts. But Culler implicitly distinguishes between the propositional *form* of an utterance and its *use* as a speech-act; that is, propositions may be used to make "statements," assertions bearing truth-claims, but they have other uses as well. Unless we examine the conventions under which they are being used, we cannot say whether a given set of propositions makes a statement or not. (For example, if I say "man will prevail," I could be making a genuine statement, but I could also be merely quoting Faulkner as part of a classroom lecture, or parodying grandiloquence, or cutting up at a party, etc.) Thus, though Culler concedes that literary meanings are propositional, he says that literary conventions release the reader from the obligation to take these propositions as statements.

Culler's concession that literary meanings are propositional, however, has potentially subversive implications for his own theory. Culler notes that even when a text tries to resist the process of naturalization by self-consciously subverting any simple general propositions that may be implied in it, its attempted resistance is itself open to naturalization by propositional means—perhaps only by such means. This, at any rate, is the implication of Culler's interesting comment that "if all else failed, we could read a sequence of words with no apparent order as signifying absurdity or chaos and then, by giving it an allegorical relation to the world, take it as a statement about the incoherence and absurdity of our own languages."[13] Followed to its conclusion, this point might turn Culler's and Ellis's theories on their heads: the way readers produce or naturalize a text *as* literary is precisely by regarding its action as possessing "an allegorical relation to the world"—*not* by disengaging it from such allegorical relation.

But we still need to go back over Culler's original statement. If we inquire why it is that thematic propositions in literature are not taken as statements about the world, we find that not much in the way of argument is presented by Culler (a sign that the position is widely held). One line of argument, however, is suggested: thematic propositions in novels "are generally indefensible or at least implausible as explicit theories." Therefore, if we were to read novels as if it were their end to express such theories as theories, we would do "scant justice to them." The most obvious objection here is that Culler has prejudged the question. *Are* the theories or views of the world presented in novels generally indefensible or implausible as such? Would this not depend on which novels we were talking about? Can we assume that novelists generally have nothing to say that is worth attending to? And what is the implication of the concept of "doing justice" to a literary work? Far from meaning that the reader should try to respect the author's apparent intentions, Culler seems to mean that he is obliged to improve on them. For it soon turns out that for Culler no less than "the major task of criticism" is the task of "making the text interesting, of combating the boredom which lurks behind every work, waiting to move in if reading goes astray or founders."[14] A possible reply to this Barthesian view is that it is the writer's job, not the reader's, to combat boredom, that a method of reading that encourages the reader to make a text more interesting than it is is condescending.

But these criticisms take us somewhat away from the issue at hand. For if we set aside his remarks on the avoidance of boredom, Culler is not arguing about how readers *ought* to make sense of texts so much as about how they *do* make sense of them, for better or worse. His aim is to describe the convention that actually operates when readers come upon thematic propositions in novels. The difficulty is that his description takes too much for granted. It assumes that we are all clear in our minds—those of us who really know how literature is read—on *what the convention is.* We are clear on it because it is built into our "literary competence," given in the rules of reading. These rules dictate that there is a kind of Limited Liability Clause covering the beliefs in literature, so that a good reader does not make the mistake of reading such beliefs as part of a "communicative project." And is this not in fact, rightly or wrongly, the way trained readers usually do behave when they read literature?

I think it is not the way they usually behave, and I shall try to support this argument by looking at Culler's own behavior as a reader in another book, *Flaubert: The Uses of Uncertainty*—a work which, according to Culler, represents a concrete application of the theory outlined in *Structuralist Poetics*. In this book, Culler suggests there are certain kinds of texts which cannot be organized in terms of thematic propositions at all. Flaubert's *L'Education sentimentale* is such a text, and Culler contrasts it in a variety of ways with another exemplary work, Balzac's *Les Illusions perdues*, a work whose action consistently submits to schematic thematization. Culler says "there are in Flaubert many passages in which details seem subject to no particular thematic determination and in which the interpretive process never even gets under way."[15] Of course any extended narrative will contain a certain amount of arbitrary detail for the sake of what Henry James called "solidity of specification," but Culler implies that Flaubert goes far beyond the usual limit. He adduces a number of passages from *L'Education sentimentale* in which "nothing is illustrated," and the reader's search for a thematic principle of organization seems to be deliberately frustrated. Thus a sentence describing Frédéric Moreau's reaction to a masked ball in Part II "leads us from one thing to another, taking contiguity rather than similarity as its law. We can do little with the details themselves, which show neither the magnificence nor the tawdriness of the gathering. The reader seeking to unify, to grasp the sense and function of this scene, has as yet little to work on." And the ensuing material only acts further "to defer meaning."[16] When, on the other hand, thematic meanings are suggested in the text, they tend to advertise their banality and their falsity, so that we get "a parody of the interpretive process as displayed in Balzac."[17] Interpretations of the action are suggested only as a prelude to giving away their "gratuitousness."[18] Flaubert creates "arbitrary and unmotivated signs, so that neither reader nor character may experience the solace of organic synthesis or of 'natural' significance."[19] He presents symbols which stand only for what Valéry called "stupidity," which is "a property of objects presenting a blank and inexhaustible face to the world," and irony, "which undermines interpretive syntheses."[20] L'Education sentimentale is thus "the most striking, most challenging example of thematic indeterminacy"—a prime case of "the uses of uncertainty."[21] Flaubert's world in the novel persistently defers interpretation, "refuses to be composed."[22] His world "is a system not in the Balzacian sense—it is not governed by laws which determine how one thing follows another in what one might call syntagmatic sequences. Its system is rather that of an immense paradigm in which everything is equivalent and could replace anything else in the syntagma of chance."[23] I have quoted at such length because Culler's analysis of this novel is an extremely agile and intelligent instance of a type of reading that has become common in recent criticism. It is, I should add, an extremely convincing reading of the novel.

And yet. . . . Having demonstrated the uninterpretability of the novel, its refusal to lend itself to thematization, Culler proceeds to read the novel in the thematic way which he declares inapplicable. Indeed, in his very exposition of the novel's refusal to be allegorized, Culler allegorizes it. What are "indeterminacy," "stupidity," the fallibility and banality of all interpretive "recuperations" of experience but the thematic concepts which, in Culler's reading, give point to the experience of the novel? My point here is best illustrated by Culler's treatment of the famous last scene of the novel, in which Frédéric and his old school friend Deslauriers attempt to sum up the content of their "education" but achieve only flatness and platitude. The expected *Bildung* of the *Bildungsroman* is hinted at only to be undermined by irony. Culler comments as follows: "Not only have Frédéric and Deslauriers learned nothing in this *Bildungsroman*, but the reader can learn little from their example, and that is perhaps the most profound tragedy: that egregious failure brings no compensatory understanding."²⁴ Perhaps so, but such a "tragic" reading can hardly be said to treat the novel as resistant to thematic recuperation, as a novel in which "nothing is illustrated."

Culler might give some ground here and concede that he has made sense of the novel by subsuming its action under a thematic proposition after all. But he might then revert to his argument in *Structuralist Poetics* that such thematic propositions are entertained only as mythical pretexts, not as genuine statements to be believed. Yet if one can judge from his use of phrases like "profound tragedy," Culler appears to treat Flaubert's meaning as a statement that Flaubert actually wished to get across to his reader, much as Balzac and other writers wish to get their statements across. And even more than this, Culler himself, far from treating this statement as a mythical pretext, seems to treat it with respect, quite as if he believed it, or at least found it plausible as a view of life. That is, Culler writes as if he *takes seriously* the view that we learn little or nothing from our experience, that egregious failure brings no compensatory understanding, and he writes as if the novel itself demands such a response from any reader.

To be sure, Flaubert's procedure in this novel is different from the procedures of Balzac, and Culler's insight into the difference is useful. But Culler misstates the nature of the difference when he describes it as a difference between novels of indeterminate and determinate meaning. Flaubert's novel is "indeterminate" only insofar as it proposes a *theory* of the indeterminacy of experience. But this theory is quite as determinate as any other. Were this not so, the novel's indeterminacies would be pointless and literally unreadable, instead of constituting a statement about the pointlessness and unreadability of things.

If one is looking for *real* freedom from allegorical or thematic meanings—for works, in Susan Sontag's words, "whose surface is so unified and clean, whose momentum is so rapid, whose address is so direct that the work can be...just what it is"—one should go not to Flaubert (or even to Robbe-Grillet, who pushes the principle of Flaubertian "stupidity" to extremes) but to works that are so innocent of meaning that they do not need to refuse it —dime novels, detective stories, Jacqueline Susann novels, comic

books, and so on.[25] Unlike works which make laborious efforts to
subvert thematic significance and thus in the very process pro-
pound it, such entertainments achieve imperviousness to interpretation without effort. The demonstrations of Northrop Frye
and other critics that the narrative structures of "elite" and
"popular" literature are identical suggest—Frye himself notwith-
standing—that what chiefly distinguishes the elite forms is precisely that they have something serious to say.

There is a disparity between our theoretical talk about literature and our actual behavior in reading and discussing literary
works. Critics and readers do not behave as the standard theories
tell us we behave—a fact which, as I have suggested earlier, owes
much to the negative constraints that operate on our theorizing.
When "statement" became stigmatized as "bourgeois" and
"mechanical," it became necessary for writers to deny that literature makes statements. At the same time, such denials could only
be communicated in the form of statements. And the critics,
while upholding the argument in theory, could hardly help vio-
lating it in practice. The Limited Liability Clause is inconspicu-
ously set aside when it becomes necessary to talk about specific
works, or else it is hedged through evasive reference to the writer's
"vision."

Can there be no distinction at all, then, between literary works
and other kinds of "communicative projects"? Obviously, there
has to be, but the kinds of distinctions which have been advanced
have been greatly exaggerated. It is possible to make purely
"intrinsic" judgments of literature, judgments that suspend all
questions of truth or belief. There may be no great novels glorifying cannibalism, but if one imagines an assortment of such
novels, one can suppose that some will be better as novels than
others. Some Nazi posters are better works of art than some
non-Nazi or anti-Nazi posters. We can grant the *donnée* of any
literary work, and judge how well it is executed; we can judge a
work according to how well it meets the requirements of the
genre, without raising the question of whether the genre is valuable or not. Internal coherence may well be a necessary condition
of literary value. But it can hardly be a sufficient condition. If
coherence were sufficient, it would be impossible to explain why

we value works such as *Moby-Dick, Crime and Punishment,* and *An American Tragedy* over the average thriller by Mickey Spillane or Agatha Christie. Judged by the test of internal coherence alone, Spillane and Christie would win hands down.

We can and do judge literature by tests of internal coherence, but we rarely stop there. Literary judgments usually involve both intrinsic and extrinsic concerns, and extrinsic concerns often impinge on intrinsic ones. Indeed, if we look at the example given above, the cannibal novel or the Nazi poster, we can see that the very distinction between intrinsic and extrinsic is often artificial. The appreciation of the intrinsic qualities of such works for most readers will be retarded by the radical violation of extrinsic norms these works entail. It is true that we conventionally allow a greater degree of tolerance to beliefs and world views in literature than in other writing, but this tolerance has its limits. The fact that we exercise it does not mean that we treat thematic propositions as fictions. The behavior of critics themselves bears these points out.

The *extreme* separation between reading a work *as* literature and reading it *as* something else, as statement about something, seems unnecessary as well as a violation of normal reading experience. It may be true enough that literary works "mean" in certain distinctive ways—specifically, through parable, drama, fiction, action made significant through thematic complication—but it does not follow that this distinctive mode of meaning necessarily possesses a special semantic status different in kind from that of ordinary propositions. Nor does it follow that literary themes make some specially softened kind of truth-claim or no truth-claim at all. Even a work which asserts that truth is totally problematic, unknowable, relative, or a function of multiple perspectives makes the same kind of truth-claim as do such assertions outside of literature.

It is true that the complications of dramatic action often undercut, ironize, or "problematize" the generalizations in literary works, but they may also be controlled by these generalizations. And even when such generalizations *are* qualified or negated by the total action of the work, this very dialectic becomes a kind of thematic proposition implied by the work as a

whole, and necessary for the reader's temporal assimilation of it.
Cleanth Brooks is right when he says of "philosophical generalizations" in poetry that "their relevance, their propriety, their
rhetorical force, even their meaning, cannot be divorced from the
context in which they are imbedded."[26] This is why it is so hazard-
ous to abstract a proposition from a literary work and treat it as
the work's message. But it does not follow, as Brooks argues,
that, because poetic or literary statements are imbedded in a
context that qualifies or even contradicts them, works of literature "never contain abstract statements"—any more than it follows that any complex argument, because it is imbedded in a
context, is not really an argument.[27] Once more, it seems that
what compels the theory that literary works make no statements is
not the nature of literary works themselves but the cultural constraints upon our theorizing about literary works.

Propagandists in Spite of Themselves

The explicators of Robbe-Grillet, Beckett, or the Theater of the
Absurd have not taken the philosophical themes of their subjects
any less directly as "theories or views of the world" than Samuel
Johnson took the philosophical ideas of Shakespeare or Pope.
One can tell that this is so from the intensity with which they
write:

> Robbe-Grillet's purpose . . . is to establish the novel on the
> surface: once you can set its inner nature, its "interiority,"
> between parentheses, then objects in space, and the circulation
> of men among them, are promoted to the rank of subjects. The
> novel becomes man's direct experience of what surrounds him
> without his being able to shield himself with a psychology, a
> metaphysic, or a psychoanalytic method in his combat with the
> objective world he discovers. The novel is no longer a chthonian
> revelation, the book of hell, but of the earth—requiring that we
> no longer look at the world with the eyes of a confessor, of a
> doctor, or of God himself (all significant hypotheses of the
> classical novelist), but with the eyes of a man walking in his city

with no other horizon than the scene before him, no other power than that of his own eyes.*

It is hard to avoid the conclusion that Roland Barthes actually finds the view of life in Robbe-Grillet's novels more plausible, less deluded, in other words *truer* and more *believable* than that found in novels that "look at the world with the eyes of a confessor, of a doctor, or of God himself." What makes the discrepancy between critical theory and critical practice so easy to overlook is the fact that the message asserted by modern and contemporary works is so frequently some kind of radical *anti*-message (like that which Barthes expounds above). And it is all too easy to mistake an anti-message (or a complex message) for a nonmessage.

Contrary to what is usually assumed, twentieth-century writing tends to be more, not less, didactic than "classical" or "traditional" writing. There are several good reasons why this is so. First, the embattled, highly politicized situation of modern culture, where the writer sees himself as an adversary of society and a competitor against other writers (if only to determine which of them can more spectacularly turn his back on society), encourages him to be more aggressively programmatic, even when he refuses all programs. Secondly, the rejection of conventional narrative organization by experimental writing necessitates a tighter thematic unity. The more firmly a work rests on a conventional narrative (or expository) structure, the greater freedom it will have to digress from thematic relevance, for digressive material can easily be naturalized by the reader as "part of the story." As long as the story remains within hailing distance of its theme, the reader will be able to tolerate generous amounts of extraneous detail without losing the thread. Modern experimental texts, by contrast, having renounced story and narrative, depend much more heavily on the reader's ability to locate thematic proposi-

---

*Roland Barthes, "Objective Literature: Alain Robbe-Grillet," Introduction to *Two Novels by Robbe-Grillet: Jealousy & In the Labyrinth,* trans. Richard Howard (New York: Grove Press, 1965), 25. As Culler says, "Much of Robbe-Grillet can be recuperated if we read it as the musings or speech of a pathological narrator, and that framework gives critics a hold so that they can go on to discuss the implications of the particular pathology in question" (*Structuralist Poetics,* 138).

tions capable of giving their disjunctive, fragmentary, and refractory details some exemplary meaning and coherence. Lacking a continuous story (or argument), images and motifs can have little unity or relevance to one another apart from the abstract concepts they illustrate—the wasteland condition of modern man, the gulf or the unity between subject and object, the interrelations of birth and death, the vanity of technocratic, usurious civilization, etc. Since the experimental method involves cutting away *explicit* thematic connections between images, allusions, and scenes, the reader has to work harder to restore these thematic connections. This means that the reader tends to become the "creator" of the work, as we somewhat misleadingly say—meaning only that he has to struggle to conceive abstract ideas that adequately subsume and connect the disparate events of the reading experience.

A precursor of experimental fiction such as *Tristram Shandy* illustrates the point well. It is relatively easy to justify the digressive sections of this novel—but only when one resorts to a thematic justification, such as the idea that the complexity of subjective experience makes it impossible to understand life in simple linear terms. As the novel as a form moves from external narrative plot to "inner plot" or stream of consciousness, its unity becomes more largely thematic. The same is true of the shift from exposition to dramatic monologue in the lyric. One can try hard to read Pound's *Cantos* as a series of ideograms, where the concrete object (or objective correlative) is, as Pound recommended, "the adequate symbol," but one will not get far in making sense of the poem until one comes upon thematic propositions about usury, democracy, technological society, the vanity of modern man, and the like. It seems that the more radically a literary work attempts to escape from thematic generalizations, the more dependent on such generalizations it becomes. For the rage to subvert general ideas is itself expressible only as a general idea.

There are all sorts of ways of dodging these conclusions, including the argument that it is not the writer but the *reader* (or critic) who imports the messages into a work which is in itself innocent of them. A sophisticated version of this strategy holds that the conceptual schemes that readers and critics apply to literary works are but useful scaffoldings, heuristic devices that should not be confused with the meaning itself. This was Cleanth Brooks's way of extricating himself from the dilemma seemingly posed by his attacks on "the heresy of paraphrase": if paraphrase is a heresy, is not Brooks a prime heretic? Brooks escapes this contradiction by arguing that although "we may use—and in many connections must use—such formulations as more or less convenient ways of referring to parts of the poem," these formulations are merely "scaffoldings which we may properly for certain purposes throw about the building: we must not mistake them for the internal and essential structure of the building itself."[28] What Brooks fails to explain is how, if the reader *needs* to build a conceptual "scaffolding," we can avoid the conclusion that the *experience* of a literary work is conceptual. Among the "certain purposes" for erecting the conceptual scaffolding would be the purpose of making sense of the poem. Why should the heuristic devices that are needed to make sense of the work not count as part of our primary experience of the work?

This tendency to regard the propositional element of literary discourse as alien to the "experience" of this discourse is the key strategy of Stanley Fish's method of "affective stylistics." Fish's argument is basically simple: we can and do, for practical purposes, treat language in terms of its net results, the propositional message we can extract from it; yet language as we actually experience it, in the temporal flow of the reading experience, is a process, not a static product; therefore, insofar as we view language propositionally (and referentially), we violate our experience of it; and in literary works, the degree of violation is significant. In at least one respect, Fish seems to turn the New Criticism on its head, for he rejects the New Critical antithesis of "literary" and "ordinary" language. But having rejected one New Critical dualism, Fish embraces another—the opposition between language as process, or experience, or "event" and language as statement. And like New Critical ironic interpretations, Fish's readings of texts as "self-consuming artifacts" operates as a means of purifying them of assertion and thus protecting the humanities from positivistic incursion.

Fish's ideas would not have attracted so much attention if there

were not at least a grain of truth in them. It is true that the
reader's unfolding experience of a discourse is not the same as his
experience of a single proposition (or a set of propositions) ex-
tracted from the whole and treated as "the message." And in
literary works, it is true, the meanings do shift, alter, and qualify
one another rapidly as one moves through the temporal process of
reading, so that any attempt to pin down the meaning of the text
in a series of propositions—as in jacket blurbs, say—is likely to
seem unsatisfactory. But none of these undeniable truths justifies
the conclusion that literary meanings are not propositional, much
less not referential, or that the experience of a discourse and what
it says are exclusive categories. To hold that the temporality of the
reading process cancels the propositional force of a discourse is in
its own way as much of a reduction as to hold that this process can
always be neatly encompassed by a proposition.

"Making Sense"

I do not want to deny that in turning the question of how a literary
work means into a question about how the reader "produces"
meaning, recent "reader-response" criticism has taken a great
step forward. For in putting the question this way, we make it
possible to overcome the difficulty, seen in New Critical discussions of "the problem of belief," of trying to resolve questions
about the nature of meaning without considering the reader's
processing of conventions. And as Culler at several points suggests—though not as consistently as one would like—this new way
of putting the question need not mean doing away with all notions
of a determinate text that exerts a prior control over the produc-
tive activity of the reader—the position that Fish in his more
recent writings has adopted. Fish says his own brand of "affective
criticism" is "a superior fiction," for "it relieves me of the obligation to be right (a standard that simply drops out) and demands only that I be interesting (a standard that can be met
without any reference at all to an illusory objectivity)."[29] Interpretations do not, according to Fish, correspond to an author's
intention objectively embodied in the conventions of the text
itself, but express only the "interpretive strategies" of the indi-

vidual interpreter or community of interpreters. Interpretive strategies are thus not only a necessary condition of producing interpretations, but a sufficient condition, unaccountable to anything outside themselves. If we ask how we can choose between competing interpretive strategies for a given text, we are told the choice is simply up to us.*

But this brings us back to the original question of literary belief: how do we "take" the thematic statements in a literary work? Culler is right to see this question as a question about conventions, but he acts as if there is no question of the nature of the convention to be applied. The anti-referential, anti-representational convention long promoted by formalist literary theory is the natural and proper convention: "in place of the novel as mimesis," Culler writes of his structuralist approach, "we have the novel as a structure which plays with different modes of ordering and enables the reader to understand how he makes

---

*Ralph W. Rader argues that Fish's "method is logically committed to discovering something like subversion in the syntax and larger features of any work that it treats because it assumes to begin with that apparent inconsistencies and incoherencies are to be accepted as positively significant. Since any semantic system becomes incoherent when the rules by which it is constituted are violated, any method of interpretation which assumes that contradiction between elements of meaning is itself meaningful can only end by proving that all discourse is meaningless. With characteristic rigor and clarity, Fish himself comes to what is in effect this conclusion: 'Perhaps, then the word "meaning" should also be discarded, since it carries with it the notion of message or point. The meaning of an utterance, I repeat, is its experience—all of it—and that experience is immediately compromised the moment you say anything about it. It follows, then, that we shouldn't try to analyze language at all. The human mind, however, seems unable to resist the impulse to investigate its own processes.'" Citing Fish's statement that these conclusions about the indeterminacy of meaning only prove "that meaning is human," Rader comments: "Fish's words really say, not that meaning is human, but that the effort to understand meaning is hopeless, that meaning does not mean. But this evades the given problem, the preexistent fact of meaning" ("Fact, Theory, and Literary Explanation," *Critical Inquiry,* 1, no. 2 [December 1974], 270–71). Jonathan Culler also calls attention to Fish's "misplaced desire to praise man as the originator of meanings," in "Stanley Fish and the Righting of the Reader," *Diacritics,* 5, no. 1 (Spring 1975), 30.

sense of the world."[30] Here structuralism quietly ceases to be a mere method of analysis and takes sides with the modernist campaign against realism.

This way of talking about "making sense" of the world by means of fictions was popularized over a decade ago by Frank Kermode's *The Sense of an Ending*. Whether this theory of making sense itself makes sense is open to question, for the very formulation seems self-contradictory: is the statement that we make sense of the world by means of fictions itself a fiction? Kermode distinguishes between good fictions (open) and bad (closed, dogmatic), and he says that the good kind are not simply "escapist," sentimental, easily consoling. "Fictions too easy we call 'escapist,'" he says. "We want them not only to console, but to make discoveries of the hard truth here and now, in the middest."[31] But it is not clear how fictions can help us make "discoveries" unless they refer to something that is not a fiction, and how anybody can refer to something that is not a fiction within Kermode's epistemological universe is not clear. Nor is it clear how we can choose intelligently between one fiction and others. As Wayne Booth points out, "Kermode stops short of giving us any way to discriminate among the various 'truths about endings' offered by the apocalyptic and millenarian works he describes. How do we decide whether a particular version of *the end* should be attended to? Kermode does not stay for an answer."[32]

Culler's above-quoted remark poses a similar problem: what is the meaning of the word *understand* in his assertion that the novel helps readers understand how they make sense of the world by playing with different modes of ordering? How can such play lead to understanding, especially if we say that the world to be understood is not a mimetic object? In order to talk about understanding, we need to have some way of determining whether one mode of "ordering" is more adequate to reality than some other mode. Merely playing with modes does not bring us down to earth in the sense suggested by "understanding" and "making sense" —normative terms that presuppose a distinction between understanding and misunderstanding, *real* and delusive sense-making. But to make such a distinction is to bring back an essentially mimetic way of speaking. Kermode and Culler want to have things both ways: they want to get rid of mimetic models without surrendering cognitive claims for literature. The result is a kind of elegant hedging.*

Culler might well reply to these objections by asserting that the novel gives "understanding" not by explaining the world but by unsettling all explanations, making us recognize the fallibility of our sense-making operations, exposing our pet certainties for the fictions they are likely to be. The novel as a self-consciously fictive construction (according to this view) calls attention to its own fictionality in order to demystify our conventional modes of seeing. It helps us to understand by making us aware of the snares and traps latent in our instruments of understanding. I am quite willing to accept this account of the novel, but my point is it is a mimetic account. It presupposes an objective world outside our conventional fictions against which we can measure them and become aware of their fictiveness. The concept of demystification or demythologizing becomes meaningless unless there is a norm of reality against which to demystify and demythologize. If we want to talk about literature as a means of understanding, we have to suppose there is something external to literature that it can understand, even if we are always wrong about whatever it is.

*Take, for example, this Kermode statement: "The show of satisfaction" given by literary fictions "will only serve when there seems to be a degree of real compliance with reality as we, from time to time, imagine it" (*The Sense of an Ending,* 63). Here Kermode takes back with one hand what he has seemingly given with the other: fictive satisfactions must comply with reality, but then only seemingly, and only with reality as we imagine it from time to time.

The same equivocation arises in Culler's formulation in his introduction to Tzvetan Todorov's *The Poetics of Prose* (Ithaca: Cornell University Press, 1977), 13: for the structuralist critic, Culler writes, "the most interesting aspect of a literary work will be what it tells us about literary signification, and how it illuminates for us the problems which literature encounters as it tries to organize and give meaning to human experience." It is not clear how literature can be said to "illuminate" problems of significance unless it can be given credit for judging these problems from an objective—i.e., realistic—point of view. Similarly, the reference to literature as "organizing" and "giving meaning" to experience begs the question.

If we reject the mimetic model, we leave unclear the position from which we are offering the rejection. How can we *know* that mimesis is a myth unless we can view from outside, mimetically?

Life as a Fiction

Yet Culler hesitates to take the final plunge. He stops short of asserting that all our sense-making procedures are fictions. In a passage on Julia Kristeva, Culler attacks as "too sweeping" the claim that "reality is a convention produced by language."[33] The effect of structuralist theory, however, with its "global expansion of the concept of the text," as Robert Alter calls it,[34] has been to give this kind of claim respectability. A recent avant-garde writer, Ronald Sukenick, declares that there has been a "cultural turnabout which has led to the discovery that all accounts of our experience, all versions of 'reality,' are of the nature of fiction."[35] The title of the essay collection from which this statement is taken, *The Life of Fiction*, suggests the nature of this "discovery." Life is fiction, fiction is life, that is all we know on earth and all we need to know. What does it mean to say that life is a fiction? Raymond Federman, another vanguard spokesman, explains:

> But in what sense is life fiction? Fiction is made of understanding, which for most of us means primarily words—and only words (spoken or written). Therefore, if one admits from the start (at least to oneself) that no meaning pre-exists language, but that language creates meaning as it goes along, that is to say as it is used (spoken or written), as it progresses, then writing (fiction especially) will be a mere process of letting language do its tricks. To write, then, is to *produce* meaning, and not *reproduce* a pre-existing meaning. To write is to progress, and not *remain* subjected (by habit or reflexes) to the meaning that supposedly precedes the words. As such, fiction can no longer be reality, or a representation of reality, or an imitation, or even a recreation of reality; it can only be A REALITY—an autonomous reality whose only relation with the real world is to improve that world. To create fiction is, in fact, a way to abolish reality, and especially to abolish the notion that reality is truth.[36]

The logic could not be spelled out more plainly: meaning does not "pre-exist" language but is created by language "as it goes along"; *therefore*, meaning in language refers not to any reality or truth external to language, but to that artificial "reality" *produced* by language. Like statements in literature, all our verbal formulations derive their meaning from systems of conventions and thus are referable only to these systems.

These statements by Sukenick and Federman may be dismissed as little more than the obligatory hyperbole of avant-garde self-promotion, the upping of the ante of extremism that seems necessary now in order to be heard above the competitive din. Yet one finds similar views, not necessarily more circumspectly phrased, in more respectable sectors. Terrence Hawkes argues, in *Structuralism and Semiotics*, that a language "does not construct its formations of words by reference to the patterns of 'reality,' but on the basis of its own internal and self-sufficient rules."[37] And Culler asserts, in *Structuralist Poetics*, "precisely because the individual signs are unmotivated, the linguist must attempt to reconstruct the system which alone provides motivation."[38] And Robert Scholes writes in "The Fictional Criticism of the Future," "it is because reality can no longer be recorded that realism is dead. All writing, all composition, is construction. We do not imitate the world, we construct versions of it. There is no mimesis, only poesis. No recording, only constructing."[39]

One could object—as I shall do in the next chapter—that the fact that we "produce" meanings does not mean this is the end of the matter and that these meanings are not answerable to anything outside their internally coherent semiological systems. But the thinkers who maintain the autonomy of these systems show little interest in dealing with such objections. They assert that it is simply naive to suppose that "the patterns of 'reality'" can have anything to say about the linguistic formulations we choose. On the contrary, all such formulations are as self-referential, "unmotivated," and, with respect to objects external to the system, as arbitrary as the statements in literary works. Like literary statements, everyday utterances are self-created (or system-created) forms of order by which human beings give coherence and meaning to experience, thus expressing their freedom against an in-

human world. (There is frequently the suggestion that anybody
who attempts to validate his statements by referring them to some
supposed external object is refusing to take "responsibility" for
them.) In this sense, "life" and our attempts to make sense of it
are fictions.

Since language is by definition incapable of referring to anything external to its own systems, it follows almost tautologically
that any talk of literary representation is senseless. It also follows
that virtually any work of any period can be read as an exemplification of the fictive relation of language to reality. This logic can
be seen in the following passage from Paul de Man's *Blindness
and Insight*:

> For the statement about language that sign and meaning can
> never coincide, is what is precisely taken for granted in the kind
> of language we call literary. Literature, unlike everyday lan-
> guage, begins on the far side of this knowledge; it is the only
> form of language free from the fallacy of unmediated expres-
> sion. All of us know this, although we know it in the misleading
> way of a wishful assertion of the opposite. Yet the truth
> emerges in the foreknowledge we possess of the true nature of
> literature when we refer to it as *fiction*. All literatures, includ-
> ing the literature of Greece, have always designated themselves
> as existing in the mode of fiction; in the *Iliad*, when we first
> encounter Helen, it is as the emblem of the narrator weaving
> the actual war into the tapestry of a fictional object. Her beauty
> prefigures the beauty of all future narratives as entities that
> point to their own fictional nature. The self-reflecting mirror-
> effect by means of which a work of fiction asserts, by its very
> existence, its separation from empirical reality, its divergence,
> as a sign, from a meaning that depends for its existence on
> the constitutive activity of this sign, characterizes the work
> of literature in its essence. It is always against the explicit
> assertion of the writer that readers degrade the fiction by con-
> fusing it with a reality from which it has forever taken leave.[40]

What this difficult passage says, in effect, is that not only are
thematic propositions in literature to be seen as fictions, but the
reason this is so is that all linguistic attempts to describe the
world are fictions. Since "sign and meaning can never coincide,"

all meaning is open and undecidable and bears no stable relation
to its apparent origin or object.

Literature differs from "everyday language," however, in its
insistence on calling attention to this fact, to which everyday
language, for practical reasons, blinds itself. That is, literature
differs from everyday language in its refusal to claim innocence,
its unwillingness to take the easy road and disguise its compromised nature. It is by thus problematizing itself that literature
becomes "the only form of language free from the fallacy of
unmediated expression." Literature is exempt from the "fallacy"
because it refuses to make the claim in the first place. All language is cut off from "empirical reality," but only literary
language knows this about itself and refuses to hide it. De Man
can thus go on to say that the literary fiction "is not myth, for it
knows and names itself as fiction."[41] That is, whereas *myth* tries
to conceal its own fictionality and undecidability, *fiction* advertises them. Joseph Riddel restates the point in summarizing
de Man (and also J. Hillis Miller and Geoffrey Hartman, who
follow de Man closely on this point): "fiction, not myth, is the
ground of all we call 'culture,' and fiction is always already
doubled and knows its doubleness."[42]

De Man is harder to argue with than Culler because he does not
so much defend a thesis as propose one as given and already
understood. Perhaps its authority is presumed to be given in
"modern thought," which no longer needs to assume the burden
of proof. In any event, it seems almost irrelevant to object that
de Man's specific illustration from Book 3 of the *Iliad* gives
dubious support to his argument. In the passage to which he
refers, Helen does indeed—in the Loeb translation—weave "a
great purple web of double fold, and thereon," we are told, "she
was broidering many battles of the horse-taming Trojans and the
brazen-coated Achaeans, that for her sake they had endured at
the hands of Ares."[43] Now supposing we assume—as I think we
reasonably can—that de Man is right in taking Helen here as "the
emblem of the narrator" of the *Iliad*, we are still hard put to find
any suggestion in the work that her weaving of the war into her
work of art is supposed to make the reader question the reality of
the action of the *Iliad*. In fact, a "self-reflecting mirror-effect"

like that seen in modern narratives which "point to their own
fictional nature" in order to call into question the epistemological
authority of the narrative itself would seem about as remote from
Homer's apparent intention as nuclear fission or jet propulsion.
One might argue that, if anything, the effect of Helen's weaving is
not to de-realize the war but to give emphasis to its reality and
importance.

Nevertheless, my point is not that de Man is necessarily wrong
about the *Iliad* but that, right or wrong, he shows no interest in
giving reasons or evidence for his interpretation. He can dispense
with reasons and evidence because he knows "the true nature of
literature," and this he knows by "foreknowledge." The *Iliad*
must necessarily know and name itself as fiction, must necessarily
assert, "by its very existence, its separation from empirical reality," because the *Iliad* is literature and it is characteristic of
literature "in its essence" to put a sign of cancellation upon its
own apparent referentiality.

A similar logical procedure is seen in J. Hillis Miller's reading
of Dickens's *Sketches by Boz* to which I referred in my introduction. The *Sketches,* Miller notes at the outset, "seem firmly
attached to the social facts of London in 1836."[44] "Here, even if
nowhere else, Dickens seems to have been practicing a straightforward mimetic realism."[45] The reader who knows enough about
recent opinion to have gathered that "straightforward mimetic
realism" is a term of abuse will not be surprised when Miller
turns and argues that this seeming realism in Dickens is merely
an "inevitable misreading" invited by literature, and that "the
Sketches by Boz, like *Oliver Twist,* express both the illusion and
its deconstruction."[46] Boz, the narrator, "must tell lies, employ
fictions, in ways which expose the fact that they are lies."[47] Miller
adduces copious textual evidence to show that the *Sketches* "do
put their own status in question"—theatrical metaphors, references to other literary works and forms, references to the imagination's tendency to impose its "romantic humor" on the facts,
hints that social reality, far from being solid and determinate, is
itself a kind of "text" that persistently eludes interpretation.[48]
Thus, "the *Sketches* are not *mimesis* of an externally existing
reality," Miller concludes, "but the interpretation of that reality

according to highly artificial schemas inherited from the past. They came into existence through the imposition of fictitious patterns rather than through the discovery of patterns really there."[49] That "artificial schemas inherited from the past" and "fictitious patterns" might themselves bear some relation to "patterns really there" Miller does not consider.

It may be true, of course, that Dickens's devices of characterization and imagery do indeed signal to the reader the literary and fictive quality of the text. But nothing in this common convention whereby fictional works concede their lack of *factual* truth justifies the conclusion that such works call attention to their inability to refer to external reality. It is only by confusing the pseudo-factual or pseudo-informational level of fictional reference with the larger thematic level that one can infer that literary works necessarily call their referential claims into question. Like de Man, Miller has resorted to the strategy, discussed earlier in this chapter, of using the fact that literary action does not present itself as literally true as an excuse to sever literature from referential claims, or to see it as invariably commenting on the futility of such claims.[50]

For all its heavy documentation, then, Miller's reading of the *Sketches* rests not on textual evidence from the work itself but on a theory that tells him in advance what this evidence must be evidence *for*. There is nothing in Dickens's use of theatrical metaphors, for example, that necessarily implies the questioning of mimetic reference. Indeed, as Miller himself suggests, such "emphasis on playacting and on the factitious calls the reader's attention *to the fact* that English society as a whole is based on arbitrary conventions."[51] As the words I have italicized suggest, Miller's own implication is that Dickens's theatrical images would seem to be a mimetic and rhetorical device by which the reader's attention is directed to the *real* aspects of English society—real aspects that happen to be elusive, unreal, and shrouded in appearances. But Miller has thought of this possible escape and taken steps to head it off. "This uncovering of the fictitiousness of the fictive is not performed, however, in the name of some 'true' language for which a space is cleared through the rejection of the fictive. Behind each fiction there is another fiction, and this new

fiction is sustained in its turn by the counterpart phantom of a
beguiling literal reading."[52] Again, one suspects that the "evidence" for such categorical assertions lies not in Dickens's text
but in Miller's theoretical hypothesis, which demands that metaphors in literature never point to reality but rather draw us back
toward their own infinite problematics. As Miller himself admits,
with unintended irony, his "double reading" of the *Sketches,* as a
work that employs realism only to deconstruct it, "would be valid
whether it was asserted explicitly or not in the text."[53] The
evidence need not be explicit in the text because it is given in the
definition of the nature of literature as "a use of language which
exposes its own rhetorical devices and assumptions."[54] This self-
deconstruction, Miller asserts, "is basic to the mode of existence
of a work of literature and constitutes it as a literary use of
language."[55] This rule applies not only to literature but to all art,
or at least to all great art: "The representative aspect, as in all
great art, tends to dissolve before the spectator's recognition of
the primacy of the medium in its meaninglessness."[56]

Again, I am not necessarily suggesting that Miller's interpretation of the *Sketches* is wrong, but only that the method he
employs establishes his case by default. There *do* exist many
literary works which call attention to the fallibility of their own
conventions—indeed, this mode has become the norm in vanguard writing. But we determine whether a work *is* in this mode
by examining its specific rhetorical intentions, not by consulting
our definition of literature. Since Miller forecloses the very possibility of language's referring to the world, any text he deals with
will naturally and automatically turn out to be a dramatization of
its own problematics. Because he sees any mediation by artificial
conventions in a text as evidence of a structure that calls its own
assumptions into question, Miller can read all texts without fail
as self-deconstructing. Thus not only Homer and Dickens, but all
other writers of all times and places will be readable as self-
reflexive writers. And not only literary works but other instances
of language, including literary criticism, will be subject to such
interpretation as well. As Miller puts it, "if the real world is a
fiction and the reflection of it in literature a fiction too, what of
the interpretation of the relation between them expressed by the

critic?" "The critic's interpretation," comes the answer, "is fiction too."[57]

I think I have said enough to show that this kind of theorist can
give us the meaning of literary works before he reads them. Since
the self-reflexive, self-consuming, "problematizing" nature of all
texts is given in advance by the critic's definition of language, it
follows that all texts *must* testify—whether self-consciously or
"blindly"—to the fictive nature of their own structures. Interpretive method is reduced to the purely instrumental job of showing
how the particular text in question, however much it may seem to
refer to something and have a determinate intention, actually
calls attention to its fallibility and undecidability.

The logical procedure of this kind of criticism is similar to that
of the New Critics. As R. S. Crane pointed out, the New Critic
"knows what the nature of 'poetic language' must be because he
has begun by dividing all language into two opposing and incommensurable kinds—the language of 'logic' and the language of
'symbolism'—and then has deduced from this initial assumption
that the 'symbolic' language of poetry must necessarily possess
the contraries of all qualities commonly asserted of 'logical discourse.' "[58] De Man, too, deduces the nature of literature by
dividing all language into two opposing and incommensurable
camps, but instead of dividing language into "paradoxical" vs.
"steno-language," de Man divides it into language that decon-
structs itself by calling attention to its own fictiveness and undecidability and language that presumes a naive confidence in its
ontological authority. This antithesis is in turn supported by a
metaphysics which holds that language cannot possibly transcend
its fictive self-enclosure.

And yet de Man's argument, surprisingly, turns out to be part
of a *defense* of literature *against* the skepticism of current decon-
structionism. This defense follows the paradoxical line that literary works cannot be *exposed* as ideological fictions if they do not
pretend to be anything else. They can be exposed, demystified,
deconstructed, only when they pretend to be something language
cannot be—referential and mimetic. Since the literary work "is
not a myth," but rather a fiction which "knows and names itself"
as such, it therefore "is not a demystification, it is demystified

from the start. When modern critics think they are demystifying literature, they are in fact being demystified by it."[59] Elsewhere de Man makes this point about the modes of irony and naiveté: "both modes are fully demystified when they remain within the realm of their respective languages but are totally vulnerable to renewed blindness as soon as they leave it for the empirical world"—that is to say, as soon as they claim to be *about* something outside their own fictive language.[60] Again, if we ask how de Man *knows* that irony and naiveté are fully demystified when "within their respective languages" but "vulnerable to renewed blindness" when advanced as references to the external world, we infer that he has deduced this conclusion from his axiomatic assumption that literary language is *always* self-demystifying, empirical language always "blind." Why this assumption is necessary or compelling is evidently beyond argument.

Note that de Man's (and Miller's) thesis defends literature against programmatic skepticism by acquiescing to it—injecting skepticism not only into the perspective of literature but into the fabric of life itself. Knowing and naming itself as fiction, literature becomes a vehicle for a nihilistic metaphysics, an anti-didactic form of preaching. In a world in which nobody can look outside the walls of the prison house of language, literature, with its built-in confession of its self-imprisonment, becomes once again the great oracle of truth, but now the truth is that there is no truth. In a curiously inverted restatement of the religion of literature, the literary work is made the sole source of truth only in the sense that it alone refuses to succumb to the delusion that truth can be spoken. Where reality has become unreal, literature qualifies as our guide to reality by de-realizing itself.

So the logic of criticism has come full circle. From the ancient view that literary fictions illustrate general truths, we moved to the view that literary fictions illustrate fictions. But having in the meantime discovered that reality itself is a fiction, we reassert that, in illustrating fictions, literary fictions reveal truth. In a paradoxical and fugitive way, mimetic theory remains alive. Literature holds the mirror up to unreality. And put on its feet, taken out of the anti-objectivist idiom in which de Man states it, such a formulation would be apt. In a distorted way, de Man's argument gets at a truth about modern if not earlier literature: that its conventions of reflexivity and anti-realism are themselves mimetic of the kind of unreal reality that modern reality has become. But "unreality" in this sense is not a fiction but the element in which we live.

Seven

How Not to Save
the Humanities

The tendencies discussed in the previous chapter point up a striking development: it has become difficult to distinguish the defenders of humanistic ideals from the attackers. Conservative humanists often share with avant-garde anti-humanists the assumption that humanism (an umbrella term, but one that serves well enough to denote a certain broad tradition of literature, culture, values, ideas, meanings, and the like) is a set of fictions which impart a shared illusion of sense to a world that is inherently senseless—or could be so described if it were legitimate to speak "inherently" of anything, as of course it is not. In the face of celebrations of cultural and literary traditions which concede that "fiction ... is the ground of all that we call 'culture,' " it is easy for would-be dismantlers of these traditions to reply that what is admitted to be groundless ought to be discarded.[1] With such arguments coming from its friends, humanism scarcely needs enemies. The polar extremes of vanguard literary thinking—on one side an exaggerated self-abasement, on the other a compensatory self-adulation—are actually one position; they follow from the same demotion of literature to the level of fiction.

In this chapter I want to look closely at the kind of reasoning out of which the self-defeating "defense" of the humanities has typically evolved and also to offer some modest recommendations on how we can avoid falling into it. I do not propose to tackle the formidable job of reconstructing the grounds of humanistic knowledge, but I shall suggest the direction which I think any such reconstruction will have to take.

Mimesis vs. Vision
A Social Melodrama

Consider the case of Northrop Frye, who remains probably the most influential exponent of the romantic theory of creative imagination. In Frye's grand vision, literature, which is to say the mythical categories and forms expressed not only in literary works but in all forms of culture, is the legislator of the world, the orderer of reality, the bringer of meaning and the sense of belonging to what would otherwise be chaos and inhuman homelessness. Those critics who have written of Frye as a kind of formalist or esthete who severs literature from the real world have missed the point of his writing. For Frye, literature does not isolate itself from the real world, it appropriates it, and thus humanizes it. "Literature," says Frye, "does not reflect life, but it doesn't escape or withdraw from life either, it swallows it. And the imagination won't stop until it's swallowed everything."[2] If Frye can be called a "formalist," his formalism does not retreat into the autonomous purity of the literary imagination but aggressively projects that autonomous imagination outward onto the external world and absorbs that external world into itself.

But Frye claims that literature makes this appropriation of the external world, this spreading everywhere of human order, value, and relationship, without soliciting belief from its readers. "The general principle is that imaginative structures as such are independent of belief, and it makes no difference to the structure whether the implied beliefs are real, pretended, or denounced as demonic...."[3] Why belief must make no difference becomes clearer when we understand Frye's general theory of culture. Over and over in successive works, Frye asserts that there are two orders of reality, an objective order in which we invest our belief, and a human order we impose on this other order in order to give it meaning. The first order is that of nature or things as they are, dead, neutral, inhuman, and unavoidable; the second is the order of things as they should be as projected by human purpose and "desire," the order of art, applied science, religion, culture, and civilization. The trouble is that Frye never locates a connection between these two orders—though he comes close to doing so in *The Critical Path,* when he says that "the vision of things as they could or should be certainly has to depend on the vision of things as they are."[4] But Frye does not go on to specify what this dependence is and finally seems to conclude that it does not exist after all. "Evidently we must come to terms with the fact that mythical

and logical languages are distinct," he writes, not noticing that
"coming to terms" with a "fact" itself seems to require the very
derivation of a "mythical" from a "logical" term that Frye is
saying cannot occur. Finally, Frye maintains the rigid disjunction
between "is" and "ought" statements that we associate with early
logical positivism. Our higher values and schemes of order rest
purely on what Frye calls "a revolutionary and transforming act
of choice," which is to say, choices rest on choices—they are
arbitrary and cannot be defended by reasons. "The notion that
our choices are inevitably connected with things as they are,
whether through the mind of God or the constitution of nature,
always turns out to be an illusion of habit."[5] Therefore it is not
valid to *believe* in statements belonging to the second of the two
orders, the order of human projection and desire.

The values and meanings on which culture is founded, then, do
not for Frye rest on any prior objective beliefs about the way
things are. Indeed, as we shall see in a moment, there are moral
reasons why they must not do so, for the dependence of human
choices of values upon objective facts would constitute for Frye an
enslavement of man to the determinism of the external world.
Given the conditions imposed by Frye's separation of the cultural
and the natural orders, culture must somehow entertain its values
without anybody's believing that anything is the case in the natural world. Values and ideas of order have to be entertained as
myths, which is to say as imaginative possibilities that do not
pretend to make reference to states of affairs in the objective
world. Though the acknowledged sources of his theories lie in
Blake, Frye divests myths of the conviction that Blake himself
had invested in them. This step has its consequences, for if we
divest myths of their claims to explain aspects of reality with some
kind of truth, we rob them of content and place our own defense
of myth in a quixotic position. Myth is supposed to humanize,
order, make sense of experience, yet its separation from any
objective ground leaves it without the authority to carry out these
functions effectively.

We have already seen that this contradiction is a familiar one in
the literary theorizing before Frye. Consider I. A. Richards, who
defined literature, in his earlier writings, as "pseudo-statement"

without cognitive value and argued that "we must cut our pseudo-statements free from belief," yet who also maintained that we must try to retain these pseudo-statements "in this released state, as the main instruments by which we order our attitudes to one another and to the world."[6] Somehow we are supposed to "order" our attitude to the world by making use of fictions whose lack of truth we recognize but decide to regard as irrelevant. As in Frye, the cognitive function ambitiously claimed for literature conflicts with the cognitive emptiness of the definition of literature. The very admission that our beliefs are founded on myths undermines their ability to generate credence.

It is possible, of course, to hold beliefs with many different degrees of conviction. We can believe tentatively, doubtfully, or provisionally, and we can believe "on faith" without objective evidence. We can also "try out" beliefs to see whether they pass the test of practical confirmation. But it is another thing to say that we can believe something while regarding it as a myth, which seems either a misuse of terms or a piece of self-deception. Michael Beldoch makes this point well in a comment on "as if" philosophies: "Although. . .we may *say* that we can believe in something 'as if' it were true, these are in fact mutually contradictory states of mind. At the moment that we *believe* in something it *is* true; the moment that we add *as if,* we cease to believe and become rationalist 'hedgers' and religious imposters."[7] It is not hard to think of instances of cultures organized around ideas that are patently not true. But it is very hard to think of any cultures which have *conceded* that the ideas that organize them are not true. Frye's vision of culture as a vast mythology seems to be up against the psychological fact that the act of designating an idea as a myth tends to deprive that idea of the pragmatic efficacy that is claimed for it. However much we may try to talk ourselves into it, the proposition that the need for objective truth is a hangover of positivism is not one we readily accept.

We are back to the question posed in my last chapter of how literature is to help us "make sense" of the world when we refuse to grant it a "mimetic" relation to the world. The contradiction seems to stem from irreconcilable requirements imposed by the cultural situation. In order to justify our humanistic claims for literature, we have to accord its visions some kind of belief. But then "belief" implies dogmas and "privileged positions," which skepticism has exposed as chimerical. Beliefs are things the wrong sorts of people put unquestioned faith in—positivists, moralists, social engineers, superpatriots, bureaucrats.

Another passage from Frye will further illustrate my point about the moral assumptions that force us into a self-defeating line of argument. In *The Critical Path,* Frye warns against what may happen when our "myths of concern" are entertained not for their imaginative "truth of vision," as Frye calls it, but for their objective "truth of correspondence":

> When a myth of concern claims truth of correspondence as well as truth of vision, and assumes that its postulates are or can be established as facts, it can hardly produce any "dialogue" except the single exasperated formula: "But can't you *see* how wrong you are?" When it renounces this claim, it acquires the kind of humility which makes it possible to see intellectual honesty on the other side too. As for one's own side, one is not renouncing its truth: what one renounces is the finality of one's understanding of that truth.[8]

There is no reason to doubt Frye's sincerity when he says that his way of disposing matters does not renounce the concept of truth. But Frye's argument commits him to something close to such a renunciation despite his good intentions. Since "truth of vision" has no definite accountability to anything outside the imagination, there is no telling what might not pass muster in its name. Frye's hand would seem to have been forced by his decision to associate truth of correspondence with the foreclosure of dialogue and the assertion of "the finality of one's understanding of... truth." Thus Frye turns the philosophical problem of knowledge into a social melodrama, with "truth of correspondence" cast as the villain and the visionary imagination as the hero. In his moderate way, Frye sets the pattern for those even more emphatic social critics who perceive a necessary connection between objective thinking, literary realism, and the dispossession of American Indians or the bombing of Asian peasants.

   This same assignment of guilt-by-association is seen in other prominent critics: in Angus Fletcher, for instance, who praises Frye's "healthy relativity in the area of human choices of what is 'good' and what is 'bad.' " "Frye makes value judgments all the time," Fletcher says, "but he does not claim they have any particular authority as such. Instead, they express his convictions of interest at any moment. . . . they have no tyrannical 'press and screw' with which to control the analogous desires of other readers."[9] Similarly, Frank Kermode, taking a page from Roland Barthes, declares that "the whole movement toward 'secretarial' realism represents a nostalgia for the types, an anachronistic myth of common understanding and shared universes of meaning."[10] Analogously, for Kermode, any movement toward objective textual interpretation implies the sentimental "pretense that everybody can agree on a particular construction of reality."[11] In a recent essay, Kermode cites Fielding's comparison of his authorial function in *Tom Jones* to "one who keeps a public ordinary, at which all persons are welcome for their money" in order to illustrate that the kind of literature that sets a preestablished meaning before its reader takes for granted "the implied passivity of the consumer." The implication is that reading conceived as a "recognition" of determinate meanings rather than the reader's free recreation is a crass sort of capitalistic transaction in which "the author's task is to cook and serve [the work] well—in exact accordance with the customer's taste."[12]
   This reasoning leads Kermode, in his most recent work, to join those critics who propose that textual interpretation is a kind of fiction-making in its own right. In *The Classic,* Kermode argues that Hawthorne's ambiguities in *The House of the Seven Gables* and *The Scarlet Letter* are "evasions of narrative authority," and "imply that each man must make his own reading."[13] "It is for the reader," says Kermode, to make sense of the many meanings of the scarlet letter "by his own imaginative collaboration."[14] "Collaboration" seems to overstate Hawthorne's role in the transaction since, according to Kermode, these meanings cannot be read as a "message" intended by Hawthorne. In such works, Kermode remarks, "the old contracts between signifier and signified, between the authoritative maker and the reader confident

that there is a right interpretation, are boldly broken. Such a text
must continually draw attention to itself as something written, as
open and plural, itself a type of things to come, in a time when all
books must be read with a difference."[15] Reading this last passage, one may wonder *why* all books must now be read with a
difference—especially if one misses the allusion to the new French
criticism. Kermode does not *argue* that we must now read in a
new way but takes it for granted that the reader, flatteringly
treated as a fellow initiate, already knows and assumes this, or at
least will not ask any questions.

In coupling "open and plural," Kermode seems to have confused the *indeterminacy* of a text with its *complexity*. A "plural"
or multisignificant text may be as much under the author's determinate control, as much an intended "message" to which the
reader's response must conform, as a univocal one. Hawthorne's
typical device of offering alternative interpretations of events
suggests the determinate point, which is surely a message intended by Hawthorne, that reality is susceptible to conflicting
views which may not be easily reconcilable. In other words,
Hawthorne is determinate *about* indeterminacy. The qualified
reader can identify the relevant alternative meanings and exclude
many meanings as irrelevant or inappropriate. Except where a
text is flawed, ambiguity does not involve any "broken contract"
between the writer and the reader, nor any "evasion of narrative
authority," and it offers no real choice to the reader, who must
either perceive the central meanings or, as we say, "miss the
point." Moreover, there is a hierarchy within the range of multiple meanings, and this too limits the reader's freedom. Thus at
the end of *The Scarlet Letter,* where one possible interpretation is
that there was no mark on the minister's chest, Hawthorne calls
into question the "highly respectable witnesses" who testify to
this version by characterizing them in a phrase that implies they
are blinded by hypocrisy.

But Kermode himself sets his theory aside when he operates as
a practical critic. Thus in *The Classic,* when he interprets *The
House of the Seven Gables,* he proceeds in the old-fashioned way,
even speculating about the books Hawthorne may have read.
Such information could hardly matter if it were really up to the

reader to make his own meaning. If this were really true, we should not need a learned gloss on what Hawthorne probably thought—or for that matter, anybody else's interpretation at all. This is not to deny that texts have to be actively interpreted and, in that sense, "constructed" by the reader. But it is misleading to suppose that this activity of construction depends upon the reader's choice, for it is itself controlled by the text. Kermode's overstatement of the truth that the reader is an active participant in the creation of meaning seems to derive from his assumption that any degree of control exercised over the reader is a kind of totalitarianism. If determinate meaning is merely a kind of capitalistic cookery, then we are morally bound to view the text as "open" and the interpreter as free and creative.

In *The Sense of an Ending,* Kermode had warned that "fictions can degenerate into myths whenever they are not consciously held to be fictive. In this sense, anti-Semitism is a degenerate fiction, a myth; and *Lear* is a fiction."* The clear implication is that if you really *believe* your beliefs, you are very likely on your way to excusing fascism. If, on the other hand, you can entertain your beliefs as fictions, you can protect them from totalitarian temptation. Yet here Kermode wavers: he concedes that some totalitarian thinkers *have* consciously held their ideas to be fictive, and in this he is right. The literature of fascism abounds in assertions of the fictive nature of truth.

Mussolini, for example, sounds exactly like a radical poststructuralist literary critic until the last clause of this statement:

> From the fact that all ideologies are of equal value, that all ideologies are merely fictions, the modern relativist infers that everybody has the right to create for himself his own ideology and to attempt to enforce it with all the energy of which he is capable.[16]

One may dismiss Mussolini's reasoning as perverse, but his apol-

*Kermode, *The Sense of an Ending,* 39. Interestingly enough, one of those who Kermode thinks "forget(s) the fictiveness of *all* fictions and thus regress(es) to myth" is Northrop Frye (41). Yet Frye's later cautionary treatment of "myths of concern" is precisely analogous to Kermode's criticism of "myths."

ogy for "might makes right" is no less logical a deduction from
the premise that "all ideologies are fictions" than the tolerance
and liberality deduced by Frye, Fletcher, and Kermode. We are
inclined to view the relativizing of belief as a liberalizing strategy
because it dissolves the authority of dogmatic and totalitarian
systems of thought. But this strategy at the same time dissolves
the authority of anything that tries to resist these systems, and
smooths the moral and psychological paths to mass manipulation.

This dimension is overlooked by current exponents of what has
come to be called the "institutional" definition of art, an approach that seeks to resolve debates over the definition of art by
invoking the shared myths of the culture. Thus for John Ellis in
his *Theory of Criticism,* literature must be defined as whatever
"the community" decides to regard as literature. "It is the agreement of the community that makes [texts] into literature," Ellis
writes.[17] But *what* community? Suppose our particular community is unsure which of many possible definitions of literature it
ought to favor? And suppose each of these definitions is being
promoted by self-interested propagandists, some of whom assert
that "literature" (or "art") is anything the individual artist, or
perhaps any other individual, chooses to regard as literature? It
may be true, of course, that communities do in fact determine the
definitions of terms like "literature" at a given historical moment, but to say this is merely to beg the question by saying that
the community believes what the community believes. The real
question is the *basis* on which the community chooses its beliefs.
To refer the determination to some abstract concept of community is to ignore the fact that such determinations are rationally
debatable and to turn the question into one of power and manipulation. Perhaps power and manipulation have always decided
such conflicts, but if we deny any scope to rational argument, we
leave the field open to them.

Clearly, writers like Frye and Kermode are afraid that unless
we cease believing that an objective order can verify our interpretations, pluralism and free debate are likely to be stifled by
dogmatism. Though this anxiety is obviously not without foundation, its particular formulation is misconceived. One does not

make the world safer for pluralism and free debate by undermining the grounds of intellectual conviction. Indeed, it can be
maintained that there can be no pluralism or free debate that
means anything unless we *can* make reference to an external
order of objects. If we cannot refer to any such order, then there is
literally nothing to argue about and no point of reference by
which disputes can be mediated. If nobody's perspective can
achieve correspondence with reality, then debate in principle
collapses into just the sort of blind clashing of arbitrary, incommensurable, untestable fictions that Frye, quite properly, deplores. Instead of a pluralism of disagreement that aims, by
collective give-and-take, to bring us closer to a common reality,
we are left with a pluralism of self-validating outlooks which
cannot even argue with one another—which is to say we are left
with a theory that rationalizes the atomized culture we now
inhabit.

Hannah Arendt makes this point in *Between Past and Future*,
noting what happens when the concept of legitimacy is reduced to
mere agreement of "the community" between arbitrarily chosen
positions. She observes that there exists "a silent agreement"
among modern political and social scientists "that everything can
eventually be called anything else, and that distinctions are meaningful only to the extent that each of us has the right 'to define his
terms.' " Yet does not this curious right, Arendt asks,

> already indicate that such terms as "tyranny," "authority,"
> "totalitarianism" have simply lost their common meaning, or
> that we have ceased to live in a common world where the words
> we have in common possess an unquestionable meaningful-
> ness, so that, short of being condemned to live verbally in an
> altogether meaningless world, we grant each other the right
> to retreat into our own worlds of meaning, and demand only
> that each of us remain consistent with his own private termi-
> nology? If, in these circumstances, we assure ourselves that
> we still understand each other, we do not mean that together
> we understand a world common to us all, but that we under-
> stand the consistency of arguing and reasoning, or the process
> of argumentation in its sheer formality.[18]

Note that this reduction of argumentation to "sheer formality" turns thinking into something like a self-referential poem.

There are those, of course, who boast that ours is a culture of scintillating "dialogue," dissonance, and pluralism, but their view is based on a delusion. Mere lack of agreement does not facilitate disagreement. Real disagreement has become rare, for the multiplicity of tongues leads not to confrontation but to incommensurability and talking at cross-purposes. The assumption that there is no common reality outside our various languages and perspectives helps to paralyze disagreement, for disagreement presupposes something "there," some third entity outside the perspectives of the debaters, though it is accessible only through a perspective. A rich pluralism would rest on an ideal of "common pursuit"—where the many differing perspectives seek, through vigorous exchange, to arrive at a common, though many-sided, truth about reality. Indeed, what else is it that vindicates all our careerism, one-upping, and competitive posturing if it is not the assumption that somewhere, somehow, there is progress in the collective struggle for truth?

Instead of such a "common-pursuit" conception of pluralism, ours is a pluralism that locks each of us into his own self-validating paradigm. Where theory teaches that there is only truth of "coherence" and no way to bring our disparate languages down to earth, we have no means of making corrections. We can always *change* perspectives of course, for the mere sake of change or to avoid boredom or to demonstrate that we are not rigid, but we cannot improve or correct them. Improvement and correction presuppose an appeal to some extra-perspectival reality against which we can measure each other and ourselves.

Humanists and
Anti-Humanists

Well-intentioned as the fictive defense of humanism is, its arguments make sitting ducks for the assaults of the anti-humanists. For example, when Frye says that art does not imitate nature but rather assimilates it to "human forms," that "literary shape cannot come from life; it comes only from literary tradition, and so ultimately from myth,"[19] his use of the word "human" invites the skepticism of a Robbe-Grillet, which is merely Frye's own skepticism carried to a bolder and more rigorously logical conclusion than Frye himself is willing to carry it. Robbe-Grillet asks whether there "is not a certain fraudulence in this word *human* which is always being thrown in our faces? . . . On the pretext that man can achieve only a subjective knowledge of the world, humanism decides to elect man the justification of everything."[20] In one important respect, Robbe-Grillet's negations are closer than Frye's hearty affirmations to the spirit of classical humanism as represented by Sidney or Johnson. His negations take objective truth seriously enough not to pretend that we can go on living by fictions in which we do not even profess to believe.

But when I speak of Robbe-Grillet's "negations," or, earlier in this chapter, of "would-be dismantlers" of literary and cultural traditions who would like to see humanism discarded, I speak loosely. Such people do of course exist, but more sophisticated anti-humanists (like Robbe-Grillet) recognize that getting rid of conventions informed by anthropocentric assumptions is easier to contemplate than to accomplish. And more recent thinkers like Derrida concede that even the most ruthless project of deconstruction must fall back at some point on the very "metaphysics of presence" or "logocentrism" that it claims to have subverted. Derrida comments more than once in *Of Grammatology* on how invariably the "heritage of logocentrism"—the belief in a real order outside language—tends to crop up in every attempt to do away with it. "Of course it is not a question of 'rejecting' these notions," Derrida writes. "They are necessary and, at least at present, nothing is conceivable without them. . . . Since these concepts are indispensable for unsettling the heritage to which they belong, we should be even less prone to renounce them."[21]

Derrida and his followers can thus be scornful of mere nihilism as a position lacking sophistication. Indeed, far from being a nihilistic project, as his critics have sometimes charged, Derrida's deconstruction of metaphysics proposes to leave intact the philosophical concepts whose lack of basis it exposes. He consoles us

that "we can always act as though none of this makes any difference."[22] And he advances a method of putting our statements
"under erasure" (*sous rature*), which permits us to cancel our
propositions without negating them. Derrida's translator, Gayatri C. Spivak, describes this technique as follows: "this is to write
a word, cross it out, and then print both word and deletion.
(Since the word is inaccurate, it is crossed out. Since it is necessary, it remains legible.)"[23] Thus if I write "~~God exists~~," I have,
by putting the existence of God under erasure, both affirmed it
and called it into question. This technique provides an extraordinary solution to the perennial problem of the modern sophisti-
cate: how can I be sufficiently aloof toward all beliefs to establish
my credentials as a qualified modern while retaining enough of
belief to get me through the business of living? By putting my
ideas under erasure, I can be skeptical and credulous at the same
time.

Thus even though Derrida's arguments constitute a frontal
attack on any sort of philosophical realism, they also propose to
recognize the inescapability of such realism. What is remarkable
is how rarely this kind of concession of the inevitability of realistic
assumptions leads those who offer it to take the next step and
reconsider the validity of these assumptions. If the logocentric
heritage is impossible to reject without in the process relying on it,
might this not be a powerful argument for its truth? If language
is incorrigibly a naive realist, how can we profess to challenge this
realism without talking nonsense?

Toward a Realist Defense
of Humanism

But here the philosophical realist is met with serious objections.
All these strategies simply evade the challenge to realism, which
asserts that we can no longer continue to see language as referring
to reality once we take seriously the fact that "reality," as we
experience it, is something that is *always already* interpreted,
already constructed, *already* constituted by the methodological
models, paradigms, sign-systems, conventions, *epistemes* through

which it is given to us? (*Always already* is a prominent phrase in the current lingo.)*

In the rhetorical world of contemporary criticism, there seems to have arisen the understanding that once somebody has pointed out that an idea rests on an "interpretation," any claims that idea may make to deal with the external world can henceforth be dismissed. Since every human experience is mediated by an act of interpretation, this strategy is quite effective in negating the truth-claims of any idea whatsoever. Thus Paul de Man believes he has scored a decisive point against Lukács's claims for his theory of realism when he notes that this theory founds the novel "on an act of consciousness, not on the imitation of a natural object"—as if it were self-evident that an act of consciousness could never bear an "imitative," or at least a referential, relation to an object. [24] Lukács sees irony as the organizing principle of the novel, de Man says, yet "irony steadily undermines [Lukács's] claim at imitation and substitutes for it a conscious, *interpreted awareness* of the distance that separates an actual experience from the understanding of this experience." [25] (Emphasis added.) Once criticism has demonstrated that a theorist's awareness is "interpreted"—and as I have said, this feat is not exceptionally difficult—it can walk away, confident it has said all that needs to be said to discredit the theorist's referential claims.

Of course the problem here is the fundamental one posed long ago by Kant: reality is not simply something we discover, something that waits for us to read its label, but something we ourselves bring into being by an active process of interpretation. And as post-Kantian thinkers have maintained, this process of active interpretation, closer to creation than to discovery, is profoundly cultural. It is determined not by things-in-themselves but by social and economic forces, by the spirit of one's time and place and condition, by the conventions of one's language, and by the drives and needs of one's psyche. Where does all this leave the appeal to a "common objective reality" outside all perspectives?

*The current world record for "always already's" may be held by Gayatri C. Spivak's Translator's Preface to Derrida's *Of Grammatology*. A rough count turns up eleven in about seventy-five pages.

Is not such an appeal merely a refusal to put our ideas in question, an all too understandable expression of nostalgia for a return to some lost paradise (which may never have existed) when literature and criticism were confident of their aims and when culture Knew Where It Was Going, when objects had not yet become estranged from consciousness but appeared to wear their meanings as their own garments?

If, as Robert Scholes says, "there is no recording, only constructing," what sense does it make to talk of a relation of reference or correspondence between language and things? And how does one answer the comment quoted earlier from Perry Meisel which declares that "semiotics is in a position to claim that no phenomenon has any ontological status outside its place in the particular information system(s) from which it draws its meaning(s)," so that, therefore, "all language is finally groundless"? Or the comment quoted from Terrence Hawkes, that a language "does not construct its formations of words by reference to the patterns of 'reality,' but on the basis of its own internal and self-sufficient rules"?[26] We can never test our various perspectives against the facts, for what constitutes "the facts" is itself always already an interpretation and thus the function of some interpreter's perspective.

Of course one can counter by asking whether "semiotics" or anything else could conceivably be "in a position" to make such claims as these, which manifestly undermine all positions and claims. One could quote Wittgenstein's observations in "On Certainty" that the act of doubting can only take place within a system of beliefs, that programmatic skepticism itself takes for granted that many things are known and established: "If you tried to doubt everything you would not get as far as doubting anything. The game of doubting itself presupposes certainty."[27] But some further response seems necessary. For it is indeed true, as recent structuralists insist, that meanings are paradigm-bound and system-constituted, that perceptions are mediated by interpretations, that perceptual reality is in a sense our construction. The question is, what follows from these assumptions? If "there is no recording, only constructing," does it follow that "realism is

· dead"? If it is true that meanings are constituted by the systems
of grammar that make them possible, does it follow that "all
language is finally groundless"?

Formidable as such questions are, I think we can make some
tentative responses to them. The first thing to be said is that the
fact that our statements do not possess meaning apart from the
codes and grammars which generate them does not mean that
what these statements *refer to* is nothing but the codes and
grammars themselves. The fact that language is always referring
to itself does not mean that is *all* it refers to. The fact that
meanings are constituted by internal systems of semantic and
syntactic rules does not mean they are constituted *only* by these
rules and are therefore not answerable to anything external. The
mediation of sign-systems is certainly a *necessary* condition of
generating meanings, but it can hardly be a *sufficient* condition.

This is not to deny what Saussure pointed out, that the particular phonetic arrangements by which languages denote concepts
are arbitrary, that conventional verbal meanings are generated
not by nature but by the play of differences within the linguistic
system. There is no necessary bond between the sound of the
word "tree" and the concept to which it refers. If we all agreed to
call this concept by some new name, our ability to talk about trees
would not be impaired. But it does not follow that, because the
signs are arbitrary, the *concepts* denoted by these signs are also
arbitrary. If they were, any coherent expression would "work" as
well as any other in covering a given situation, yet we do not find
that this is the case. We do not choose *any* internally coherent
collocation of signs when attempting to refer to a situation, but
devote some care to choosing some collocations over others, and
we attempt to fit the collocation to the situation. This fact suggests there is more to the matter of "motivation" than the internal workings of our semiological systems. Indeed, it is the
inability of structuralist theory to explain why we choose some
patterns over others that marks its most serious limitation.

Jonathan Culler argues that when a community of readers
happen to agree on the meaning of a text, this is not because
there is something *in* the text that causes them to have this
agreement. Rather, their finding a common element in the text is

itself the consequence of their prior agreement, established by
their having learned common conventions of reading. "Far from
appealing to 'the text itself' as a source of objectivity," Culler
writes, "one must assert that the notion of 'what the text says'
itself depends upon common procedures of reading."[28] Though it
is obviously true that a group of readers could not agree on a
text's meaning unless they possessed common conventions of
reading, it does not follow that this is the *only* thing their agreement depends upon. For it is not enough that readers be equipped
with common conventions; they need to know which of these
common conventions is to be applied in a particular case—why
this convention should be invoked in *this* instance. Conventions
themselves do not tell us in what circumstances they, as opposed
to other conventions within the same system, should be put into
play. There has to be something external to the convention that
determines that this and not some other is the convention to be
applied.

   For example, the expression "Keep off the grass" can function
either as an injunction not to walk on a lawn or as a warning
against narcotic stimulants. How do we know which of these two
conventions of interpretation to apply? The fact is we cannot
know unless we can guess the intention of the user of the expression, a guess we make on the basis of the referential situation in
which the expression is made (whether it is normally the type of
situation in which green grass or marijuana would be referred to),
the habitual concerns of the speaker, and so on. If we have none
of these clues, we may not be able to guess the meaning at all. In
any event, the fact that a group shares these two potential conventions of interpretation through a common inheritance of linguistic competence would not in itself be sufficient to compel their
agreement on one over the other or to explain this agreement
when it occurred. The group would agree *not only* because they
shared interpretive conventions, but also because the speaker or
writer of the message caused them to invoke the same convention
by intending that they do so and by building this intention into
the circumstances of his speech act. Of course, some structuralist
could object that what causes the agreement is not the intention
of the speaker or writer but the fact that the members of the

group share conventions for resolving semantic ambiguity. This might be valid, but the fact would remain that conventions are not self-activating but require external agency. Culler himself seems to concede the force of this argument when, abandoning the position he has taken above, he says that a "work has structure and meaning...because these potential properties, *latent in the object itself,* are actualized by the theory of discourse applied in the act of reading."[29] If there are properties "latent in the object itself" prior to the "theory of discourse" applied in interpreting these properties, then the interpretation is codetermined by the text as well as by an arbitrary system of conventions.

It is difficult to see how any theory of the arbitrariness of language with respect to its referents can account for that passion to "call things by their right names" that animates serious speakers and writers, conscientious teachers, and good editors. Of course this is no argument against such a theory, for this passion may well rest on a delusion. But it is not necessary, in defending the concept of "right names," to invoke some magical "prose of the world" that can be read off from natural objects or some "metaphysics of presence" which sees "a moment of original plenitude" behind every sign. It is this red herring—the charge that *every* attempt to locate an order of reality to which language is answerable conceals an appeal to transcendental mysticism—that has permitted current theorists to get away with rejecting all theories of external motivation out of hand.

The Genetic Fallacy

The fallacy here is a version of the so-called genetic fallacy, the assumption that the *conditions* under which concepts and terms originate determine their logical and ontological status, or, to put it more simply, their truth. Knowledge about the origin of our formulations in language, consciousness, or social conditions has no necessary bearing on the question of the truth of these formulations. Of course, genetic analysis is often very helpful, but it serves to tell us how and why ideas have developed as they have, not whether they are true or false. It is explanatory, not evaluative. This is why it is not a philosophical refutation of the anti-

mimetic position to show, as I tried to do above, that it has arisen
historically through "guilt by association." At best, such a
demonstration suggests that we should look again at the position,
but the demonstration cannot prove the position wrong.

The recognition that our concepts are constructions of language systems, then, or of psychological or social processes, tells
us nothing about their relation or lack of relation to reality. It
follows that the antithesis between "constructing" and "recording" (or matching or representing) is unreal, for it opposes a
genetic category to a logical one; it confuses the process by which
formulations come into being (constructing) and the logical status of these formulations (recording). The opposition becomes
unreal as soon as we recognize how much constructing is required
in the process of recording. The fact that a reader's interpretation
of a text is, in a sense, his construction is no argument against (or
for) its adequacy to that text. Similarly, the fact that a literary
work is constituted by the imagination, or by a system of literary
conventions, does not prevent it from qualifying as a record or
representation of reality.

At the risk of laboring the obvious, it seems necessary to point
out that an idea may arise from the most *irrational* psychological
sources and yet be true and in this sense *rational:* for example,
suppose after I dream that there will be a blizzard on Thursday
there proceeds to be a blizzard on Thursday, though snow has not
been predicted. The process by which I arrived at my prediction
was irrational but the prediction, whose truth does not depend on
the process by which it originated, ended up being a rational one.
Knowing that a prediction originated in a dream may be a good
reason for checking it with more than usual caution and rigor,
but such knowledge has no bearing on the truth of the prediction.
The same principle applies to literary creation: the fact that a
literary work is constituted by an intuitive or unconscious psychological process, by the dominant social ideology, by the conventions of literature and language, or by all these things working
together, tells us nothing about the work's adequacy or inade-
quacy as a representation of reality. Similarly, the fact that a text
calls attention to its conditions of production, to its "textual"
nature, for example, does not mean that it is not referential. On

the contrary, this self-reflexive device, which has become so much
the stock-in-trade of recent fiction, frequently operates as a
means of referring beyond the textuality of the work to the
general crisis of modern culture. As I try to suggest in my next
chapter, "anti-realistic" methods constitute a kind of rhetoric
whose purposes and assumptions ultimately presuppose mimetic
objects.

E. H. Gombrich's analysis in *Art and Illusion* of the problem
of representation in the visual arts suggests a way of overcoming
the disabling antithesis between interpretation and objective representation, both in art and in talk about art. "There is no reality
without interpretation," says Gombrich, "just as there is no
innocent eye, there is no innocent ear." But he adds, "this need to
organize and interpret does not mean that we are helplessly
caught in our interpretation. We can experiment and through
trial and error learn something about such impressions. An alternative interpretation may drive out the accepted one and reveal a
glimpse of the reality behind it."[30] "The undeniable subjectivity
of vision does not preclude objective standards of representational accuracy."[31] To put this in the terms I have been employ-
ing, the subjectivity of vision is a fact about its genesis, not about
the adequacy of its truth-claim. The artistic process for Gombrich is a process of "schema and correction," "making and
matching." The "schema" or "making" is an active process, a
projection of the artist's will and imagination mediated by artistic
conventions, but this projection can be tested and corrected as a
"matching" of the objective world. This is not to say that "visual
truth alone will make a picture into a work of art,"[32] but rather
that visual truth is not an empty criterion that is irrelevant to
esthetic judgment. But none of this will make the slightest sense
if we assume that statements about the genetic aspect of the
process ("making") can count as refutations of the truth-claims
of the process ("matching").

Unlike many current critics (some of whom cite him as agreeing with their view), Gombrich does not use the concept of artistic
convention as an excuse to give up on the theory of representation. On the contrary, Gombrich tenaciously detects a representational element even in highly abstract forms of art. Farfetched as

it may seem at first, Gombrich argues that even an abstract
canvas like Mondrian's "Broadway Boogie-Woogie" refers to
some objects more than to others:

> ...if anyone should ask me seriously if Mondrian had repre-
> sented a bit of boogiewoogie so accurately that I could now
> recognize the style if you played it to me, I would have to point
> to...the need...for the context in which the communication
> takes place. If you made the context sufficiently specific I
> could. I trust myself to plump for the right piece if one played
> two contrasting pieces to me—one slow and blue, one fast
> and noisy. For here the Mondrian would give me a pointer—
> a pointer for that game which psychologists call "matching."
> Given a simple choice, Mondrian tells me in what class or
> category or pigeonhole of music to seek for the equivalent.[33]

Gombrich notes that there is surprising agreement among members of an audience in their ability to receive such "pointers."
Indeed, the ability to be directed to the same external referent by
a work of art is one of the conditions that constitute what we call
an "audience." And it is a source of confusion in modern-art
audiences that no common referent can be located.

Gombrich comments in his preface to the second edition of *Art
and Illusion* that some readers of the first edition misinterpreted
the book as a defense of "fidelity to nature as the standard of
artistic perfection," whereas others mistakenly saw it as asserting
"the opposite view according to which the demand for fidelity to
nature must always be meaningless, since everybody sees nature
differently."[34] The latter misreading seems the more common
among recent critics, who choose to dwell on the "making" and
ignore the "matching." Thus J. Hillis Miller, in the course of
demonstrating that realism is a "fiction," writes that "Gombrich
has shown how any tradition of graphic representation involves
complex conventions whereby three-dimensional objects are signified by marks on a flat surface. These conventions are *in no
sense realistic* but come to be taken for granted as adequate
mirrorings of reality by artists and viewers of art who dwell within
the conventions."[35] (Italics added.) Gombrich's point, however,
is that the conventions not only "come to be taken for granted" as
adequate mirrorings of reality but may actually *be* adequate (or

inadequate) mirrorings, though the matter of adequacy is hardly simple, and no single convention or group of conventions has a monopoly on reality. Unlike Miller, Gombrich does not suppose that "convention" and mimetic "correspondence" are mutually exclusive concepts, and he preserves that "glimpse of the reality behind" conventions that permits us to test and justify them.

That experience is "always already interpreted"—and in this sense is our "construction"—is true by definition. But terms like "interpretation" and "construction" conceal a vagueness that cries out for clarifications and distinctions. The room in which I now write and the arguments I compose are both perceptual constructions. Yet clearly, there is a sense in which they are very different kinds of constructions. My perceptual construction of the room is one that I cannot choose *not to make.* It may be true, as Wittgenstein says, that all seeing is *seeing as,* and that the aspect under which we see things is determined by our "language games." But I cannot decide to see my four walls or my typewriter or this page in front of me as something wholly other than what they are—as the Pacific Ocean, say—or not to see them at all, whereas I can decide, if I like, not to be a philosophical realist in my interpretation of these experiences. My experience of my room is *given* and *unrefusable* in a way that my attempt to interpret this experience philosophically cannot be, though both my experience and my interpretation of it are constructions. Such unrefusable experiences (one might term them "the Godfather Effect") constitute "the facts" in a sense that distinguishes them from interpretations.

It makes perfect sense to appeal to the facts when we assess the merits of conflicting interpretations, even though it is true enough that what "the facts" are is something that can be determined only by an act of interpretation. That we cannot conceive of a fact without *some* interpretive paradigm does not mean that this fact can have no independent status outside *the particular paradigm we happen to be testing at the moment.* In other words, while conceding the view that facts do not exist in some naive state prior to interpretation, we do not have to go along with the relativist, who infers from this that "the facts" are always tautologically self-confirmed by the paradigms that constitute them. For these facts *do* exist independently of *some* paradigms, and these paradigms achieve credibility when they can be successfuly cross-checked with these facts.

This argument for the separability of some facts from some paradigms or interpretations has been most thoroughly developed by Karl Popper. As summarized by Ralph Rader, Popper's philosophy argues that

> all our knowledge is inherently and permanently hypothetical, that knowledge can never begin with "the facts" but only with a conjecture about the facts, and that the test of a conjecture (read hypothesis or theory) is not the degree to which it finds confirmation in facts—the significance of which it effectively constructs—but the degree to which it risks refutation by independent facts which it does not have immediately in view. . . . The more disparate the independent facts that general premises can be shown logically to entail, the more the premises may be assumed to reflect the actual underlying structure of the facts, and the more worthy they accordingly are to be taken tentatively as an approximation to the truth.[36]

The assumption here is that though all facts are paradigm-bound, any set of individual facts will be "disparate" with respect to certain paradigms. It is these disparate facts that provide, by a test of falsification, an independent test of these paradigms. The facts which we have come to regard as "unrefusable" (or as "brute facts") are those which cross-check successfully with so many possible paradigms and conflict with so few of those that we have yet encountered that we feel safe in concluding that they correspond to the way things are. This does not mean that new evidence cannot arise which will disconfirm them but that, so far as we have been able to determine, they hold up.

If the paradigm-bound nature of facts meant that no facts could ever be independent (or "disparate") with respect to *any* paradigms whatsoever, then all paradigms would indeed be self-confirming and we would be imprisoned in our guesses without any means of testing them. Popper has advanced this point in his controversies with Thomas S. Kuhn and others, but the quarrel goes beyond contemporary controversies to Kant himself. By conceding Kant's premise—that our minds are constitutive of the world we perceive—but denying the inference that we cannot therefore test our ideas against the world, Popper shows us a way out of the paralysis of post-Kantian thought: "Kant was right that it is our intellect which imposes its laws—its ideas, its rules—upon the inarticulate mass of our 'sensations' and thereby brings order to them. Where he was wrong is that he did not see that we rarely succeed with our impositions, that we try and err again and again, and that the result—our knowledge of the world—owes as much to the resisting reality as to our self-produced ideas."[37]

It is this "resisting reality" that the current way of talking about fictions fails to respect. Certain common experiences of this resisting reality possess so high a degree of unrefusability that they have the force of givens in our everyday experience. It was doubtless these experiences to which Henry James referred when he described "the real" as "the things we cannot possibly *not* know, sooner or later, in one way or another."[38] The reality of the physical world, the inevitability of death, the social nature of man, the irrevocability of historical events and changes—these are facts we cannot possibly *not* know, though we can argue infinitely about their significance and how we ought to understand them. Nobody can restrict literary truth to this narrow level of the given, yet literature does not have infinite license to abrogate it.

The literary way of talking about fictions pretends that no such unrefusable facts exist. This way of talking has endowed not only literature but all communication and discourse with an unaccountability that would be terrifying if its implications were taken seriously. No problem seems more pressing in the humanities right now than the radical unaccountability that infects its talk. It is as if we see poets and critics as licensed to say anything they please, since their talk is weightless and without consequences. Yet even weightless ideas have consequences: literature, despite all sorts of utopian claims that continue to be made for it, settles all the more deeply into its familiar role as our vehicle and exemplar of socially sanctioned narcissism. A corrective is needed.

As important as it was for critics to learn that literature and
language are systems of humanly created conventions and not
simple mirrors or photographic copies, it is now at least as
important that they rescue some sense in which these conventions
are accountable to something beyond themselves.

Eight

Babbitt at the Abyss

My assumption throughout this book has been the simple one that writing requires a convincing understanding of the world, and that to be without such understanding is as much a liability to a creative writer as it would be for a political scientist, a social scientist, or an editorialist. One aspect of the crisis of modern literature is that writers have had such great difficulty understanding their world that some have come to feel that the world is intrinsically resistant to understanding, and this crisis is deepened by the fact that those who do profess to have understanding in our world often inspire the keenest distrust. T. S. Eliot was concerned with this problem in his 1923 review of Joyce's *Ulysses*, when he speculated that narrative realism, which had sufficed for dealing with the relatively coherent society of the nineteenth century, was useless as a means of ordering the chaos of the twentieth, "the immense panorama of futility and anarchy which is contemporary history." In suggesting that fictional realism was obsolete, Eliot was really declaring that the world view of liberal bourgeois individualism, with its optimistic belief in progress and the rational intelligibility of experience, could no longer be accepted as an explanation of history.

Eliot went on to say that in exchanging "the narrative method" for "the mythical method"—that is, "the manipulation of a continuous parallel between contemporaneity and antiquity"— Joyce had taken "a step toward making the modern world possible for art."[1] Henceforth, Eliot implied, novelists interested in seriously coming to terms with the modern world would have to abandon realism and take up the mythical method. This view has not lost its hold on us. The classics of modern fiction self-consciously overturned the conventions of bourgeois realism, registering in their form as well as their content a comment on the bankruptcy of the bourgeois social order and its world view.

207

Modern fiction radically disrupted the linear flow of narrative, frustrated expectations about the unity and coherence of human character and the cause-and-effect continuity of its development, and called into question, by means of ironic and ambiguous juxtapositions, the universalizable moral and philosophical "meaning" of literary action. It shifted the focus of attention from the objective unfolding of events to the subjective experiencing of events, sometimes to the point of enveloping the reader in a solipsistic universe. Often this fiction contained a tone of epistemological self-mockery, again symptomatic of the waning explanatory power of bourgeois rationality. The assertion that we need a mythical method to make the modern world possible for art presupposes that modernity cannot be made intelligible as part of a continuous evolutionary process. It also implies that the fiction writer cannot hope to *understand* the modern world, that the best he can do is "order" it by arranging its various constituents in structural patterns.

Postmodern Fiction

Since World War II it has seemed necessary to speak of a postmodern mode of fiction, which departs not only from realistic conventions but from modernist ones as well. In retrospect we can see that it took postmodern fiction to carry to its logical extreme the break with traditional realism which critics like Eliot ascribed to classic modern fiction but which modern fiction had actually executed only in part. Indeed, one of the strengths of modern fiction was that it could often incorporate within its own structures much of the bourgeois realism which it was undermining. To put it another way, modern fiction, except in a few instances, did not actually effect the total subjectivization and privatization of human experience called for by modernist theories which defined literature as an expression of inward "consciousness" set over against the rational discourse of the public, objective world. By contrast, postmodern fiction tends to carry the logic of such modernist theories to their limit, so that we have a consciousness so estranged from objective reality that it does not even recognize its estrangement as such.

The weakness of much postmodern fiction lies in its inability or refusal to retain any moorings in social reality. For once it slips those moorings, the fictional imagination, in Robert Alter's words, tends to "go slack."[2] It indulges in a freedom of infinite fabulation that is trivializing in that the writer is not taken seriously enough to be held accountable to an external standard of truth. Though apparently a sign of high respect for literature, the deference we extend to the writer's "vision," our tendency to grant the creative writer his *donnée* (in a far more permissive sense than Henry James had in mind in laying down this dictum), is a form of indirect condescension, a way of saying that it can make no real difference to anybody what the writer says, or whether he adopts this vision of life rather than that. This critical permissiveness has the short-run virtue of protecting works whose lack of serious intellectual content would otherwise be all too obvious. If writing has been ridden by crisis in the postwar decades, one reason may be that writers have encountered special difficulties arriving at statements about the way we live now, a deficiency which cannot be indefinitely concealed by the theory that fiction has no obligation to offer statements or that creative writers do not need to know how society works in order to get on successfully. One reason for this deficiency may be that the kind of society which has emerged in the last several decades poses special problems of understanding.

However, the absence of a theory of society and history by which literary action can be arranged and disposed can itself be a theory, especially when the project of conceptual understanding comes to seem either so futile or so discreditable that it is the target of programmatic assaults. Contemporary fiction is often highly programmatic in its very revolt against programmatic concepts of fiction. In chapter 1, I cited Alain Robbe-Grillet's assertion that "the world is neither significant nor absurd. It *is*, quite simply." Yet one could argue that this view bears the same relation to Robbe-Grillet's and other contemporary fiction as Samuel Johnson's Christian stoicism bears to *Rasselas*. The contemporary novel, in its very determination to demystify all ideology and escape from programmatic content, bears the same allegorical relation to ideology as the most didactic of traditional fiction.* The contemporary novelist's emphasis on life's resistance to any single interpretation is predicated on his knowing in advance, with dogmatic certainty, that the old ways of making sense of life are false. Disillusionment is a rare emotion in contemporary fiction, for before he even begins the writer knows all too well the vanity of those systems of belief that make it possible to have illusions.

It is one thing to reject bourgeois values, as classic modern novelists often did, and another thing to come on the scene when these values have been so thoroughly eroded that it is unnecessary and pointless to reject them—the position I take to be the point of departure of postmodern fiction. If modern writers aimed at unmasking official illusions about the material and moral progress of civilization, postmodern writers begin at a point after this myth has been exploded and such demolition is needless—though certain writers continue, anachronistically, to demolish what no longer exists, as if unable to break their dependency on ingrained literary habit. Whereas modern fiction could still locate a distinct ideology held by social authorities, these authorities no longer present so clear and visible an ideological target. The social context of modern fiction was a nineteenth-century middle class that still upheld the austere morality of production and the respectable manners embodied in Victorianism and the American genteel tradition. The social context of postmodern fiction is an amorphous mass society that has lost contact with these earlier traditions and beliefs.

This mass society presents nothing approximating the stubborn resistance to cultural innovation, personal freedom, and individual self-definition which marked earlier bourgeois society and therefore nothing like the sharply dramatic model of social and economic struggle upon which the novelistic presentation of conflict has thrived. In much modern fiction, the hero struggles

*Much the same claim can be made about contemporary poetry. As Paul Breslin notes, "the poetry of the 1970s. . .has a stock rhetoric of portentousness, and all too often its mysteries are only the trivial mystifications of cant and code. To crack the code is to realize that the poetry comes, not from a vast otherness, but from a perfectly intelligible literary ideology" ("How to Read the New Contemporary Poem," 358).

against a social order that is presented as the mere dead weight of a once living past. Nevertheless, the social order and its ideology are amply and solidly *present* as a coherent resisting force, a setting which makes the delineation of character intelligible. As Erich Auerbach pointed out in *Mimesis:*

> As recently as the nineteenth century, and even at the beginning of the twentieth, so much clearly formulable and recognized community of thought and feeling remained [in Europe] that a writer engaged in representing reality had reliable criteria at hand by which to organize it. At least, within the range of contemporary movements, he could discern specific trends; he could delimit opposing attitudes and ways of life with a certain degree of clarity. To be sure, this had long since begun to grow increasingly difficult. Flaubert (to confine ourselves to realistic writers) already suffered from the lack of valid foundations for his work; and the subsequent increasing predilection for ruthlessly subjectivistic perspectives is another symptom.[3]

Perhaps the fact that a vestige of "recognized community of thought and feeling" remained explains why the "ruthlessness" of the modern writer's subjectivism was checked by his ability to place subjectivism in its historical context—to dramatize it as a social and historical problem. In a representative novel like *The Counterfeiters,* for example, Gide presents a series of characters, most of them avant-garde intellectuals, who feel little affiliation with the public world of institutions and ambitions. These characters inhabit prisons of unfulfilled homosexual longing, narcissism, and idleness. But at the same time as the novel depicts the privatized consciousness of these characters from the inside, it also presents the institutionalized deterioration that is bringing this condition about. The "counterfeit" character of the economic, social, and spiritual "currency" is shown as the source of the destruction of intersubjective community and the production of a counterfeit selfhood which can make no connection with the world. The work is thus able to give a realistic social explanation of the alienation from social reality that besets its characters.

Both the defenders and the attackers of classic modern fiction have tended to take modernist literary theory literally and have thus exaggerated the subjectivist, anti-realistic character of this fiction. They have overlooked the extent to which its subjectiviza- tion of experience was held in check not only by what Eliot calls "the mythical method" and by various devices of "spatial form" but also by the retention of a realism of setting. When a hostile critic like Georg Lukács equates the "ideology of modernism" with the reduction of experience to subjectivity and "psycho- pathology," he adopts the same view of this fiction as those defenders who praise it for its indifference to mimesis. Lukács's own examples reveal the shortcomings of his argument. He points out, for instance, that Ulrich, the hero of *The Man Without Qualities,* aims by his own admission "to abolish reality," "sub- jective existence 'without qualities,' " being "the complement of the negation of outward reality." Lukács quotes Musil's state- ment that "I have not, I must insist, written a historical novel. I am not concerned with actual events.... I am interested...in what one might call the ghostly aspect of reality."[4] It is surpris- ing, though, to turn to the novel itself and find how much less "ghostly" it is than later "anti-novels" motivated by the same anti-realist esthetic theory. In this novel, Vienna, "that ancient capital and imperial city," is as dominating a presence as is the London or Paris of nineteenth-century realistic novels—though, in contrast to them, it is a city whose physical and spiritual coherence is in process of disintegration. The confused dynamism and discontinuity of the postbourgeois city, that which will dom- inate the imagination of later writers, has at this point not yet displaced the containing background of historical tradition—as Musil's imagery suggests:

So no special significance should be attached to the name of the city. Like all big cities, it consisted of irregularity, change, sliding forward, not keeping in step, collisions of things and affairs, and fathomless points of silence in be- tween, of paved ways and wilderness, of one great rhythmic throb and the perpetual discord and dislocation of all opposing rhythms, and as a whole resembled a seething, bubbling fluid in a vessel consisting of the solid material of buildings, laws, regulations, and historical traditions.[5]

Almost literally, the "solid material" of traditional social order is
still sufficient in this novel to *contain* the irrational, seething
fluid of discord and dislocation which will soon burst it asunder.
One need not force Musil's novel into the category of realism in
order to point out that it is a type of novel which includes realistic
representation in the process of questioning realism—quite a
different procedure from that of postmodern writing, which begins at a point beyond realism. In the former case, the presentation of change has a background of continuity which lends change
significance and permits us to see loss of order *as* a loss; in the
latter, change often appears only against the unresisting background of earlier change, and the ability to present distortion as
such is impaired.

Novels such as *The Counterfeiters* and *The Man Without
Qualities* present a bourgeois society in disintegration, yet still
solid, specific, and comprehensible enough to furnish the material of drama. In contrast, the type of society which has emerged
since the end of World War II, for all the overpowering weight of
its technology and its bureaucratic organization, is a more elusive
and shadowy entity. It is a society where boredom is more con-
spicuous than poverty and exploitation, and where authority encourages hedonistic consumption and a flabby, end-of-ideology
tolerance. Such a society does not present the type of sharp
resistance requisite for individual self-definition. In saying this, I
do not mean to imply that censorship and repression would be
desirable, but rather that the patronizing of diverse viewpoints in
contemporary society is a reflection of contempt for ideas, which
are seen as impotent, and not of a disposition to take them
seriously. Though there is some truth to the complaint that this
society "processes" and "indoctrinates" individuals, the typical
product of this processing is not the indoctrinated conformist of
anti-utopian science fiction and radical folklore, but a diffuse,
unfocused, protean self which cannot define issues in any determinate way. A confused self is as good as an indoctrinated self
from the ruling-class point of view—though the situation is complicated by the fact that the "ruling class" itself often shares the
confusion. If one excepts the oppressed racial minorities, the

obstacle to individual freedom is no longer the stifling weight of inherited institutions and beliefs but the anomic meaninglessness and triviality of a "freedom" without content or direction. (Even the oppression of minorities is increasingly a purely economic matter without any particular ideological rationalization. The language and symbolic motifs of the black ghetto were long ago absorbed by advertising and popular entertainment.) Despite all the talk about "future shock," it is actually the surprising *absence* of shock, the amiable passivity in the face of change, which has characterized the culture of the seventies.

Gide, Kafka, Musil, and other writers of the modernist generation had the advantage of being able to take for granted *what it was that they were opposed to*. The opinions, values, institutions, and aspirations of bourgeois society were sufficiently well defined so that the representation of external setting, action, and manners could serve as a symbolic or typological shorthand for exemplary psychological, social, and historical conflicts. This holds true, too, for American fiction of that period. For example, when Nick Carraway, in his climactic conversation with Gatsby, says, "They're a rotten crowd.... You're worth more than the whole damn bunch put together," it is clear that Fitzgerald knows who "they" are—not only Tom and Daisy Buchanan but the whole class of spoiled wealth for which Tom and Daisy stand. As Irving Howe points out, writers of Fitzgerald's generation could take for granted, without necessarily being highly aware of them, "various theories concerning capitalism, the city, and modern industrial society.... These ideas had so thoroughly penetrated the consciousness of thinking men, and even the folklore of the masses, that the novelists could count on them without necessarily being able to specify or elaborate them."[6] These explanatory social theories, as Howe says, are what enable the novel to achieve that "symbolic compression of incident, the readiness to assume that X stands for Y," through which it translates particular actions and settings into typifications of society at large.[7] But Howe notes that with the advent of postwar mass society such theories "are no longer quite so available as they were a few decades ago." That is, "modern theories about society—theories that for novelists have usually been present as tacit assumptions—have partly broken

down," and for younger writers this presents both "new difficulties" and "new possibilities."[8]

Howe has here touched upon a significant point, yet one that
critics have neglected, possibly because the assumption that
theoretical understanding of society is a prerequisite of novel-
writing offends their axioms about the nature of literature. As
theoretical understanding has deteriorated, it has become more
difficult for novelists to give representative social significance to
the presentation of character and action, for writers no longer
know what characters and action "represent" or typify. As a
consequence, subjectivism and solipsism have so invaded the
novel's point of view that eventually these characteristics have
been normalized as part of the very definition of fiction. Just as
the alienation of poetry from a social function and a world view
that would connect it to objective reality has been normalized by
the doctrine of the ideal autonomy of poetry, the similar alienation of the novel has been normalized by the doctrine that omniscient novels are necessarily false to experience. For some time in
criticism, any attempt on the writer's part to transcend the limited perspective of limited characters through an omniscient perspective has been stigmatized as an "intrusion" upon the organic
form of the novel as well as an act of bad faith.

From Mythologies to Games

The thesis I have developed here—and will try to extend further—was applied to American fiction in the late fifties and early
sixties by critics such as Lionel Trilling, Richard Chase, Alfred
Kazin, John W. Aldridge, and Irving Howe, from whose 1959
essay, "Mass Society and Postmodern Fiction," I have already
quoted. These critics noted that in much of the fiction of the
fifties, society seemed to have become so abstract, remote, and
amorphous that writers found it unusually difficult to delineate
highly individual characters. Characters in fiction seemed either
to inhabit a kind of narcissistic isolation (Holden Caulfield, the
Invisible Man, Dangling Man), totally estranged from society, or
they had to contrive artificially to stimulate situations of conflict
and adventure that their society had failed to provide (Sal Para-

dise, Augie March, Henderson). To quote Howe once more, "the theme of personal identity, if it is to take on fictional substance, needs some kind of placement, a setting in the world of practical affairs. And it is here that the postmodern novelists ran into serious troubles: the connection between subject and setting cannot always be made, and the 'individual' of their novels, because he lacks social definition and is sometimes a creature of literary or ideological fiat, tends to be not very individualized."[9] Alfred Kazin had made a similar point in an essay published in 1958 entitled "Psychoanalysis and Literary Culture Today." Writers like John Osborne, Jack Kerouac, Allen Ginsberg, and Norman Mailer, Kazin said, strained to find objects adequate to their need for dramatic and ennobling intensities of feeling. It was not anger their writing expressed, for anger presupposes a focused understanding of one's object, but rather a groping for some "cause to be angry about," or, in Mailer's case, "something to be revolutionary about." In Mailer's essay, "The White Negro," Kazin comments, we see a forced attempt to reimagine the conditions and the feeling of actual social struggle by an "adaptation to the hipster of the myth of the proletariat." A consequence of this is the glorification of hoodlum violence as one of the last forms of "daring the unknown." In all this violence, Kazin says, "nothing is really taking place except theoretically. . . . Nothing here is taken from the real life of struggle, from life as actual conflict; it is an attempt to impose a dramatic and even noble significance on events that have not genuinely brought it forth."[10] This quality of forced melodrama—of searching out pretexts for dramatizing the self in actions large and heroic enough to justify language of heightened intensity—is found in works such as Burroughs's *Naked Lunch* (1959), Kesey's *One Flew Over the Cuckoo's Nest* (1962), and Mailer's *An American Dream* (1965) and *Why Are We in Vietnam?* (1967). Underlying the ostensibly iconoclastic mood of these works is nostalgia, nostalgia for a period in which the pitting of a heroic protagonist against a hostile, persecuting bourgeoisie corresponded roughly to social fact. If one drew one's conclusions about the history of the last twenty-five years strictly from a reading of these (often best-selling and highly popular) works, one would think that the reciprocal enmity between the creative and conventional factions of society was as live an issue as ever.

Mailer's case seems particularly symptomatic, since in the sixties he was ambitiously trying to make his fiction a testing ground of the historical and social forces of his age. What obstructed this effort was Mailer's inability to arrive at an analysis of history that went beyond crude schematization or mere confusion. On the one hand, Mailer reduced contemporary history to an apocalyptic myth of liberation, counterposing the hipster and the square, the id and the rational consciousness, the "existential" individual and the plastic, life-denying power of "Technologyland." The content of the social criticism contained in this scheme was summed up in *Advertisements for Myself* (1959): "The shits are killing us."[11] Embodied in the novels, this simple diagnosis became the principle of characterization of such corporate establishment figures as D. J.'s "asshole" father, Rusty, and his "medium asshole" associates in *Why Are We in Vietnam?* Scatology, in other words, tried to do the work of sociology. On the other hand, the element of schematic moralism in Mailer's fiction—as in that of Kerouac, Burroughs, and later Pynchon—was confused, though not really mitigated, by a diffuse, semi-mystical enthusiasm for the vibrating electrokinetic dynamisms of technological society itself. Thus Mailer's point of view was simultaneously distant from the society which he sought to understand and insufficiently separable from the confused processes of that society.

"Social communication is the doom of every truly felt thought," Mailer writes in *Advertisements for Myself.* In this sentence Mailer rationalizes the subjectivistic turn of his own novels of the sixties, novels which reject conventional novelistic typology in favor of privately cooked-up languages of obscenity and personal voodoo. Mailer's reasoning is worth examining:

> To communicate socially (as opposed to communicating personally or humanly) means that one must accept the sluggish fictions of society for at least nine-tenths of one's expression in order to present deceptively the remaining tenth which may be new....
> To communicate socially is to communicate by way of the

mass-media—movies, radio, television, advertising, newspa-
pers, best-selling novels, etc—which is to communicate by
way of the largest and most debased common denominator—
which in turn is equivalent to communicating very little, for
procedurally one becomes part of a machine which is antithetical to one's individual existence. Antithetical, I say, because
this machine attempts to direct the fortunes of men by the
obsolete and hence impractical results of the past.[12]

Two striking reductions are accomplished in this statement: first,
"social communication" as such is made synonymous with cor-
rupt and dishonest modes of manipulation.* Mailer does not
simply reject the type of social communication that characterizes
a system in which messages have become commodities. He rejects
collective symbols as such, which would be tantamount to rejecting language itself if we took the statement literally. Secondly,
Mailer represents the mass media and the technological bureau-
cracies as forms of traditionalism—as if they were not in their
own way expressions of radical revolt against inherited forms.
Since the collective language and the collective past have disintegrated into a form of merchandised cant, and since there is
evidently no hope of rehabilitating them, the writer has no choice
but to improvise a private typology. Again, we see a tendency
already present in classic modern fiction carried by a postmodern
writer to an unprecedented extreme.

In *Advertisements for Myself*, Mailer writes that obscenities
are "our poor debased gutturals for the magical parts of the
human body, and so they are basic communication, for they
awake, no matter how uneasily, many of the questions, riddles,
aches, and pleasures which surround the enigma of life."[13] Obscenities, that is, having been protected by taboos from the
inauthenticity that results from general social use, remain an
uncorrupted way of speaking about what Mailer calls "the mysterious dualities of our mysterious universe."[14] This last phrase is
suggestive of the vague Manichaean theology which is never far
from the surface of his writing. How it all works out in fiction is
seen in *An American Dream*, whose protagonist, Rojack, mythol-

*The tactic is similar to the repudiation of socialized discourse by Roland
Barthes and other new French critics. See above, 89–90.

ogizes his alternating penetrations of the vagina and the anus of
the maid Ruta as an "existential" encounter with the dualism of
Heaven and Hell. Mailer's attempt to elevate Ruta's private parts
into symbols of the metaphysical axes of reality results in one of
the more memorable examples of unintentional comedy in American literature, and in the process illustrates the difficulty a writer
encounters when he attempts to make an improvised typology
take the place of a plausible system of concepts.

This difficulty plagues the novel's conclusion. There Rojack is
made to sense, through the telepathic intuition that seems to be
his routine means of receiving information throughout this novel,
that only by making a circuit around three sides of the parapet—
"*All* three sides"—of the penthouse apartment of his antagonist,
Kelly, millionaire representative of the public world of institutions, can he prevent the death, elsewhere in the city, of his lover,
Cherry.[15] Rojack fails to make the circuit and Cherry, subsequently, is found dead. Since nothing in nature or established
convention connects the act of walking a parapet with the preser-
vation of the life of a mistress, there is no connection between
Rojack's actions and the significance attributed to these actions
except the arbitrary circumstance that the two things happened to
come together in the author's mind. Such arbitrariness of connection follows from the rejection of "social communication," which
suspends preestablished assumptions about how things are connected and what follows from what. Rojack conceives his actions
in this scene as a defiance of Kelly and all that his type stands for,
but Kelly has no apparent awareness of the significance of this
defiance. Perhaps he can have none, since the authenticity of
Rojack's act depends by definition on its significance remaining
unassimilable to any publicly shareable system. The projection of
the writer's arbitrary subjective fantasies upon the world compen-
sates for the lack of a convincing vision of how things actually
connect in that world.

In Mailer's journalisite work, which has drawn his attention
away from fiction since the late sixties, many of these problems
persist. *Miami and the Siege of Chicago* is organized around an
implausible contrast between Chicago (and Mayor Daley), hon-
estly brutal and violent and therefore authentic, and Miami

Beach (and Richard Nixon), plastic, antiseptic, and therefore
life-denying. The contrast is typical of the arbitrary schematism
of the later journalistic works. This schematism falsifies social
reality in the interest of a dramatic clash of moral and social
polarities. American life might indeed be more intensely colorful
if Miami and Chicago (or any other pairing) really justified their
placement in a Manichaean scheme of symbolism—as Paris and
the American manufacturing town had done, say, for Henry
James. Unfortunately, the fundamental differences between these
cities—as distinct from the kind of differences that are exploited
in publicity releases—have been largely effaced by the uniformi-
ties of the economic and social system. One can appreciate
Mailer's urban contrasts if one puts one's sense of truth to sleep,
but only on this condition. The same objection applies to Mailer's
attempts to depict innocent figures like Marilyn Monroe and
Muhammad Ali as symbols of the contradictions of American
culture. Since the real people cannot support the weight of such
symbolism, the effect is bathos. On the other hand, the most
successful of Mailer's journalistic works, *The Armies of the
Night,* achieves its power and humor through the confessed bewil-
derment of the central observer—a device reminiscent of *The
Education of Henry Adams.* The theory that history is senseless is
in its own right an intelligible and unpretentious theory, and it
creates the possibility of comedy.

The alternative to Mailer's forced mythology is the abandon-
ment of mythology, the self-consciously parodic treatment of
myth-making as a kind of game whose arbitrariness is freely
conceded and advertised by the writer. The writer who knows he
has no convictions to impart excuses the self-indulgence of continuing to write by making his confession of futility a chief end of
his writing. In this way he presumably converts the exhaustion of
the fictional impulse into the principle of its rebirth. So argues
John Barth in one of the most influential statements about the
new fiction, "The Literature of Exhaustion." Exhaustion goes
about as far as it can go in the vein of affectedly apologetic
self-hatred in works such as Barthelme's "Sentence," a single,
three-page sentence commenting about itself, and in several of
the pieces in Barth's *Lost in the Funhouse,* one of which avoids

the finality of a conventional ending by breaking off in mid-sentence:

> O God comma I abhor self-consciousness. I despise what we
> have come to; I loathe our loathesome loathing, our place our
> time our situation, our loathesome art, this ditto necessary
> story. The blank of our lives. It's about over. Let the *denoue-
> ment* be soon and unexpected, painless if possible, quick at
> least, above all soon. Now now! How in the world will it ever[16]

In lieu of a *representation* of the social world we have the *phrases*
"our place our time our situation" and "the blank of our lives."
We infer that contemporary life is too insignificant and trivial to
merit any richer characterization. But what *is* our place, our
time, our situation? In what sense are our lives a "blank" and
how did they come to be this way? The assumption is that these
questions have been answered, and in a sense of course they have,
by the ideology of modernism, itself here boiled down to a hand-
ful of self-mocking generalizations. Estrangement from an intelligible reality seems to have become so extreme that it can only be
treated as a sort of joke; and it has blotted out the awareness of
its causes—or perhaps merely the writer's interest in them.

Alienation, Inc.

In summary, then, novelists after World War II found difficulty
adjusting their perspectives to a society which did not fit inherited
categories of explanation. They were thrown back on willed
mythologies which they themselves could hardly take seriously
very long, and soon began to parody. The new society was not so
much antagonistic to their visions as indifferent, a diffuse,
protean, yielding mass society whose often maddening compla-
cency concealed its uncertainty about its beliefs and its appre-
hensions about its future. By the beginning of the sixties,
however, a new phase had appeared: the passivity and loneliness
of the fifties had crystallized, become something more self-
conscious and, in some respects, more clearly defined. To be
lonely in the fifties—as those who came to maturity in the decade
will recall—was merely a personal problem. In the sixties, to be

lonely came to mean being "alienated." This constituted a
liberating advance in one respect, for the discovery that one's
problems could be traced to deficiencies in the social process
might alleviate personal guilt and prepare the way for positive
action. But the new self-consciousness about alienation, "growing up absurd," and so forth, might invest alienation with an
element of self-dramatization or even self-congratulation. The
honest pathos of the genuine sufferer might give way to the
strident theatrics of the professional victim. In the fifties, though
sociological writers might describe disaffiliated groups of the
period as a Lonely Crowd, the actual members of this group had
no awareness of figuring in a significant social tendency, and
certainly saw no charm in the fact. The pose of the "rebel without
a cause" epitomized by James Dean and Elvis Presley did lend a
certain heroism to the aimlessness of youth in the fifties, but this
pose was ahistorical, apolitical, and nonideological. In the sixties,
alienation ceased being a mere predicament, prosaically coped
with as best one could, and became a historically conscious *style*,
a mode of ideological and moral symbolism. Its target was traditional "bourgeois values" themselves, as if these values were still
fully intact.

Philip Rieff has written of "the triumph of the therapeutic"
social type over the legendary "inner-directed" individualist in
the moral mythology of modern Western society. The older bourgeois melodrama conceived life as a struggle to master nature and
the disciplines of work and morality and to emulate public
models of authority and achievement. Therapeutic man, by contrast, sees himself as engaged in a new kind of melodrama, a
struggle for private "self-realization," unique "identity," and
"meaningful" personal relations. "Role-playing" behavior, dis-
approved of by therapeutic man when it is predetermined by
bourgeois social forms, is viewed as a form of authentic liberation
when dictated by spontaneous impulse. Moral sensitivity—seen
as the antithesis of bourgeois insensitivity—comes to be measured
by one's consciousness that one has "problems," that one is
"vulnerable," and that one is willing to be "open" about them
with others. One's very selfhood is understood as a problem, if
not as a grievance, a condition of acute vulnerability defenseless

against even the slightest disturbance and requiring permanent ministration and "caring." Good and bad are redefined as willingness to admit (and share) one's vulnerability and refusal to do so. The enemy is not external society so much as the socially induced repressions which frustrate one's attempts to be wholly open. A pathetic groping for "warmth" in the outer world tends to become the highest imaginable ideal of collective enterprise. The triumph of the therapeutic, in short, might be described as the Lonely Crowd come to self-consciousness.

It is a logical step from the victimized self-conception of the therapeutic type, with his problems, to the more optimistic and often aggressively self-assertive styles of "liberation." The collective solipsism of the encounter group is proposed as the remedy for the solipsism of the individual. The modest goals of "self-realization" and "interpersonal relating" are given utopian and Dionysian reformulations, and the Lonely Crowd, undergoing yet another change of costume, reemerges as a postrevolutionary brotherhood or sisterhood. The retreat into private subjectivity is redescribed as a form of visionary and apocalyptic "transcendence." Ideas which, in a more innocent period of American history, had been couched in the naive rhetoric of self-help and positive thinking are repackaged in chic, "existential" brands and trimmed up with Eros and myth, somewhat as if William Blake, Friedrich Nietzsche, and Wilhelm Reich had entered into partnership with Dr. Norman Vincent Peale. The radical therapies do little more than lend a euphemistic coloration to the philosophy and psychology of alienation, since they all begin by taking it for granted that the external world is so irrational, menacing, and unmanageable that the private self has become the only area of experience subject to control.

But our consumer society not only popularizes ideologies of alienation; to an increasing extent it invests its capital in them. As Saul Bellow's Herzog observes, people have begun "touting the Void as if it were so much salable real estate"[17]—now a description of literal fact with the ready marketability of the literature, entertainment, and symbolic appurtenances associated with "alternative life-styles." Joseph Schumpeter, in his *Capitalism, Socialism, and Democracy* (1942), suggested that such a turn of events followed the logic of capitalism itself. "Unlike any other type of society," Schumpeter wrote, "capitalism inevitably and by virtue of the very logic of its civilization creates, educates and subsidizes a vested interest in social unrest."[18] Yet Schumpeter's prediction that this process would eventually do away with capitalism now seems more problematical. A formidable conglomerate of publicists, theoreticians, musicians, bards, prophets, therapists, mystagogues, sexualogues, and ideological dieticians and haberdashers has formed a kind of alienation industry, supported by the expanding segment of society which predicates its very sense of community on the type of "disinherited mind" that was once the monopoly of the antagonists of bourgeois society. The success of this industry testifies to the ability of modern capitalism to profiteer off the very psychopathology that it brings about.

Postmodern Comedy

The social context of postmodern fiction, then, is a middle class which by the fifties had not only become alienated from its earlier traditions but in the sixties and seventies has absorbed and commercialized the self-consciously alienated ideologies, rhetorics, and personal styles of literary and cultural modernism. The consequence is that it is not only the explanatory paradigms of bourgeois culture which have been compromised but the revisionary counterparadigms of vanguard culture as well.

The crisis of vanguard culture lies in the fact that it stops short of one kind of revision, the revision of the modern revisionary ethos itself. At the core of our postmodern modes, as I argued in chapter 2, are familiar formulas given the appearance of novelty by exaggeration: perpetual formal revolution, perpetual "renewal" of the forms of perception, perpetual assault on the objective reality principle, perpetual going beyond alienation to further extremes of alienation. Weary though we have become of modernist experimental modes, and wryly cynical about the quasi-theological claims that used to be made in their name, we do not know how to break out of them. The very formulas through which modernism is repudiated derive from modernism.

It is therefore not surprising that frustration and self-hatred (often expressed as self-exaltation) have descended on the cultural scene, and that the commentators on this scene make extensive use of terms like "exhaustion," "belatedness," "secondariness," and so on. The exhaustion of the experimental mode is mistaken for the exhaustion of literature. "Everything has already been done," goes the refrain. "*Our* history not only repeats itself as farce, it *is* farce. Self-parody is the only authentic, the only possible, style. We have lost our innocence and know that the very concept of novelty is a delusion. There is no breaking out of the constrictions of the already written. Like characters in a Borges story, we are doomed to rehearse the same plots repetitively and without end, drawing whatever vitality we can from the playful self-awareness that everything has been done before."

And yet, the newly heightened awareness of the changed situation has caused certain patterns to emerge more clearly. The recognition of the "decline of the new," when accompanied by a sense of the social causes which have led to it, itself suggests a way out of the current crisis. With greater understanding of the social transformations described above, something approaching the enabling theoretical idea of society which had previously been unavailable begins to cohere. Intrinsically, it is a theoretical idea which makes for comedy rather than high seriousness, social farce and caricature rather than documentary realism. Viewed from a certain angle, the recognition that "radical" modernism, not puritanism and respectability, is the natural cultural counterpart of advanced capitalism has potential for social comedy. For novelists as diverse in outlook and method as Bellow, Barthelme, Barth, Philip Roth, and Stanley Elkin, the recognition of these changes and a critical view of what Bellow calls "the solemnity of complaint" have given a peculiar shape to their work. Because their perspective is informed by an understanding of what has happened to modernist ideology, they are able to avoid some of the pitfalls of postmodern subjectivism.

To see "self-reflexive" writers such as Barthelme and Barth not only in sociological terms but as actually concerned with society requires some defense. Both the apologists of the new fiction and its detractors tend to agree that this fiction is hermetic and asocial. For example, Barthelme's *Snow White* is seen by both a sympathetic critic, Albert Guerard, Jr., and a hostile one, Gore Vidal, as a kind of pop Americanization of the French *nouveau roman*—"a book about language," as Guerard calls it.[19] But this work might be more profitably compared with works by Sinclair Lewis than with those by Alain Robbe-Grillet. For in some respects *Snow White* is *Babbitt* brought up to date for an age of consumerized alienation and self-consciousness. Barthelme's parody of the jargons of psychology, esthetics, educationese, political and cultural radicalism, and existentialism fulfills a satiric function comparable to Lewis's parody of the language of realtors, patriots, and civic boosters. Lewis's satire on moralistic versifying, through the figure of the poetaster "Chum" Frink, is matched by Barthelme's parodic weaving of quotations throughout his novel from such somber modernist writers as Kierkegaard, Eliot, Malcolm Lowry, and others, whose anguish today seems almost as formulary as the optimistic pieties of Edgar Guest had been in the twenties. Snow White's seven hapless suitors are self-estranged Babbitts: "Whereas once we were simple bourgeois who knew what to do," they reflect together at one point, "now we are complex bourgeois who are at a loss. We do not like this complexity. We circle it wearily, prodding it from time to time with a shopkeeper's forefinger: What is it? Is it, perhaps, *bad for business?*"[20]

What has altered everything for the seven is their having encountered the personified Spirit of Alienation herself, Snow White, the woman who can find no heroes in her life (only "prince-figures"), who is bored by everything, most of all her own boredom ("Oh I wish there were some words in the world that were not the words I always hear!"),[21] and who is unable to discover any "meaningful role." A chapter listing Snow White's college courses provides some clue to the origin of her condition:

> Beaver College is where she got her education. She studied *Modern Woman, Her Privileges and Responsibilities*: the nature and nurture of women and what they stand for, in evolution and in history, including householding, upbringing,

peace-keeping, healing and devotion, and how these contribute
to the rehumanizing of today's world. Then she studied *Classical Guitar I*, utilizing the methods and techniques of Sor,
Tarrega, Segovia, etc. Then she studied *English Romantic
Poets II*: Shelley, Byron, Keats. Then she studied *Theoretical
Foundations of Psychology*: mind, consciousness, unconscious
mind, personality, the self, interpersonal relations, psycho-
sexual norms, social games, groups, adjustment, conflict,
authority, individuation, integration and mental health. . . .
Then she studied *Personal Resources I and II*: self-evaluation,
developing the courage to respond to the environment, opening
and using the mind, individual experience, training, the use of
time, mature redefinition of goals, action projects. . . . [22]

The irony of this jargon is that the more pretentious it becomes,
the more it contributes to the disabling self-consciousness and
self-estrangement it is supposed to explain and help us overcome.
The self-parodic form of *Snow White* as a whole, in which
ostentatiously "literary" language is used to tell the story as a
means of ridiculing the pretensions of literary communication, is
finally a form of cultural statement: it emphasizes the disjunction
which has set in between genuine feelings of alienation and the
fashionable literary and cultural languages which pretend to
explain them. As Dan, one of the seven suitors, says, "analogies
[i.e., languages] break down, . . . but the way I feel remains."[23]

In Barthelme's novel, the normal expectations about the relationship between class or occupation and ideology have been
turned on their heads. The key device here is the representation,
often comically exaggerated, of characters in prosaic occupations
as self-conscious connoisseurs of esoteric forms of *angst*. This
device, the principle on which Snow White and her suitors are
created, is employed to even more elaborate effect in Barthelme's
short story "A Shower of Gold" (collected in *Come Back, Dr.
Caligari*). The story inverts the conventional conflict between a
struggling young artist and an unsympathetic mass public. The
conflict remains, but the characteristics of the antagonists have
been transposed. It is the public which burns for discussion of the
Existential Crisis of Modern Man and the artist who must flee
from it in order to save his sanity as well as his art. "Everybody

knows the language but me," says the artist, Peterson, when his
barber, "a man named Kitchen who was also a lay analyst and
the author of four books titled *The Decision to Be*,"[24] lectures
him in the barber's chair about I-Thou relationships, Pascal,
Nietzsche, and the problem of Self and Other. This barber concludes by advising Peterson that what he really needs is "to break
out of the hell of solipsism. How about a little more off the
sides?"[25] Because Peterson needs money in order to support his
art, he agrees to appear as a guest on a popular television quiz
program, *Who Am I?*, the aim and format of which is described
to him by Miss Arbor, a program representative:

> "*Who Am I?* tries, Mr. Peterson, to discover what people
> *really are*. People today, we feel, are hidden away inside them-
> selves, alienated, desperate, living in anguish, despair and bad
> faith. Why have we been thrown here, and abandoned? That's
> the question we try to answer, Mr. Peterson. Man stands alone
> in a featureless, anonymous landscape, in fear and trembling
> and sickness unto death. God is dead. Nothingness everywhere.
> Dread. Estrangement. Finitude. *Who Am I?* approaches these
> problems in a root radical way. . . ."[26]

Peterson, primarily interested in the amount of his fee, hesitates
to commit himself. Miss Arbor presses him:

> "What I want to know now, Mr. Peterson, is this: are you
> *interested* in absurdity?" "Miss Arbor," he said, "to tell you
> the truth, I don't know. I'm not sure I believe in it." "Oh, Mr.
> Peterson!" Miss Arbor said, shocked. "Don't *say* that! You'll
> be. . . ." "Punished?"[27]

Peterson *is* punished. For disbelieving in it, absurdity revenges
itself through a series of surreal intrusions into his garret studio
by initiates of the new *Zeitgeist*. These intruders attempt to
induct him into the fellowship of corrosive self-consciousness that
has become the official philosophy. Among them are "the three
girls from California," who quote Pascal, prepare a dish called
veal engagé from their rucksacks, and declare they "need love."
Peterson escapes to his neighborhood bar, presumably not yet
infiltrated by the advancing ethos.

On the air at last, Peterson rebels against this absurdist consensus, blurting out defiance before he can be cut off. The world may indeed be absurd, he says, and absurdity may punish one for disbelieving in it, but finally "absurdity is itself absurd." In such a world, "possibilities nevertheless proliferate...and there are opportunities for beginning again.... Don't be reconciled. Turn off your television sets...cash in your life insurance, indulge in a mindless optimism. Visit girls at dusk. Play the guitar...."[28]

Peterson's attainment of the status of anti-anti-hero or anti-existential hero is a variation on one of Barthelme's favorite themes, the comic impossibility of heroism in a world paralyzed by self-consciousness. Typically, Barthelme dramatizes the pathetic diminution of the hero in the contemporary world by attributing a kind of agonized yet commonplace self-consciousness to some of the more fragile heroes of American popular mythology: Snow White, Batman and Robin, King Kong, the Phantom of the Opera, etc. In "The Joker's Greatest Triumph," Batman is foiled, knocked unconscious, and unmasked by his archfoe, the Joker. Revived afterward in the Batmobile and told that the Joker now knows his true identity, Batman expresses his dismay in a pastiche of comic-book and literary styles:

> "Great Scott!" Batman said. "If he reveals it to the whole world it will mean the end of my career as a crime-fighter! Well, it's a problem."
> They drove seriously back to the Bat-Cave, thinking about the problem.[29]

In a story entitled "The Party" (in *Sadness*), King Kong reappears, "back in action." But the setting is a cocktail party, Kong "is now an adjunct professor of art history at Rutgers," and if he still occasionally performs feats of terror, "he is simply trying to make himself interesting."[30] Like Snow White's suitors, Batman and King Kong are cases of that increasingly common social type that Barthelme is cruelly adept at depicting—the person who is *aware* that everything he thinks is banal yet can do nothing about it, and who therefore adopts a posture of perpetual ironic self-deprecation, which he also senses to be banal.

Barthelme's parody of intellectual languages points to a connection between the crisis of language and the crisis of society. It suggests that the general dissemination of the concepts of advanced intellectual culture has deluded people into believing that all the mysteries of human nature can be explained by the simple act of affixing verbal labels on them. The sudden availability of the diagnostic vocabularies of sociology, psychoanalysis, and literary criticism seems to have implanted in mass society a vast delusion, simultaneously fatuous and pathetic, of self-understanding. Herzog calls this "the delusion of total *explanations*."[31] In *Herzog* and *Mr. Sammler's Planet,* terms like "alienation" are part of the arsenal of cant wielded by false "explainers" and "reality-instructors," cultural opportunists who capitalize on unearned theories of despair and revolution—in what they are quick to recognize as a seller's market for such "cultural canned goods." As one explainer, Lionel Feffer, candidly tells Sammler:

> "I'm convinced that knowing the names of things braces
> people up. I've gone to shrinkers for years, and have they cured
> me of anything? They have not. They have put labels on my
> troubles, though, which sound like knowledge. It's a great
> comfort, and worth the money. You say 'I'm manic.' Or you
> say, 'I'm a reactive-depressive.' You say about a social
> problem, 'It's colonialism.' Then the dullest brain has internal
> fireworks, and the sparks drive you out of your skull. It's
> divine. You think you're a new man. Well, the way to wealth
> and power is to latch onto this. When you set up a new enter-
> prise, you redescribe the phenomena and create a feeling that
> we're getting somewhere. If people want things named or
> renamed, you can make dough by becoming a taxonomist."[32]

As both Sammler and Herzog recognize, such "explanations" purvey knowingness, not knowledge.

The central theme of *Mr. Sammler's Planet* is the degeneration of the ideology of modernism, and this is presented as an aspect of the more general collapse of Western liberal individualism and its ideal of personal autonomy. Sammler's past makes him a nexus of the historical forces, both hopeful and destructive, whose collision has created the present-day world. A former democratic-socialist and heir of the progressive Enlightenment, Sammler is also a victim of the Holocaust and in a wartime act of revenge he has participated in its murderous brutality. His past places him at the intersection of Western liberal individualism and the forces which have destroyed it—or, rather, perverted it. For ironically, as it now comes home to Sammler, in his meditations, liberal individualism has survived the Holocaust, but in forms which parody its original inspiration. Originating as part of a noble dream of uniting science with morality and liberating the mass of humanity from the nightmare of historical circumstance, liberal individualism has detached itself from its motivating ideas of good and evil and divided into opposing but collaborating factions: "an oligarchy of technicians, engineers, the men who ran the grand machines," tolerates a culture of hedonistic self-indulgence and "symbolic wholeness."[33] This historical vision gives Sammler's criticism an authority and clarity lacking in Herzog's comparatively sentimental whining. It is no doubt easier for us to like Herzog, who is lovably mixed up and therefore not superior to us. A character like Sammler, who clearly *is* superior, in wisdom if not in ability to carry it into action, requires more risks on the part of his creator. He does not win our affection by the standard pose of being in the dark about everything.

The characters surrounding Sammler are possessed by a neurotic "fever of originality," at once arrogant and desperate, which issues in exhibitionistic playacting, and the quest to be "interesting": "theater of the soul" performed "with hair, with clothes, with drugs and cosmetics, with genitalia, with round trips through evil, monstrosity, and orgy. . . ."[34] Life has begun to imitate bad experimental art:

> Life looting Art of its wealth, destroying Art as well by its
> desire to become the thing itself. Pressing itself into pictures.
> Reality forcing itself into all these shapes. Just look (Sammler
> looked) at this imitative anarchy of the streets—these Chinese
> revolutionary tunics, these babes in unisex toyland, these
> surrealist warchiefs, Western stagecoach drivers. . . .[35]

If the middle class was once aloof or hostile to the dreams of artists, it now rushes to act out the artist's most visionary fantasies.

One measure of the transformation of bourgeois culture in

America is the disappearance of debate over the alleged "provincialism" of American life, a term once hotly argued about and now scarcely ever heard. Much nineteenth-century American literature rests on a dramatic formula that poses an "advanced" minority against the stubborn inflexibility of a provincial majority—an inflexibility which, depending on the point of view, may be judged as narrow-minded rigidity and philistinism or as honest, unaffected plain-dealing. As urban cynicism has eroded this provincialism, the old-fashioned, unalienated provincial bourgeois character-type has begun to take on a new kind of corrective value. In recent social comedy, the classic situation sometimes reappears in inverted form: the advanced mentality is depicted as a kind of reverse provincialism of the majority. And wherever the old-style, stubborn provincial turns up—that is, wherever he is shown as not having succumbed to the advanced modes which surround him—he is presented as a model of an alternate life-style, so to speak. That is, fashionable alienation itself becomes the resisting background against which individual character is dialectically forged. In this reversal, the businessman, the perennial target of the derision and contempt of literary culture, reappears suddenly as a figure of refreshing nonconformity.

Thus Bellow locates the central morality of *Mr. Sammler's Planet* in the wealthy doctor-businessman and paterfamilias, Elya Gruner, a tough operator with underworld connections. Gruner's off-stage Mafia associates are presumably genuine criminals, not Byronic poseurs dabbling in evil in order to make themselves interesting. This does not mean that Bellow endorses either organized crime or big business. The "oligarchy of technicians" *is* amoral. What Bellow values are the pre-technological virtues of honor, loyalty, accountability, and plain-speaking, for which the language of contracts and bookkeeping, a continuous stylistic motif in the novel, is an appropriate image. Gruner, Sammler reflects at the novel's close, has remained faithful to "the terms of his contract,"[36] those binding human loyalties which are the enabling basis of civilization. These contractual obligations have been violated by free-floating seekers of "limitless demand," who recognize no scarcity of satisfactions, claim exemption from moral debts, and present to the world "a full bill of demand and complaint.... Non-negotiable."[37] Contractual relations have a basis in human solidarity; to revolt against them in the name of an amorphous humanity may eventually be to revolt against humanity itself.*

In a parallel fashion, Philip Roth actually invokes the name of George F. Babbitt at a crucial point in his novel *My Life as a Man*, in order to define the quality of saving common sense which his protagonist, a young novelist named Peter Tarnopol, singularly lacks. The novel teems with literary allusions, parallels, and parodies. Tarnopol, like such earlier fictional victims of romantic illusion as Don Quixote, Emma Bovary, and Isabel Archer, has acquired his romantic view of life from his reading. Unlike the illusions of his predecessors, however, Tarnopol's have been induced not by escapist romances but by the complex masterpieces of European modernism from Flaubert to Dostoevsky, which he has studied at the university and hopes to emulate in his own novel. From these writers Tarnopol has acquired a contempt for ordinary bourgeois life and a hunger for "moral ambiguity" and "complexity." So thoroughly does Tarnopol romanticize the Abyss that he ends up marrying into it—only to discover that its fascinations are overrated. Like Isabel Archer, he disastrously rejects an uninterestingly stable partner for an intriguingly alienated one—Maureen Johnson, a marvelous creation who embodies almost every cliché of cosmopolitan rootlessness and pseudo-artistic emancipation. Her repeated demand—the ultimate slogan of contemporary populist narcissism—is that she be treated "as a *human being*, not as a *thing*." Reflecting on his mistake years later, Tarnopol imagines that a "worldlier fellow than myself—George F. Babbitt, say, of Zenith, Minnesota," would not have been susceptible to her temptations.†

---

*Compare Bellow's mode of "literary economics" with that of Barthes and the new French criticism, as discussed above, 67ff.

†Philip Roth, *My Life as a Man* (New York: Holt, Rinehart and Winston, 1974), 185. But perhaps Babbitt *would* have been susceptible. Lewis's Babbitt is himself in some ways nearer to the recent "therapeutic" social type than to the traditional hard-nosed businessman. He suffers from vague discontents, feels his authority over his children is slipping,

To choose one final example, I suggest that the extraordinary linguistic vitality which Stanley Elkin has unleashed in such works as *A Bad Man*, *The Dick Gibson Show*, "The Bailbondsman" (collected in the recent *Searches and Seizures*), and *The Franchiser* owes something to Elkin's choice, for narrators and protagonists, of aggressive, unsentimental, often vulgar and bullying businessmen, who *love their work* and are not alienated from it. To be sure, these entrepreneurs invest their businesses with dimensions of romance, mystery, and metaphysics that go far beyond the mere pursuit of profits. And yet the intricate, concrete facts of the business in question—running a department store, radio announcing, making bail bonds, operating a string of franchises—are always profusely and lovingly particularized, and this specificity lends to Elkin's characters a more than hypothetical individuality. Perhaps the talk of these characters is so full of energy because they are not wholly overcome by their self-contradictions, identity crises, attenuating self-consciousness, and the diffusions of the protean self.

Take the protagonist of "A Poetics for Bullies" (collected in *Criers and Kibitzers, Kibitzers and Criers*), a reversal of the type of story which pits a "sensitive" young man against a callous society. Far from desiring love and understanding, Push makes war on them:

> I'm Push the bully, and what I hate are new kids and sissies, dumb kids and smart, rich kids, poor kids, kids who wear glasses, talk funny, show off, patrol boys and wise guys and kids who pass pencils and water the plants—and cripples, *especially* cripples. I love nobody loved. . . .
> A kid is going downtown on the elevated train. He's got his little suit on, his shoes are shined, he wears a cap. This is a kid going to the travel bureaus, the foreign tourist offices to get brochures, maps, pictures of the mountains for a unit at his school—a kid looking for extra credit. I follow him. He comes out of the Italian Tourist Information Center. His arms are full. I move from my place at the window. I follow him for two

---

and gives himself over to infatuations with quasi-artistic women such as the widow Tanis Judique.

blocks and bump into him as he steps from a curb. It's a *collision*—the pamphlets fall from his arms. Pretending confusion, I walk on his paper Florence. I grind my heel in his Riviera. I climb Vesuvius and sack his Rome and dance on the Isle of Capri.[38]

Push receives his proper comeuppance, but this does not negate the pungency of his character—he knows who he is and what his work is.

But "A Poetics for Bullies" also illustrates some of the difficulties inherent in revaluing toughness as a corrective virtue. Our admiration for an individualism expressed in an honest commitment to hardness and work requires us to suspend questions about the morality of the hardness and about the social ends to which the work is directed. Pressed far enough, the glorification of the no-nonsense businessman becomes only a new version of the idealization of the primitive or the cult of the hard-boiled. The toughness that preserves Elkin's protagonists from fashionable esthetic hypersensitivity verges on cruelty. Elkin's "kibbitzers" delight a bit too much in exercising power over his "criers." His Bad Man, his Bailbondsman, and his Franchiser share a common worship of power exercised in tyrannizing over their wives, associates, and underlings. This quality is not quite mitigated by the fact that these characters are themselves finally victims, who suffer from their contradictory need for the love they repel.

In Bellow's fiction, the alternative to sentimentality about the self is not cruelty so much as anti-intellectualism, a latent impulse in all his fiction that becomes obtrusive in the recent *Humboldt's Gift*. In this novel, Von Humboldt Fleisher, Charlie Citrine, Renaldo Cantabile, and Ulick, Citrine's brother, form a spectrum ranging from Humboldt's artistic vulnerability at one end to Ulick's counterartistic hardness at the other. Even Ulick, a variant of Elya Gruner, is touched just enough by the disease of sensibility to request that Citrine purchase a painting for him in Europe. And Cantabile, otherwise an embodiment of the life force, is ingloriously married to a Ph.D. candidate in English. Citrine belongs somewhere in the middle of this spectrum. He has been commercially tough enough in his own career to be a public success, yet he is poetic enough to share Humboldt's vulnerability and to lack the unselfconscious ferocity of Cantabile and Ulick.

Unlike Mr. Sammler, who is a refugee from another world and knows it, Citrine has neither the exemplary history nor the social placing needed to give his character density and plausibility. He is unconvincing both as a public figure and an estranged intellectual, a fact heightened by his religiosity, which has no necessary connection with either realm. Citrine's philosophical views, displayed by Bellow as copiously as he displays Mr. Sammler's, are less incisive and more irrelevant. In place of history as a ground of criticism we get theosophy and diatribes against thinking. Bellow's long-standing attack on *explainers* here ceases to be restricted to *bad* explainers. Evidently tired of all explanations, Citrine turns to his vague theosophy, which even he recognizes to be only another explanation, and which Bellow apologizes for with self-protective slapstick comedy. The low point of this rejection of the intellect takes place when Citrine furnishes a new kind of proof for the existence of God. "If there is nothing but nonbeing and oblivion waiting for us," Citrine muses, "the prevailing beliefs have not misled us, and that's that. This would astonish me, for the prevailing beliefs seldom satisfy my need for truth."[39] Fashionable intellectuals deny God's existence; but these intellectuals are always wrong; *ergo*, God must exist after all.

Despite these limitations, the fiction I have discussed may suggest a way toward the recovery of society by the artist, a way of making "the modern world possible for art" that does not require substituting structural myths for theoretical understanding. To be sure, it is important to distinguish between Bellow's and Roth's reliance on conventions of traditional realism and Barthelme's overturning of these conventions. And it is necessary to acknowledge the differing views of language and its debasement which underlie these opposed methods. Barthelme's irony toward official, institutional, professional, and artistic jargon does not stop at these targets but spreads and envelops *all* language, including Barthelme's own authorial prose. His stories call attention to their own inability to overcome their imprisonment in the artifices of language and the solipsism of consciousness, though it should not be forgotten that this very strategy itself makes a statement. Bellow, for his part, is no less aware than Barthelme of the immense deterioration of the traditional languages of cultural authority: "It was not the behavior that was gone," Sammler thinks at one point. "What was gone was the old words...the terms beaten into flat nonsense." But Bellow wishes to affirm the substance for which the old words had stood: truth, honor, compassion, virtuous impulse: "About essentials, almost nothing could be said. Still, signs could be made, should be made, must be made."[40]

Barthelme's protagonist at the end of "A Shower of Gold" reaffirms a Shakespearean ideal of human nobility, but the language in which he does so is self-parodic:

> "My mother was a royal virgin," Peterson said, "and my
> father a shower of gold. My childhood was pastoral and ener-
> getic and rich in experiences which developed my character.
> As a young man I was noble in reason, infinite in faculty, in
> form express and admirable, and in apprehension...." Peter-
> son went on and on and although he was, in a sense, lying, in
> a sense he was not.[41]

Compare this with the conclusion to *Mr. Sammler's Planet*, where the affirmation is not qualified by irony. Of his friend Gruner, whose death he has just witnessed, Sammler thinks:

> "He was aware that he must meet, and he did meet—
> through all the confusion and degraded clowning of this life
> through which we are speeding—he did meet the terms of his
> contract. The terms which, in his inmost heart, each man
> knows. As I know mine. As all know. For that is the truth of
> it—that we all know, God, that we know, that we know, we
> know, we know."[42]

Sammler himself, as he realizes, has failed to live up to his standards due to his limited compassion for the frailty that surrounds him. But the authority of the standards themselves is not compromised by this fact. Bellow acknowledges Barthelme's skepticism about man's ability to know truth, but he attacks the perverse tendency of such skepticism to become an excuse for self-pity and self-indulgent despair. And for Bellow, affirmation survives "the confusion and degraded clowning" of contemporary life which is included so richly in the texture of his novel, whereas for Barthelme it does not.

These recent works by Bellow and Barthelme, then, in many ways exemplifying the antithetical poles in the current literary debate between tradition and innovation, look at the plight of "advanced" consciousness from distinctly different perspectives. And yet their views of the plight itself, one might say their definitions of it, have much in common. Both writers perceive that it is not only the traditional moral and artistic languages that have forfeited their power, but the counterlanguages of modernist adversary culture as well. Both expose the hollowness into which the cult of creative autonomy has degenerated.

The writer's problem is to find a standpoint from which to represent the diffuse, intransigent material of contemporary experience without surrendering critical perspective to it. Since critical perspective depends on historical sense, on seeing the present somehow as part of a coherent historical process, this task demands a difficult fusion of the sense of contemporaneity with the sense of the past that gives contemporaneity distinct definition. To quote Irving Howe once more, "a novelist unaware of the changes in our experience to which the theory of mass society points, is a novelist unable to deal successfully with recent American life; while one who focused only upon those changes would be unable to give his work an adequate sense of historical depth and social detail."[43] The examples discussed above represent an approach to a standpoint both "inside" contemporary society yet critically detached from it. This approach restores that state of balance between unchecked fabulation and objective social realism without which fiction, in Alter's phrase, must "go slack," degenerating into a trivial playing with the infinity of imaginative possibilities. What makes this recovery possible is a theoretical picture of modern historical reality which, though far from comprehensive, is considerably more coherent than any picture that was available only a few decades ago, and more plausible than any of the willed mythologies on which so many writers have been forced to depend.

The degeneration of public language into cliché as a consequence of propaganda, publicity, advertising, and academese has
had far-ranging consequences for modern literature. The immediate consequences of this situation—in which literature finds
itself virtually deprived of uncontaminated language—have been
negative: literature either depends excessively on private myth
and the structures of the "mythical method," or else, turning
against myth, becomes anti-literature, venting scorn on itself as a
kind of punishment for its continued dependence on an ex-
hausted and discredited language. One way of avoiding this dead
end is to make the deterioration of language one of the objects of
the fictional criticism of society, to infuse it into the typology of
character and setting. The corruption of language then ceases to
be merely an occasion for novelistic introversion or wordplay but
becomes seen as a social fact, spreading into personal and collective relations. By this route, fiction reestablishes a connection
with recognizably central patterns of individual and social
experience.

The problems of recent fiction are emblematic of the larger
problems of current culture which have been discussed in earlier
chapters of this book. Our increasing inability to comprehend our
reality, combined with our growing suspicion of modes of comprehension that seem reductive, dogmatic, or tied to a coercive
politics, has provoked a crisis of rational understanding. The
crisis is seen in our despair of the possibility of such understanding or our desire to celebrate its impossibility as a kind of
release from social and philosophical determinisms. Not only the
literature and the literary theory of the vanguard but its political
and educational thinking as well illustrate this ambivalence
toward reason. By a combination of circumstance and design,
leading forces in our culture have severed their connection with
indispensable forms of social and historical understanding. To
restore the connection, we will have to revise our literary assumptions. But we will also have to revise our received ideas of revision.

Notes

Chapter One

1. Irving Howe, *Decline of the New* (New York: Harcourt, Brace and World, 1970), 259. Other analysts of "the decline of the new" to whom I am particularly indebted in this book are: Hans Magnus Enzensberger, *The Consciousness Industry*; Harold Rosenberg, especially *The Tradition of the New* (New York: Horizon Press, 1959) and *The De-definition of Art: Action Art to Pop to Earthworks* (New York: Horizon Press, 1972); Richard Chase, "The Fate of the Avant-Garde," *Partisan Review*, 24, no. 3 (Summer 1957), 363–75; Lionel Trilling, *Beyond Culture: Essays on Literature and Learning* (New York: Viking Press, 1968) and *Sincerity and Authenticity* (Cambridge: Harvard University Press, 1972); Renato Poggioli, *The Theory of the Avant-Garde,* trans. Gerald Fitzgerald (New York: Harper and Row, 1971); Hilton Kramer, *The Age of the Avant-Garde* (New York: Farrar, Straus and Giroux, 1974), 3–19. On Daniel Bell's *The Cultural Contradictions of Capitalism,* see above, 94 n.

2. I have provided reasonably full documentation throughout when referring to what the New Critics and others have held. But the reader interested in more will find it in my *Poetic Statement and Critical Dogma* (Evanston: Northwestern University Press, 1970).

3. José Ortega y Gasset, *The Dehumanization of Art and Other Essays on Art, Culture, and Literature,* trans. H. Weyl (New York: Anchor Books, 1956), 119.

4. William H. Gass, *Fiction and the Figures of Life* (New York: Vintage Books, 1972), 23–24.

5. Georg Lukács, *The Theory of the Novel,* trans. Anna Bostock (Cambridge, Mass.: M.I.T. Press, 1971), 53.

6. Frank Lentricchia, "The Historicity of Frye's *Anatomy,*" *Salmagundi,* 40 (Winter 1978), 119.

7. Immanuel Kant, *Critique of Judgment,* in *Critical Theory Since Plato,* ed. Hazard Adams (New York: Harcourt Brace Jovanovich, 1971), 397.

8. Stéphane Mallarmé, "The Evolution of Literature," in Adams, *Critical Theory Since Plato,* 690.

9. Oscar Wilde, *The Decay of Lying,* in Adams, *Critical Theory Since Plato,* 683.

10. Ibid., 680.

11. Ibid.
12. Philip Rieff, *The Triumph of the Therapeutic: Uses of Faith after Freud* (New York: Harper Torchbook, 1966), 258.
13. Gerard Genette, "Vraisemblance et motivation," quoted and translated by Robert Alter, "Mimesis and the Motive for Fiction," 234.
14. Edward Said, *Beginnings: Intention and Method* (New York: Basic Books, 1975), 38.
15. J. Hillis Miller, "The Fiction of Realism: *Sketches by Boz, Oliver Twist,* and Cruikshank's Illustrations," in *Dickens Centennial Essays,* ed. Ada Nisbet and Blake Nevius (Berkeley: University of California Press, 1971), 85.
16. For my analysis of Miller's interpretation, see above, pp. 175–78.
17. Said, *Beginnings,* 9.
18. Ibid., 11–12.
19. George Steiner, "The Lost Garden," *New Yorker* (June 3, 1974), 106. This essay is a review of Lévi-Strauss's *Tristes Tropiques.*

Chapter Two

1. George Steiner, *Language and Silence: Essays on Language, Literature, and the Inhuman* (New York: Atheneum, 1967), 162.
2. Richard Poirier, *The Performing Self: Compositions and Decompositions in the Languages of Contemporary Life* (New York: Oxford University Press, 1971), xii.
3. Harry Levin, "What Was Modernism?" *Refractions: Essays in Comparative Literature* (New York: Oxford University Press, 1966), 292.
4. Donald Barthelme, *Snow White* (New York: Bantam Books, 1968), 82.
5. Alain Robbe-Grillet, *For a New Novel: Essays on Fiction,* trans. R. Howard (New York: Grove Press, 1965), 87. Unless indicated, italics in quotations are not added.
6. Susan Sontag, *Against Interpretation* (New York: Delta Books, 1967), 7.
7. Leslie Fiedler, *Waiting for the End* (New York: Stein and Day, 1964), 227.
8. Jacob Brackman, *The Put-On: Modern Fooling and Modern Mistrust* (Chicago: Regnery, 1971), 68.
9. Fiedler, *Cross the Border—Close the Gap* (New York: Stein and Day, 1972), 64.
10. Ortega y Gasset, *The Dehumanization of Art,* 46.
11. Poggioli, *The Theory of the Avant-Garde,* 66.
12. On this ambiguity of the romantic theory of autonomy, probably the most helpful analysis is still that of Raymond Williams, *Culture and Society, 1780–1950* (New York: Harper Torchbooks, 1966), 30–48.
13. Murray Krieger analyzes this antinomy in the New Criticism and

other literary theories in *The New Apologists for Poetry* (Minneapolis: University of Minnesota Press, 1956) and other works.

14. P. B. Shelley, "A Defence of Poetry," in Adams, *Critical Theory Since Plato*, 502.

15. Henry David Aiken, ed., *The Age of Ideology* (New York: Mentor Books, 1956), 23.

16. Immanuel Kant, *Prolegomena to Any Future Metaphysics*, trans. Mahaffy, revised L. W. Beck (New York: Bobbs-Merrill, 1950), 46.

17. René Wellek, "Romanticism Reconsidered," *Concepts of Criticism* (New Haven: Yale University Press, 1963), 201–2.

18. Erich Heller, *The Disinherited Mind: Essays in Modern German Literature and Thought* (New York: Meridian Books, 1959), 172.

19. William James, *The Varieties of Religious Experience* (New York: New American Library, 1958), 153.

20. Friedrich von Schiller, *Naive and Sentimental Poetry*, trans. J. A. Elias (New York: Frederick Ungar, 1966), 100.

21. Ibid., 101.

22. Shelley, *Defence*, 511.

23. Northrop Frye, *The Critical Path: An Essay in the Social Context of Literature* (Bloomington: Indiana University Press, 1971), 94.

24. W. H. Auden, *The Dyer's Hand and Other Essays* (New York: Vintage Books, 1968), 78–79.

25. Kant, *Critique of Judgment*, in Adams, *Critical Theory Since Plato*, 383, 384.

26. Auden, "In Memory of W. B. Yeats," *The Norton Anthology of Modern Poetry*, ed. Richard Ellmann and Robert O'Clair (New York: Norton, 1973), 742.

27. Leonard B. Meyer, "Concerning the Sciences, the Arts, AND the Humanities," *Critical Inquiry*, 1, no. 1 (September 1974), 166.

28. T. S. Eliot, "The Social Function of Poetry," in *Critiques and Essays in Criticism, 1920–1948*, ed. R. W. B. Stallman (New York: Ronald Press Co., 1949), 107; Susanne K. Langer, *Feeling and Form* (New York: Charles Scribner's Sons, 1953), 234.

29. Eliot, *The Use of Poetry and the Use of Criticism* (London: Faber and Faber, 1933), 151.

30. Once again, further documentation can be found in my *Poetic Statement and Critical Dogma*.

31. R. W. Emerson, "Self-Reliance," *Selected Writings* (New York: Modern Library, 1950), 157.

32. Robbe-Grillet, *For a New Novel*, 19.

33. Northrop Frye, *The Secular Scripture: A Study in the Structure of Romance* (Cambridge: Harvard University Press, 1976), 45–46.

34. This point is elaborated above, 181ff.

35. Barthelme, *Snow White*, 18–19.

36. Henry James, "The Art of Fiction," in *Criticism: The Foundation of*

Modern Literary Judgment, revised edition, ed. Schorer et al. (New York: Harcourt Brace and World, 1958), 49.
37. Ibid., 47.
38. Eliot, "From Poe to Valéry," *To Criticize the Critic* (New York: Farrar, Straus and Giroux, 1965), 39.
39. James, "The Art of Fiction," in Schorer, *Criticism: the Foundation of Modern Literary Judgment,* 48.
40. James, *The American Scene* (Bloomington: Indiana University Press, 1968), 273.
41. Eliot, " 'Ulysses,' Order, and Myth," in *Selected Prose,* ed. Frank Kermode (New York: Harcourt Brace Jovanovich, 1975), 177.
42. Georg Lukács, *The Meaning of Contemporary Realism,* trans. J. and N. Mander (London: Merlin Press, 1963), 33.
43. Jorge Luis Borges, *Labyrinths: Selected Stories and Other Writings,* trans. J. Irby (New York: New Directions, 1964), 57.
44. Ibid., 17.
45. See above, 220–21.
46. Sontag, *Against Interpretation,* 27.
47. Poirier, *The Performing Self,* 40.
48. On Mailer, see above, 216–20.
49. Poirier, *The Performing Self,* 40.
50. Ibid., 93.
51. John Cage, "Diary: How to Improve the World (You Will Only Make Matters Worse) Continued," *TriQuarterly,* 18 (Spring 1970), 101.
52. Calvin Tomkins, *The Bride and the Bachelors: Five Masters of the Avant-Garde* (New York: Viking, 1965), 194.
53. Sontag, Introduction to Roland Barthes, *Writing Degree Zero* (New York: Hill and Wang, 1953), xx.
54. Robert Scholes, "The Fictional Criticism of the Future," *Tri-Quarterly,* 34 (Fall 1975), 233. Scholes's last sentence echoes a remark of T. S. Eliot's: "The poet makes poetry, the metaphysician makes metaphysics, the bee makes honey, the spider secretes a filament; you can hardly say that any of these agents believes: he merely does" ("Shakespeare and the Stoicism of Seneca," *Selected Essays* [New York: Harcourt Brace and World, 1960], 118).
55. Raymond Federman, ed. *Surfiction: Fiction Now and Tomorrow* (Chicago: Swallow Press, 1975), 7.
56. William Gass, *Fiction and the Figures of Life,* 8.
57. Perry Meisel, "Everything You Always Wanted to Know About Structuralism but Were Afraid to Ask," *National Village Voice* (September 30, 1976), 43–45.
58. Ibid.
59. Jonathan Culler argues in this vein against the *Tel Quel* critics in *Structuralist Poetics: Structuralism, Linguistics, and the Study of Literature* (Ithaca: Cornell University Press, 1975), 247–50.

60. Derrida, "Structure, Sign, and Play in the Discourse of the Human Sciences," quoted and translated by Jonathan Culler, *Structuralist Poetics*, 247. I have used Culler's translation of this passage, which is more accurate than the standard English translation by Mackscy and Donato in *The Structuralist Controversy: The Languages of Criticism and the Sciences of Man*, ed. Richard Macksey and Eugenio Donato (Baltimore: Johns Hopkins University Press, 1972), 264.

61. Derrida, "Structure, Sign, and Play," in Macksey and Donato, *The Structuralist Controversy*, 264.

62. Nietzsche, as quoted by Gayatri C. Spivak, Translator's Preface to Derrida, *Of Grammatology* (Baltimore: Johns Hopkins University Press, 1976), xxx.

Chapter Three

1. Joyce Carol Oates, "New Heaven and Earth," *Saturday Review of the Arts* (November 1972), 53.

2. Roland Barthes, *Mythologies*, trans. A. Lavers (New York: Hill and Wang, 1972), 75.

3. Sontag, *Styles of Radical Will*, 203.

4. Theodore Roszak, *The Making of a Counter Culture* (New York: Anchor Books, 1969), 215.

5. Richard Gilman, *The Confusion of Realms* (New York: Random House, 1969), 19.

6. Herbert Marcuse, *Eros and Civilization: A Philosophical Inquiry into Freud* (New York: Vintage Books, 1962), 113.

7. Poirier, *The Performing Self*, 144.

8. Leo Bersani, *A Future for Astyanax: Character and Desire in Literature* (New York: Little, Brown, 1976), 56.

9. Robbe-Grillet, *For a New Novel*, 160.

10. Barthes, *Writing Degree Zero*, trans. A. Lavers (New York: Hill and Wang, 1953), 32.

11. Ibid., 49.

12. Ibid., 26.

13. Marcuse, *Counterrevolution and Revolt* (Boston: Beacon Press, 1972), 89.

14. Ibid., 90.

15. Ibid., 93.

16. Marcuse, *Eros and Civilization*, 169. "The norms which govern the aesthetic order are *not* 'intellectual concepts'" (*Counterrevolution and Revolt*), 95.

17. Marcuse, *Counterrevolution and Revolt*, 125.

18. Marcuse, *Eros and Civilization*, 162.

19. Fiedler, *Cross the Border—Close the Gap*, 63.

20. Terry Eagleton, *Criticism and Ideology: A Study in Marxist Literary Theory* (London: New Left Books, 1977), 161.
21. Terry Eagleton, *Marxism and Literary Criticism* (Berkeley: University of California Press, 1976), 74.
22. Ibid., 83, n.16.
23. Kant, *Critique of Judgment*, in Adams, *Critical Theory Since Plato*, 397.
24. Marcuse, *Counterrevolution and Revolt*, 92.
25. Ibid., 94–95.
26. Marcuse, *Eros and Civilization*, 130.
27. Marcuse, *Counterrevolution and Revolt*, 92.
28. Marcuse, *Eros and Civilization*, 131.
29. Marcuse, *Essay on Liberation* (Boston: Beacon Press, 1969), 48.
30. See Robert Scholes's discussion of this concept in Russian formalist criticism in *Structuralism and Literature: An Introduction* (New Haven: Yale University Press, 1974), 83–85, 173–76.
31. Marcuse, *Essay on Liberation*, 30.
32. Ibid., 38–39.
33. Marcuse, *Counterrevolution and Revolt*, 98.
34. Quoted by James Stupple, "Fiction Against the Future," *American Scholar*, 46, no. 2 (Spring 1977), 219.
35. Ibid.
36. Scholes, "The Fictional Criticism of the Future," 246.
37. Ibid., 243.
38. Barthes, *Writing Degree Zero*, 48.
39. Ibid.
40. Marcuse, *One-Dimensional Man: Studies in the Ideology of Advanced Industrial Society* (Boston: Beacon Press, 1964), 68.
41. Marcuse, *Counterrevolution and Revolt*, 118n.
42. Marcuse, *Essay on Liberation*, 37.
43. Marcuse, *Counterrevolution and Revolt*, 101.
44. Gilman, *Confusion of Realms*, 49.
45. Ibid., 264.
46. Ibid., 48, 72.
47. Gilman, "The Idea of the Avant-Garde," *Partisan Review*, 39 (Summer 1972), 395.
48. Poirier, *The Performing Self*, 31.
49. Poirier, *A World Elsewhere: The Place of Style in American Literature* (New York: Oxford University Press, 1966), 7.
50. Sontag, *Against Interpretation*, 7.
51. Poirier, *The Performing Self*, xv.
52. Fiedler, *Cross the Border—Close the Gap*, 64.
53. Ihab Hassan, "Joyce, Beckett, and the Postmodern Imagination," *TriQuarterly*, 34 (Fall 1975), 181.

54. Cary Nelson, "Reading Criticism," *PMLA*, 91, no. 5 (October 1976), 804.
55. Roland Barthes, *S/Z*, trans. R. Miller (New York: Hill and Wang, 1974), 44–45.
56. Verena Conley, "Missexual Misstery," *Diacritics*, 7, no. 2 (Summer 1977), 82.
57. Roland Barthes, "What is Criticism?" *Critical Essays*, trans. Richard Howard (Evanston: Northwestern University Press, 1972), 260.
58. Derrida, "Structure, Sign, and Play," in Macksey and Donato, *The Structuralist Controversy*, 264.
59. Frank Kermode, "Novels: Recognition and Deception," *Critical Inquiry*, 1, no. 1 (September 1974), 119.
60. Fiedler, *Cross the Border—Close the Gap*, 64.
61. Ibid., 78.
62. Richard Wasson, "From Priest to Prometheus: Culture and Criticism in the Post-Modern Period," *Journal of Modern Literature*, 3, no. 5 (July 1974), 1201.
63. Ibid., 1195.
64. Ibid., 1197.
65. Ibid., 1201.
66. Ibid., 1197.
67. Eldridge Cleaver, quoted in epigraph to Anthony Wilden, *System and Structure: Essays in Communication and Exchange* (London: Tavistock Publications, 1972), v.
68. Mark Poster, *Existential Marxism in Postwar France* (Princeton: Princeton University Press, 1975), 7.
69. Ibid., 276.
70. Poirier, *The Performing Self*, 29.
71. J. H. Plumb, *The Death of the Past* (New York: Houghton Mifflin, 1969), 14–15.
72. Lasch, *Haven in a Heartless World*, 19.
73. Paul de Man, *Blindness and Insight: Essays in the Rhetoric of Contemporary Criticism* (New York: Oxford University Press, 1971), 145.
74. Marcuse, *Counterrevolution and Revolt*, 85. See also Barthes's remarks on the political innocuousness of avant-garde theater: "Whose Theatre? Whose *Avant-Garde?*" in *Critical Essays*, 67–70.
75. Marcuse, *Counterrevolution and Revolt*, 103.
76. Marcuse, *One-Dimensional Man*, 103.
77. Stupple, "Fiction Against the Future," 219.
78. Marcuse, *Counterrevolution and Revolt*, 101.

Chapter Four

1. Richard Ohmann, *English in America: A Radical View of the Pro-*

fession, with a chapter by Wallace Douglas (New York: Oxford University Press, 1976), 58.

2. Ibid., 59.

3. Louis Kampf and Paul Lauter, eds. *The Politics of Literature: Dissenting Essays on the Teaching of English* (New York: Vintage Books, 1973), 8.

4. Ohmann, *English in America,* 63.

5. Ibid., 167.

6. Ibid., 62.

7. Ibid., 148.

8. Ibid., 158.

9. Ibid., 302.

10. Ibid., 301-2.

11. Ibid., 94.

12. Ibid., 167.

13. Ibid., 88.

14. Ibid., 221.

15. Ibid., 243.

16. Charles Baudelaire, *Selected Writings on Art and Artists,* trans. P. E. Charvet (London: Penguin Books, 1972), 33-34.

17. Ohmann, *English in America,* 68-69.

18. John McNamara, "Teaching the Process of Writing," *College English,* 34, no. 5 (February 1973), 661.

19. Ibid.

20. James M. McCrimmon, "Writing as a Way of Knowing," in *Rhetoric and Composition: A Sourcebook for Teachers,* ed. Richard L. Graves (Rochelle Park, N.J.: Hayden Book Co., 1976), 3.

21. Donald C. Stewart, "Rhetorical Malnutrition," 163.

22. Ibid., 165.

23. Ibid., 163. Christensen's statement appears in "A Generative Rhetoric of the Sentence," in Graves, *Rhetoric and Composition: A Sourcebook,* 131.

24. Christensen, "A Generative Rhetoric," in Graves, *Rhetoric and Composition,* 138.

25. David H. Hill, "The Dead Letter Office: Composition Teaching and 'The Writing Crisis,'" *College English,* 39, no. 8 (April 1978), 885, 893, 889.

26. Ibid., 888.

27. Ibid., 893.

28. Richard A. Lanham, *Style: An Anti-Textbook* (New Haven: Yale University Press, 1974), 10.

29. Ibid., 12.

30. Ibid., 25.

31. Patrick Story, "Being and Writing: A Review," *College English,* 38,

no. 2 (October 1976), 201. I am personally indebted to Professor Story for calling Lanham's book to my attention.
32. Lanham, *Style: An Anti-Textbook,* 82.
33. Ibid., 91.
34. Ibid., 10.
35. Ibid., 11.
36. Ibid., 131.
37. Alexis de Tocqueville, *Democracy in America,* vol. 2, trans. H. Reeve (New York: Vintage Books, 1945), 165, 170.
38. Frederick Engels, *Anti-Dühring,* trans. E. Burns (New York: International Publishers, 1972), 304.
39. Karl Marx and Frederick Engels, *The Communist Manifesto,* authorized English trans. (New York: International Publishers, 1948), 12.
40. Karl Marx, *Capital: A Critical Analysis of Capitalist Production,* vol. 1, trans. S. Moore and E. Aveling (New York: International Publishers, 1967), 85.
41. D. S. Carne-Ross, "Scenario for a New Year," *Arion,* 8, no. 2 (Summer 1969), 227.
42. René Wellek, *Concepts of Criticism,* 37–53.

Chapter Five

1. Susan Sontag, *Against Interpretation,* 7.
2. Richard Poirier, *The Performing Self,* xv.
3. Bruce Franklin, "The Teaching of Literature in the Highest Academies of the Empire," in Kampf and Lauter, *The Politics of Literature,* 113, 122.
4. Louis Kampf, "Culture Without Criticism," *Massachusetts Review,* 11, no. 4 (Autumn 1970), 638.
5. Richard Coe, "Contemporary Critical Method, Science, Ideology, and Reality," paper delivered and distributed at annual meeting, Midwest Modern Language Association, Chicago, Ill., November 1973, 2–3.
6. Sarah Lawall, *Critics of Consciousness: The Existential Structures of Literature* (Cambridge, Mass.: Harvard University Press, 1968), 2.
7. Murray Krieger, "Mediation, Language, and Vision in the Reading of Literature," in Adams, *Critical Theory Since Plato,* 1232.
8. Richard Palmer, *Hermeneutics: Interpretation Theory in Schleiermacher, Dilthey, Heidegger, and Gadamer* (Evanston, Ill.: Northwestern University Press, 1969), 247.
9. Ibid., 7.
10. Ibid., 247.
11. Ibid., 4.

12. Ibid., 4–5.
13. Ibid., 159.
14. Ibid., 7.
15. Ibid., 249.
16. Ibid., 252.
17. Ibid.
18. Geoffrey Hartman, "Literary Criticism and Its Discontents," *Critical Inquiry*, 3, no. 2 (Winter 1976), 218.
19. Ibid., 217.
20. Ibid., 213.
21. Palmer, *Hermeneutics*, 225.
22. Cleanth Brooks, *The Well Wrought Urn* (New York: Harvest Books, 1947), 211.
23. John Crowe Ransom, *The World's Body* (New York: Charles Scribner's Sons, 1938), 115–16.
24. Brooks, *Modern Poetry and the Tradition* (New York: Oxford University Press, 1965), 147–48.
25. Ibid., 148.
26. Ransom, *The World's Body*, 198, n. 1.
27. Ibid., 124.
28. Murray Krieger, "The Existential Basis of Contextual Criticism," *The Play and Place of Criticism* (Baltimore: Johns Hopkins University Press, 1967), 239–51.
29. See my discussion of this issue in *Poetic Statement and Critical Dogma*, 54–61.
30. I. A. Richards, *Coleridge on Imagination* (New York: W. W. Norton, 1950), 228.
31. Coe, "Contemporary Critical Method, Science, Ideology, and Reality," 3.
32. Israel Scheffler, *Science and Subjectivity* (New York: Bobbs-Merrill, 1967), 19.
33. See above, 193ff.
34. C. G. Jung, *Modern Man in Search of a Soul*, trans. W. S. Dell and C. F. Raynes (New York: Harcourt Brace, 1933), 168, 172.
35. Brooks, *The Well Wrought Urn*, 213.
36. Ibid., 190–91.
37. R. P. Blackmur, "The Later Poetry of W. B. Yeats," *Form and Value in Modern Poetry* (New York: Anchor Books, 1957), 33–58; Allen Tate, *The Man of Letters in the Modern World*, 113–32.
38. Richards, *Principles of Literary Criticism* (New York: Harcourt, Brace and World, 1928), 253.
39. Brooks, *The Well Wrought Urn*, 255.
40. Ibid. See also Graff, *Poetic Statement and Critical Dogma*, 94–103.
41. Alfred Kazin, *On Native Grounds* (New York: Anchor Books, 1956), 311–49.

42. Hazard Adams, *The Interests of Criticism: An Introduction to Literary Theory* (New York: Harcourt, Brace and World, 1969), 141.
43. Harold Bloom, *Kabbalah and Criticism* (New York: Seabury Press, 1975), 109.
44. Hartman, "Literary Criticism and Its Discontents," 211.
45. Ibid., 212. Compare Hartman's comments here with Barthes's remark above that "the language each critic chooses does not come down to him from heaven" (81).
46. See above, 173–78.
47. T. S. Eliot, *Christianity and Culture* (New York: Harvest Books, 1949), 99.
48. Eliot, *The Use of Poetry and the Use of Criticism,* 30.
49. Ibid., 151.
50. I. A. Richards, *Science and Poetry* (New York: W. W. Norton, 1926), 72.
51. Ibid.

Chapter Six

1. Sir Philip Sidney, *The Defense of Poesy*, ed. A. S. Cook (Boston: Ginn, 1890), 11. See my discussion of modern critical misreadings of Sidney's statement that "the poet nothing affirmeth, and therefore never lieth," in *Poetic Statement and Critical Dogma*, 180–83.
2. Samuel Taylor Coleridge, *Selected Poetry and Prose*, ed. Donald A. Stauffer (New York: Random House, 1951), 264.
3. René Wellek and Austin Warren, *Theory of Literature* (New York: Harvest Books, 1956), 14.
4. Jonathan Culler, *Structuralist Poetics*, 145–46.
5. John Ellis, *The Theory of Literary Criticism: A Logical Analysis* (Berkeley: University of California Press, 1974), 43.
6. Ibid., 48.
7. Herman Melville, *Moby-Dick* (New York: Riverside Editions, 1956), 222.
8. Ibid.
9. See Richard Ohmann, "Speech Acts and the Definition of Literature," *Philosophy and Rhetoric*, 4, no. 1 (Winter 1971), 1–19; Barbara Herrnstein Smith, "Poetry as Fiction," *New Literary History*, 2, no. 2 (Winter 1971), 259–81. For some excellent criticisms of the speech-act position, see Michael Hancher, "Beyond a Speech-Act Theory of Literary Discourse," *Modern Language Notes*, 92, no. 5 (December 1977), 1081–98.
10. Barbara Herrnstein Smith, "Poetry as Fiction," 271.
11. Ibid.
12. Ibid.
13. Culler, *Structuralist Poetics*, 138.

14. Ibid., 262.
15. Culler, *Flaubert: The Uses of Uncertainty* (London: Paul Elek, 1974), 106–7.
16. Ibid., 95.
17. Ibid., 98.
18. Ibid., 103.
19. Ibid., 108.
20. Ibid., 109.
21. Ibid., 147.
22. Ibid., 151.
23. Ibid.
24. Ibid., 149.
25. Sontag, *Against Interpretation*, 11.
26. Brooks, "Irony as a Principle of Structure," in Zabel, *Literary Opinion in America*, 731.
27. Ibid.
28. Brooks, *The Well Wrought Urn*, 199.
29. Stanley E. Fish, "Interpreting 'Interpreting the *Variorum*,'" *Critical Inquiry,* 3, no. 1 (Autumn 1976), 195–96.
30. Culler, *Structuralist Poetics*, 238.
31. Frank Kermode, *The Sense of an Ending*, 179.
32. Wayne Booth, *Modern Dogma and the Rhetoric of Assent* (Notre Dame, Ind.: University of Notre Dame Press, 1974), 188n.
33. Culler, *Structuralist Poetics*, 141.
34. Robert Alter, "Mimesis and the Motive for Fiction," 233.
35. Ronald Sukenick, *The Life of Fiction*, ed. Jerome Klinkowitz (Urbana: University of Illinois Press, 1977), 154.
36. Raymond Federman, *Surfiction*, 8.
37. Terrence Hawkes, *Structuralism and Semiotics* (Berkeley: University of California Press, 1977), 16–17.
38. Jonathan Culler, *Structuralist Poetics*, 18. I am grateful to Anton van der Hoven for calling my attention to this remark, and to the fact that Culler repeats it almost verbatim in *Ferdinand de Saussure* (New York: Penguin Modern Masters, 1977), 106.
39. Robert Scholes, "The Fictional Criticism of the Future," 236.
40. De Man, *Blindness and Insight*, 17.
41. Ibid., 18.
42. Joseph Riddel, "A Miller's Tale," *Diacritics* (Fall 1975), 62. On the phrase "always already," see above, 194 and n.
43. *The Iliad,* trans. A. T. Murray (London: Loeb Classical Library, 1928), 125–27.
44. Miller, "The Fiction of Realism," 89.
45. Ibid., 86–87.
46. Ibid., 120.
47. Ibid., 122.

48. Ibid., 115.
49. Ibid., 116.
50. See above, 152.
51. Miller, "The Fiction of Realism," 111.
52. Ibid., 121.
53. Ibid., 116.
54. Ibid., 121.
55. Ibid., 116.
56. Ibid., 150.
57. Ibid., 122–23.
58. R. S. Crane, "Criticism as Inquiry; or, The Perils of the 'High Priori Road,' " *The Idea of the Humanities and Other Essays* (Chicago: University of Chicago Press, 1967), 34.
59. De Man, *Blindness and Insight*, 18.
60. De Man, "The Rhetoric of Temporality," in *Interpretation: Theory and Practice*, ed. Charles Singleton (Baltimore: Johns Hopkins University Press, 1969), 207.

Chapter Seven

1. Joseph Riddel, "A Miller's Tale," 62. See above, 174.
2. Northrop Frye, *The Educated Imagination* (Bloomington: Indiana University Press, 1964), 80.
3. Frye, *The Secular Scripture*, 13.
4. Frye, *The Critical Path*, 104.
5. Ibid., 104 5.
6. I. A. Richards, *Science and Poetry*, 72.
7. Michael Beldoch, "The Therapeutic as Narcissist," in *Psychological Man*, ed. Robert Boyers (New York: Harper Torchbooks, 1975), 117.
8. Frye, *The Critical Path*, 107–8.
9. Angus Fletcher, "Northrop Frye: The Critical Passion," *Critical Inquiry*, 1, no. 4 (June 1975), 744.
10. Frank Kermode, "Novels: Recognition and Deception," 112.
11. Ibid., 118.
12. Ibid., 104.
13. Kermode, *The Classic: Literary Images of Permanence and Change* (New York: Viking, 1975), 107.
14. Ibid., 108.
15. Ibid.
16. Quoted by Henry B. Veatch, *Rational Man: A Modern Interpretation of Aristotelian Ethics* (Bloomington: Indiana University Press, 1964), 41. My argument here is indebted to Veatch's thesis.
17. John Ellis, *Theory of Literary Criticism*, 47.
18. Hannah Arendt, *Between Past and Future: Eight Exercises in Political Thought* (New York: Viking Press, 1960), 95–96.

19. Frye, *Fables of Identity: Studies in Poetic Mythology* (New York: Harcourt, Brace and World, 1963), 36.
20. Robbe-Grillet, *For a New Novel*, 53.
21. Jacques Derrida, *Of Grammatology*, 13–14.
22. Jacques Derrida, *Speech and Phenomena and Other Essays on Husserl's Theory of Signs*, trans. David B. Allison (Evanston: Northwestern University Press, 1973), 131.
23. Gayatri C. Spivak, Translator's Preface, *Of Grammatology*, xviii.
24. Paul de Man, *Blindness and Insight*, 56.
25. Ibid.
26. Scholes, Meisel, Hawkes, see above, 60–61, and 172.
27. Ludwig Wittgenstein, *On Certainty*, ed. G. E. M. Anscombe and G. H. Von Wright, trans. D. Paul and G. E. M. Anscombe (New York: Harper Torchbooks, 1969), 18e.
28. Culler, "Stanley Fish and the Righting of the Reader," 29.
29. Culler, *Structuralist Poetics*, 113.
30. E. H. Gombrich, *Art and Illusion: A Study in the Psychology of Pictorial Representation* (Princeton: Princeton University Press, 1961), 363.
31. Ibid., xi.
32. Ibid.
33. Ibid., 368.
34. Ibid., xi.
35. J. Hillis Miller, "The Fiction of Realism," 135.
36. Ralph W. Rader, "Fact, Theory, and Literary Explanation," 245.
37. Karl Popper, *Objective Knowledge: An Evolutionary Approach* (London: Oxford University Press, 1972), 68, n. 31.
38. Henry James, "Preface to 'The American,'" *The Art of the Novel: Critical Prefaces*, with an Introduction by Richard P. Blackmur (New York: Charles Scribner's Sons, 1934), 31.

Chapter Eight

1. T. S. Eliot, *Selected Prose*, 177.
2. Robert Alter, *Partial Magic: The Novel as a Self-Conscious Genre* (Berkeley: University of California Press, 1975), 224.
3. Erich Auerbach, *Mimesis: The Representation of Reality in Western Literature*, trans. W. Trask (Princeton: Princeton University Press, 1953), 550–51.
4. Quoted by Lukács in *The Meaning of Contemporary Realism*, 25.
5. Robert Musil, *The Man without Qualities*, trans. E. Wilkins and E. Kaiser (New York: Capricorn Books, 1965), 4.
6. Howe, *Decline of the New*, 195.
7. Ibid., 194–95.
8. Ibid., 196.

9. Ibid., 203–4.
10. Alfred Kazin, "Psychoanalysis and Literary Culture Today," in *Psychoanalysis and Literature*, ed. H. M. Ruitenbeek (New York: Dutton, 1964), 3–5.
11. Norman Mailer, *Advertisements for Myself* (New York: G. P. Putnam's Sons, 1959), 21.
12. Ibid., 155.
13. Ibid., 268.
14. Ibid., 269.
15. Norman Mailer, *An American Dream* (New York: The Dial Press, 1965), 248.
16. John Barth, *Lost in the Funhouse* (New York: Doubleday, 1968), 113.
17. Saul Bellow, *Herzog* (New York: Viking, 1966), 93.
18. Joseph Schumpeter, *Capitalism, Socialism, and Democracy* (New York: Harper Torchbooks, 1950), 146.
19. Albert J. Guerard, Jr., "Notes on the Rhetoric of Anti-Realist Fiction," *TriQuarterly*, 30 (Spring 1974), 28; Gore Vidal, "American Plastic: The Matter of Fiction" and "The Hacks of Academe," *Matters of Fact and Fiction: Essays, 1973–76* (New York: Random House, 1977).
20. Donald Barthelme, *Snow White*, 88.
21. Ibid., 6.
22. Ibid., 25.
23. Ibid., 137.
24. Barthelme, "A Shower of Gold," *Come Back, Dr. Caligari* (New York: Anchor Books, 1965), 132. The title is evidently suggested by Lord Raglan's enumeration of the marks of the hero in *The Hero: A Study in Tradition, Myth, and Drama* (New York: Vintage Books, 1956), 177, 187.
25. Ibid.
26. Ibid., 129–30.
27. Ibid.
28. Ibid., 137–38.
29. Barthelme, "The Joker's Greatest Triumph," *Come Back, Dr. Caligari*, 119.
30. Barthelme, *Sadness* (New York: Farrar, Straus and Giroux, 1972), 58.
31. Bellow, *Herzog*, 166.
32. Bellow, *Mr. Sammler's Planet* (London: Weidenfeld and Nicolson, 1971), 111.
33. Ibid., 182.
34. Ibid., 229.
35. Ibid., 148–49.
36. Ibid., 313.
37. Ibid., 34.

38. Stanley Elkin, *Criers and Kibbitzers, Kibbitzers and Criers* (New York: Random House, 1973), 197, 199–200.
39. Bellow, *Humboldt's Gift* (New York: Viking, 1975), 357.
40. Bellow, *Mr. Sammler's Planet*, 261.
41. Barthelme, *Come Back, Dr. Caligari*, 138.
42. Bellow, *Mr. Sammler's Planet*, 313.
43. Howe, *Decline of the New*, 197.

Index